Joining

THE RELATIONSHIP GARDEN

Joining

THE RELATIONSHIP GARDEN

Jock McKeen and Bennet Wong

THE HAVEN INSTITUTE PRESS 2013

THE HAVEN INSTITUTE PRESS

240 Davis Rd
Gabriola Island, BC
V0R 1X1 Canada

www.haven.ca

Joining: The Relationship Garden

First edition (*The Relationship Garden*) 1996.

ISBN 978-0-9784618-4-3

Designed and typeset by Toby Macklin
www.tobymacklin.com

Original cover artwork by Mary Sullivan Holdgrafer, photographed by Seann Childs of LightArt Photography.

To our family, and friends,
and those who have participated
in The Haven's project.
You are all part of
our relationship garden.

Contents

Editor's Foreword

By Toby Macklin

This book is a thoroughly revised edition of Jock McKeen and Bennet Wong's *The Relationship Garden*, which was originally published in 1996. The new edition appears in 2013, the 30th anniversary year of The Haven, the centre which Jock and Ben founded, and 43 years after they embarked together on the relationship project that informs this book.

Also in 2013, their book *The New Manual for Life* is appearing in a brand new edition. It has been my privilege to work closely with Jock and Ben in revising these new books. In this process, it became very clear to us that the two books are intrinsically related to one another and should now appear as complementary volumes. Their new titles mark this fact: *Being: A Manual for Life* and *Joining: The Relationship Garden*. Together they outline the core of Ben and Jock's work together, which underlies Haven programs such as Come Alive, Living Alive Phases I and II, and the Couples Alive series.

One of the biggest tasks we set ourselves for these new editions was organizational. Both the original books were packed with important and useful ideas, but we heard repeatedly from readers that sometimes they did not hang together well and in places were hard to follow. As we revisited the books, we had to agree. In part, this came about through historical circumstance. The books were based on notes that Ben and Jock were making as they taught, often responding to particular issues that came up in programs, and included a good deal of material that had originally been published elsewhere. Consequently, topics were sometimes not clearly ordered, there were repetitions, inconsistencies, and so on. We realized that this wasn't only the case inside each book, but also across the two of them.

The new editions are much better organized. We have grouped the chapters differently, we have combined material in places, reduced it in places, filled it out in others. We've even moved some material from one book to the other, where we think it is more at home! The books also have new indexes so that it will be much easier to find what you're looking for if you're using them as reference books.

We have also paid close attention to the content, style and tone of the writing. Much of the material is substantially rewritten in order to clarify the ideas and to reflect the authors' current thinking on important topics. For example, Jock and Ben have for a while now been saying that they wanted to do a better job of explaining in writing the concepts of power and strength. So in *Being: A Manual for Life* the chapters on this topic have been completely reworked. In *Joining: The Relationship Garden*, the chapters entitled Sexuality and The Family Garden have received a thorough make-over. But these are just examples – anyone who knows the original books will realize as they read the 2013 editions that there is scarcely a page where the text has not been substantially revised.

You will find in this book a thought from the *Yi Jing* that in many ways sums up the challenge and possibilities of relationship as Ben and Jock conceive and live it:

> *In order to find one's place in the infinity of being, one must be able both to separate and to unite.*

Oddly enough, that sentence also describes quite well the process we have been through with these two books. They stand together now, both separate and united.

Joining

THE RELATIONSHIP GARDEN

The day will come when, after harnessing the winds, the tides, and gravitation, we shall harness for God the energies of love. And on that day, for the second time in the history of the world, man will have discovered fire.

– Pierre Teilhard de Chardin[1]

PART I

Contexts

1 Our Relationship Project

BEN: *The year was 1970. After a decade of private psychiatric practice, specializing in problems of adolescence during the heady days of the "Hippie Revolution," I was filled with excitement over what seemed to be a possible dream. My teachers were the youth themselves; my colleagues were too baffled by the rebellious energy to offer much information or support in my struggle to understand the phenomenon that was sweeping society. Much of the time, I felt isolated in my professional community; some of the time, I was obviously rejected by them. The situation reawakened my inner childhood angst, which found some relief in the emotional sharing of the endless numbers of teenagers that flowed through my office.*

JOCK: *After a childhood of loneliness and rejection by my peers, my academic and social successes at university were welcome relief. Now, newly married and heading to the west coast for my medical internship, I was filled with excitement over the prospects of being able to make a difference in people's lives. During the senior years of my medical training, I had discovered a meaningful existence while working with the street gangs of youth, helping them with their problems of drugs and dropout behaviours. My intention was to complete my medical internship, then study psychiatry so that I could be more effective. Wishing me well as I left our street clinic, many of the youth advised me to look up the psychiatrist Ben Wong in Vancouver. After settling into the responsibilities of my internship at the Royal Columbian hospital in New Westminster, BC, I arranged to visit this Dr. Wong to discuss the possibility of an elective time studying with him in his office. I was confident that he would accept me as all of my mentors had done throughout my training. I knew how to impress. With my fashionable clothes, long wavy hair and de rigueur moustache, he would immediately know that I was "with it" in the youth culture that he knew so well!*

BEN: *I wondered, "Just what does this young doctor hope to learn from me? I guess that I will soon learn as he is due to arrive here at my office any minute now." My receptionist announced the arrival of Dr. McKeen, and I asked her to send him down the corridor to my office. In response to his knock, I invited him to "come on in!" As the door swung open, I rose to offer my handshake. But I was struck dead in my tracks! To my astonishment, this young Dr. McKeen was a dead-ringer copy of singer Tony Orlando, moustache, sideburns and all! Completely losing all control, I broke into a hilarious laugh, exploding with the words, "You gotta be kidding!" After settling down, I was able to carry on a decent discussion with Jock, whom I soon discovered to be a paragon of narcissism. However, he also quickly revealed a most nimble mind, full of curiosity and adventure, willing to experiment and expand, while yearning to be in touch through his self-involvement. He was an old soul in a youthful, agile body! Within fifteen minutes of our initial contact, I knew that we were destined to create something together. In language that he might understand without becoming defensive, I told him that I believed that we could work together sometime in the future. That seemed to please him.*

After that momentous meeting, we planned our subsequent learning situations. Knowing that the field of psychiatry had little to offer in the areas in which Jock was particularly interested, Ben discouraged him from pursuing postgraduate training in that discipline. Eventually, Jock went to England to study acupuncture and traditional Chinese medicine in Oxford. Since then, we have devoted our attention to combining our understanding of Western and Eastern philosophies and healing traditions.

You might well ask, "Why are *two men* writing a book about loving and the development of intimacy? What could they possibly know about such matters, which usually involve a man and a woman, or members of a family?" As we publish this second edition of *The Relationship Garden*, we have been together for 43 years; during this time we have made the study of loving and intimacy our central concern. Both of us were trained as scientists: Ben studied psychiatry and psychoanalysis following his medical degree; Jock trained in traditional Chinese medicine and acupuncture, after he graduated from medical school. Both of us had been fascinated with religions and spirituality, and were very involved in working closely with people as they delved into the concerns of their lives. It seemed that relationship and loving were central concerns of most people we met. And yet, we could not find any authorities who could answer "What is love?", "What is intimacy?", and "How can I deepen in relationship without losing myself?" These are the questions we set out to answer.

The Project

Over the years, we have been involved in a project of self-exploration together. In the spirit of the investigative seventies, we made an agreement with each other to explore intimacy together. By "intimacy" we mean knowing one another deeply, being revealed to one another; the Latin root of the word is *intimus*, meaning "inside." From the beginning, we approached the whole endeavour as two scientists, interested in discovering as much as we could. Our ground rules were simple, but rigorous. We each agreed to grant "access" to the other; this meant that upon request, one person could ask "What are you thinking?" and the other would agree to tell as much as he knew at that time. We did leave a provision for censoring; it was an appropriate response to say, "I choose not to tell you." This was humorously important when Ben was carefully holding back saying what he had bought for Jock as a birthday gift; the fun of a surprise could be dampened by the scientific rigour of being forced to tell. So honest revelation included being able to openly censor.

As well, we agreed to share our feelings, perceptions and judgments with each other, spontaneously, as soon as we could. Thus, there was no requirement for questioning; each person's responsibility was to willingly offer the information, so that the other could be included in his world. At the beginning, Jock was not too good at this. He was ready to offer the bare facts; however, he did not realize that Ben wanted *details!* So, we began to distinguish between factual, cool reporting of editorialized summaries, and embodied revelations. What we wanted to share to go deeper was the *experience* – the thoughts, feelings, sensations and impressions of moment by moment. As trained scientists, this was a struggle for us, to move deeper, into the layers where we *personally* lived. We were moving from the *objective* world of reporting, into a realm where we needed to develop our language and communication to share the *felt experience* of our lives.

It was in this project that we developed and honed the Communication Model which we explore in this book and elsewhere. The ground rules are simple, but rigorous and stringent. Deception is the enemy of intimacy. Jock discovered that he was a liar – not by conscious intent, but certainly through a lifetime of trying to put on the most appropriate presentation to win the affection and approval of others. We were not practised at *revelation*; we were programmed to deceive, to withhold, to minimize, to deflect. In other words, we found that we had adopted many socially established programs that interfered with open communication. The Communication Model helped us to patiently work through this.

A significant attitude we took from the beginning was that there was no truth, no objective reality. We each had our own experiences, coloured by our past, and our built-up prejudices, and there was no "truth" outside of this. So we could share our perspectives without one having to be right or wrong. This helped to lay a structure to develop a relationship without blame, and with full *responsibility* by each party. Since neither person would be *right or wrong*, we would only be sharing viewpoints, perspectives; we did not have to decide who was "correct" in any circumstance. Hence, we avoided the legalistic structures in which many people become mired.

In this project, we found that most of what we had previously believed about loving, and relationships, and sex and intimacy simply were not so for us. We gradually built up a language to describe our experience together. We investigated further by comparing our results with the findings of many people who were around us. We talked openly with friends, colleagues and clients, with the intention of finding out what was so, rather than what was supposed to be so, or what other people said was so. We discovered many unexpected elements of relationships; these principles that we found continue to hold up to scrutiny over the years.

> JOCK: *What we were discovering about ourselves specifically, and about relationships in general, was breathtakingly beautiful! At the same time, I felt an uncomfortable gnawing somewhere deep in my gut, some unspeakable and unrecognizable fear for which I could find no explanation. My unconscious needs for survival would often overpower me. I began to recognize that whenever I would feel especially close to Ben, I would discover many reasons why I had to curtail my visits to him – I would become too busy or have conflicting appointments. Then I would not phone him for weeks. In past relationships, the other person would ultimately contact me to renew contact. Ben never would. How puzzling!*

At the beginning, each of us was living in our respective marriage, and we only had a social relationship with each other, as well as a collegial interest in matters psychological. We found our times together to be stimulating and provocative. When Jock returned from his acupuncture studies in England, he set up an office next door to Ben's, sharing a common waiting room. We would meet each day to discuss our approaches with our patients (yes, they were "patients" in those days – we had not moved from the medical model of the therapist and patient yet). And we would talk about what we were doing with people, and what approaches seemed to bring the most benefit. Certainly, our perspective with our patients was psychological; each of us had adopted a belief that peoples' lives could only change when their attitudes and lifestyles changed. So, even when the patients' complaints were physical in nature, we were most interested in how these people related to their world. Our medium of investigation was often the relationship that we established with them. It was apparent that people were openly sharing many of the intimate, painful details of their lives, and were thus opening themselves to us, in the therapeutic relationship.

As we met in our clinical conferences to discuss our patients, we were interested in how we could deepen our contact with them; it was apparent that the more significant the contact we had with them, the more ground they could gain in working with their concerns about their lives. In other words, if we could know them more, they could know themselves more, and they could see their lives in a different perspective; thus their healing would be facilitated. Consequently, we wanted to learn what stood in the way of our getting to know them more deeply.

We could see that one of the barriers was the professional distance into which we had been indoctrinated. It was acceptable for the patients to share their lives and concerns with us; we were supposed to keep an objective distance from them. And this was obviously (to us) an obstruction to the therapeutic endeavour. In the spirit of the times, we decided to try to open up ourselves, and become more personal with our clients (when we opened up and shared, the "patient" became a "person" instead of an object – hence the word "client" now applied). But we found that we had our own defences, and limited the relationship with each client with our own prejudices, and fixed attitudes about how things "should" be, rather than simply appreciate how they were.

In our morning meetings together, where we were now discussing our "clients," we began to be more interested in how our own limitations as people restricted the relationship with them. We wanted to find out about *our* walls and defences, to overcome our habitual ways of keeping distant, so that the healing process could deepen. We decided in this spirit to investigate how we kept ourselves barricaded and distant from each other. In short, we decided to see how close we could get with each other, and to work through each defence that prevented such closeness.

We began to talk about our feelings with and about each other. We found we were shy and inexperienced in giving words to them. We were comfortable at picking up a tab in a restaurant, or praising each other, as expressions of interest and affection. But to directly say "I like this about you" was very difficult. And even more difficult were the negatives that inevitably came up; we were too polite to say, "I don't like this about you." We realized that in order for our intimacy to deepen, we had to give voice to these feelings, positive and negative. And as we did, we would find breakthroughs in our morning meetings. Soon, we were not talking much about our clients; increasingly, we were involved in talking about our feelings for each other, and for ourselves. This process took more time, and we began to come to the office an hour ahead to "process." This grew into an hour and a half, and then into two hours pre-client time. We would also meet at the end of the day to talk about what we had thought and felt during the day, to keep in touch with each other. As well, we spent an hour on the phone each night.

As we became more familiar with each other, we also began to know ourselves and our own processes more. As we would discover something new in the morning meeting, we would be surprised to find that we saw this same issue in many of the clients during the day. It was as if the issue could not be seen until we faced it in ourselves, and in our own relationship. We began to theorize that professionals could only go with their clients where the professionals were prepared to go themselves.

Our clients were fascinated, if somewhat taken aback. They began to practise the interpersonal skills that we introduced in the clinical hour with their families and friends. We found that they were coming early to their appointments, to talk with the secretary, who also was involved in this style of interpersonal communication. And the clients were talking with each other, developing friendships in the waiting room! Because our client populations were quite different, this made for some interesting dynamics. Ben's clients were mostly adolescents dealing with life directions and parental and school issues; Jock's were elderly folk with chronic pain and idiosyncratic complaints that Western medicine did not seem to touch. These two groups met in the melting pot of the waiting room, and really came to appreciate each other, and to learn from the relationships that they developed. The little old ladies brought cookies for the young hoodlums; we were never quite sure what substances the youngsters brought to initiate the older folk!

To our surprise, we found that people were becoming more interested in each other, and less interested in the "doctor." They even invited each other to their appointments, and took increasing charge of their hour. By the end of the day, we often had stacked up several people in our offices, who had simply stayed after their appointment was over, and flowed into the next client's hour. We were having group communication process, and in the midst of it people's troubles were getting better!

Then we began to leave our practices for brief periods to lead residential experiential learning programs in a rural setting; all our work there was done in group process. From our experiences with our waiting room and office, we had already seen the benefit of people working together in groups. We were thrilled with the gains that people could make in the group setting – so much more extensive and more substantial than the limited work in private counselling. Group process helped to avoid what Carl Whitaker used to refer to as the "emotional incest" of individual psychotherapy.[1] We began to dream about having a farm or rural facility that would serve as a large version of our waiting room, where people could come together, to meet, to get to know one another, to help one another to heal.

Then we faced living together, and sharing personal time, as well as the professional hours of the day. We had each separated from our wives by this time, and our sons were living with their respective mothers. So we were unattached, and decided to live together as two bachelors. As we worked out our domestic situation, we made everything grist for the mill. Nothing was too small to investigate. In Zen tradition, every minute is eternity, and every small action contains the entire universe. We would talk, examine, argue about the smallest details. We learned to observe grace or heavy-handedness in how we washed the dishes together. When we would have our meals together, there was an aesthetic as to how we would share the tasks involved in selecting and preparing the food. If Jock brought Ben a spoon he did not need, this would be cause for a long discussion and investigation into the lack of presence.

In short, we were learning to be *present* with one another, and to acknowledge when we fell out of presence. We were becoming sensitive to each other, acknowledging when we departed from this sensitivity.

> BEN: *Our project was enjoying a large measure of success! Often, I could tangibly feel the contact that was growing between Jock and myself! I suddenly flashed back to my senior high school days when, for an assignment, I had written an essay titled "My Best Friend." In it I had described in detail the kinds of things that would be felt between myself and an imagined true friend. My teacher was apparently uncomfortable with the revealing of my inner wishes; although she gave me an "A" for my writing, she appended a brief note cautioning me never to reveal the contents of the essay to anybody else! Jock and I were now living out in detail all that I had described some twenty-two years before.*

So, although we happen to be two men who have lived through this experiment, we see ourselves as two persons trying to determine the parameters of loving, *to discover intimacy*. In our living and exploring together, we have discovered many elements in relationship. Also, we have learned that these principles apply to any relationship. In our seminars, we have taught that there are common processes and issues that occur in relationships of any length; hence, people can come together for a weekend, never having met each other, and work on the patterns of relating that they bring to this short-term relationship. In a similar fashion, people who have been together for many years have the same issues to contend with as those who are simply newer in their interactions.

Neither does the nature of the relationship particularly matter. As long as any two people are willing to commit themselves to being honest and curious with each other, they can work on a deepening intimacy. Thus, while the principles are very important to both same- and opposite-sex couples, they also apply to friends, parents in relation with children (and vice versa), siblings, and business partners.

Overcoming Control

Early in our relationship, we recognized the urgent desire to *control* one another: the greater the control, the higher the level of safety experienced. Yet we could also see that all such control leads to the ultimate destruction of any relationship; so we became determined to always unearth any underlying motives or means of control that might arise. How would we know when we were controlling and not just desiring? If we did not get what we wanted, we felt fine if all we were doing was wanting something to happen; if we had been controlling, we would feel resentful and angry.

> JOCK: *Now I understand that my pattern of withdrawing from intimacy is a symptom of fear. All of my life, I have been afraid of being captured. I believed that all of my human contacts had always wanted something from me, something for their own pleasure and not mine. To beat them all to the punch, I developed extraordinary means of capturing them before they captured me, using seduction, pleasing, succeeding and acting – all to get my own way. Ben was totally different – he appeared to want nothing from me, and never would pursue me, no matter how hard I tried! I didn't know what to make of this.*

> BEN: *My friends were concerned about me in relationship to Jock. They believed that he was out to use me, to get what learning he could from me and ultimately dump me, leaving me heartbroken and hurt. I could only reassure them that I knew that certainly he was trying to do just that, but that I understood myself well enough to know that I would never give away anything that I did not want to give, and that I could only be manipulated in areas in which I wanted to be manipulated. I knew that we only have to fear that which we want to do, and that if we participate, we are responsible for the consequences. With Jock I was finding a sense of fulfilment that I had hitherto only fantasized about in my youth.*

Relationships built on need are always controlling relationships. Controlling people tend to locate their centre in others. At separation, the controlling person becomes a victim, full of resentment and anger. On the other hand, a whole person experiences sadness over the loss, devoid of resentment. Needy people become enmeshed with one another, without effective boundaries; they do not grow. Whole persons in relationship become more of themselves. The relationship serves as a garden that provides nurture for everyone (children as well as adults) to flourish and grow into the full potential of themselves. Even if they separate, they continue to appreciate one another for what they have learned together.

JOCK: *Ben has been a shepherd to my process, for the transformation and revelation of my soul. I went through several stages in discovering what it was that I was seeking. When I was a child, my statement would have been, "My soul wants to be seen." Later, after I was less afraid of close contact, I would have said instead, "My soul wants to be touched." Once I had moved through much of my dependency needs, and realized that I didn't need to be loved, but rather I need to love, I would then say, "My soul needs to be born."*

The Relationship Garden

Since the beginning of our relationship, we set as our goal the care and maintenance of a relationship garden in which each of us could best grow. Even though this task has necessitated an incredible investment of time and energy, with our rarely being outside of one another's vision for more than a few days a year over a span of 43 years, we believe that what we have discovered can help others to manage the same within their own time frame. We have lived the principles in this book for over four decades, during which time we have experienced marriages and divorces (with other people), raising children, developing our careers and the school at The Haven, issues of succession and retirement, and aging, illness, decline and loss. The principles have held up, and we have lived them with equanimity and joy and pleasure in being together. Our friends have been concerned that we may have become enmeshed in this project, and that we may be deceiving ourselves in our assessment of our individual autonomous growth. Perhaps that may be so; the real test will occur if and when we are ever separated. We feel a sense of confidence that we will successfully pass such a test. However, as we have grown older and wiser, we have come to believe in the eternal aspects of loving; hence, we are beginning to believe that we will *never* be separated. We know of no earthly test of that!

What thou lovest well remains, the rest is dross. – Ezra Pound[2]

2 Life in the Garden: A Fable

Once upon a time, the entire Universe was filled with unrestricted, free-flowing energy that danced joyously and chaotically in all directions in the Garden of Energy. For eons, the Universe enjoyed this existence, this freedom. However, since everything was so perfect and predictable, the Universe gradually began to feel a disquieting sense of boredom. Then, one day while at play, just for fun, it decided to create some beings. Separating out pieces of its own energy, it shaped and embodied one pattern of a being into a triangle, and another into a circle. These were coloured with the pigments of the rainbow and were named "Triangulus" and "Circula" so that they could be easily identified. Although both of their energy flows remained connected to the source and thus to one another, the Universe allowed them unrestricted freedom to move, travel and play in order for them all to enjoy life to its maximum. And so they did!

Triangulus and Circula enjoyed their existence together with one another and with the Universe, exploring all the nooks and crannies of the Garden of Energy that was bathed in a warm, glowing light. The sky, the earth and all beings in them which were connected to one another and to them were theirs to discover. What delight! Since the energy that flowed through Triangulus and Circula was the same energy that flowed through the Universe and all the other Beings therein, they felt no fear. Curiosity was their gift.

Just as had occurred to their creator previously, after eons of play all things became known to them. Circula and Triangulus began to feel a sense of sameness that gradually grew into a disquieting sense of boredom. Wanting some unpredictability to provide spice, they developed a game of hide-and-go-seek which they played not only with one another but also with the Universe and all of the other Beings therein. What fun!

Over more eons of time, the playing of hide-and-go-seek became other than fun – it became compelling! As it became more competitive, they discovered that the hiding became more effective when their connection with one another and with All Beings was disrupted and hidden. Soon, they were experiencing more disconnection than connection, and each began to feel isolated and alone. Since they no longer knew what each other was thinking or doing, the game of hide-and-go-seek began to take on aspects of anxiety and desperation. The fun turned into fear and the business of life became serious!

Now that they could no longer depend upon the basic connection of the flow of energy between themselves and other Beings, Circula and Triangulus desperately developed means of controlling one another and the Universe. They were unable to tolerate the dreadful sense of isolation that they felt even in the company of one another! So each began to develop ways of manipulating, seducing and bargaining with the other; together they began to bend the Universe to their will, overcoming and destroying much of the rest of the Universe so that they could feel more secure. The more that they did this, the more they lost the connection of their energy with all else and the more suspicious they became of one another and the entire Universe. The light turned harsh and piercing.

As they looked across to one another and to the Universe, they now experienced a frightening abyss between them. Instead of returning to their roots where their energy was already connected (although forgotten), they focused upon building bridges across that chasm in order to contact one another. Such bridges included social skills, fantasy diversions, religions, scientific discoveries, new and better ways of communication and transportation, and groupings into common languages, families and couples. All of these were jealously protected, for fear of losing advantage and control over one another. Out of this fear grew experiences of jealousy, hurt feelings and ultimately, vengeance and violence. The Universe felt sad!

In spite of all of this, they retained a concern for one another – since at root, they were one another! Unable to feel the flow of energy connecting them, they instead began to make connections at a more superficial level. Instead of feeling at one with one another, when they were not competing they began to feel a sense of sympathy for others. They developed a desire to take care of one another. In such a way, they managed to maintain control of their relationships, and began to feel secure again. Institutions and religions were developed around moral systems, and smugness and pride in righteousness were natural outcomes.

Now, across the great abyss, Triangulus and Circula expressed to one another their great need for one another, and each swore to take care of the other. Of course, what they had forgotten was the fact that each of them was already whole and already connected to one another. So the belief in needing one another was a Big Lie. However, since they were able to dress up the Big Lie with hearts and flowers, they made it very appealing indeed, calling it their "Romance!" Now, they wanted each other to swear allegiance for life, even though by doing so they were committing themselves to a death of their own individual selves. The price that they had to pay was the sacrifice of their own personal potential of being! However, that did not matter to them, because to submit to the control of the other was exciting and full of the promise of security. Now, they did not have to stare across the big abyss. Rather, they spent their time in the movie house and fun palaces that made them forget about Reality! They could spend their time taking care of one another instead of having to care about one another. Although they no longer could feel their connection with one another, they worked hard to get to know one another so that they could please one another.

In fact, what Circula and Triangulus now felt for one another was the certainty of possessiveness and control. For a long time, that did not matter – at least not until the control stopped working! Eventually, the stark realism of being alone tended to leak out, sometimes because of natural aging, or loss of roles, or the falling out of Romance by one of them. When that happened to either Circula or Triangulus, each would feel the pain of loneliness. Finding that pain too difficult to bear, they converted it into hurt feelings and anger and each began to blame the other. This manoeuvre was a desperate attempt to prevent the self from falling into the abyss. So long as the other was to blame, this angry energy provided a temporary sense of meaning to an otherwise horrifying experience of nothingness and depression. Out of this tendency to blame arose a whole new approach to life – becoming a victim in which the other became responsible! Now life became not only serious, it became irresponsible!

Gradually, the institutions took over the responsibility for everybody, leaving each person only the right to do what was politically correct. To make life more predictable, Triangulus and Circula were forbidden to look triangular and circular; each was made to look like a grey box. Spontaneity, individuality and personal freedom became a thing of the past! The light of the Universe dimmed in the Garden of Energy as all movement, sound and colour became legislated.

However, Circula and Triangulus, trapped in their politically correct grey box, yearned to return to their original shapes and colours – to be themselves! When they saw each other's personal pain, they felt sorry for one another and wanted to help one another. Realizing the original trap of wanting to take care of one another, they refused to do that any longer; they knew that they could not take away the other's pain. Instead, they learned how to be responsible for their own pain, to be present to witness the pain of the other, to share rather than blame. While so doing, they began to feel the connection of their energy at their roots, discovering that their hurt was the pain of their separation. When they felt their connection, they knew that each of their pain was one another's pain – that it was not just similar, it was the same! Now, they were able to resonate with one another's feelings, and no longer felt alone.

With that resonance, colour and aliveness returned to the lives of all Beings. The Garden of Energy began to flower and energy flowed freely again. For Triangulus and Circula, life again became liberated, full of light and movement. They danced and sang, played and worked with full hearts. And the Universe smiled!

The beginning ...

3 Resonance and The Nature of Loving

Love is the drive towards the unity of the separated. – Paul Tillich[1]

Our Connection to Universal Energy

The story of Circula and Triangulus we told in the previous chapter is of course a kind of myth. However, it reflects ideas that are consistent both with modern physics and contemporary psychology, as well as ancient Chinese philosophy and medicine. In our work and lives together we have drawn on all these sources. In this chapter, we explore a model that is also described in the story of Circula and Triangulus and that can be seen as a backdrop against which we have worked out many of our ideas about relationship. Known as the Resonance Model or sometimes as the Self and Connections Model, it contains ideas that can make an enormous difference to the way people think about and live their lives and relationships.

In this model, we assume that people are born out of a sea of energy that we refer to as universal energy; some might call it *qi* or *prana* or God. Each being is unique at conception, yet also connected to this pulsating energy. As each person is born and grows up he or she tends to experience a progressive separation from universal energy, in ways we describe below. People continue to yearn for this original connection throughout their lives, and yet some imperative appears to ordain that we also experience separation in order, ideally, to individuate – to become our individual selves – before we are able to achieve again a greater sense of that universal connection. Such is the dual task set before us. As the *Yi Jing* puts it, we must learn "both to separate and unite."

In the diagram on the facing page the unique patterns of two individuals emerging from universal energy are represented by a circle and a triangle. At conception, we imagine that the universal energy flows freely in these beings. However, their energetic connection can be disrupted even in utero. Then, at birth, the child is clearly separated from its mother physically, and to varying degrees both psychologically and energetically. This experience of separation is fundamental and continues as the child grows in interaction with its environment.

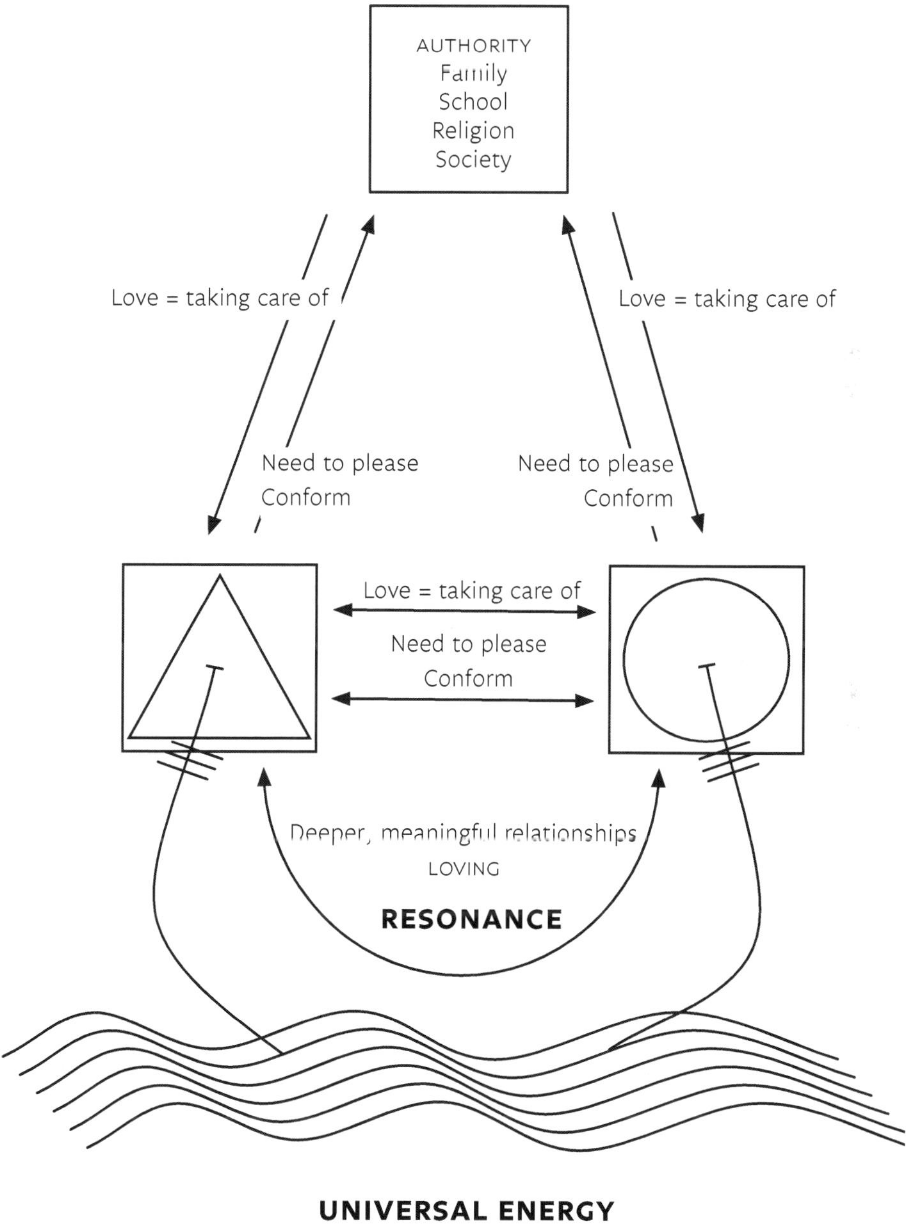
AUTHORITY
Family
School
Religion
Society
Love = taking care of
Love = taking care of
Need to please
Conform
Need to please
Conform
Love = taking care of
Need to please
Conform
Deeper, meaningful relationships
LOVING
RESONANCE
UNIVERSAL ENERGY

Becoming Appropriate

The two individuals represented in our diagram by the circle and the triangle are born into a world in which they must be protected and taken care of if they are to survive. The square at the top represents the authority figures – family, school, religion, society – that will be their caretakers. The square caretaker, representing the demands of the environment in which the children are raised, motivates them to abandon (largely unconsciously) much of their individual difference. They learn to please and to conform by becoming "square" themselves. In this way they fit in and survive.

The process of teaching appropriate behaviour is both desirable and necessary – toilet training, healthy eating patterns, and appropriate interpersonal social behaviour are all necessary in any society. However, in order to conform, developing children must abandon or repress much of their own true nature. In order to be more "square," they must create walls around themselves (represented in our diagram by the boxes around the triangle and the circle). In this way they curtail and control the pulsating energy within them, which therefore diminishes in amplitude. With this rigidification or "freezing" of the box around them, people lose their sense of connection with the sea of universal energy. The restriction of energy in this way is shown in the diagram by the three small lines below the boxes. This continued sense of separation determines much behaviour in life. In particular, it accounts for people's basic inner feeling of isolation, and the many strategies they develop in order to avoid this.

In place of experiencing a connection to universal energy, and hence with one another, people learn instead to "take care of" or "look after" one another; this is what society calls "love." Such "love" – taking care of and looking after – meets many needs of the developing (square) child as well as of the caretaking (square) parent. It is socially acceptable and highly conditional ("If you take care of me, I will take care of you"). This is the kind of love that builds societies and cultures. It is necessary, convenient and practical for people's survival in society; at the same time, however, it is the source of many emotional problems. In conforming to the expectations of the square culture, people are cut off from themselves and the source of universal connection with one another. They are in this way caught in a dilemma. On the one hand they want the security and rewards of being looked after and taking care of others, and hence "belonging"; on the other, they yearn for deeper relationships and a sense of meaning and connection beyond what society's paradigm of "love" can offer.

The Possibility of Loving: Revelation, Thawing and Resonance

Many people find themselves chronically trapped in this dilemma, caught between either using better strategies to ensure that someone will take better care of them, or developing some means of reconnecting with their universal energy. Most relationships appear to be based largely on the former; most spiritual practices and religions claim to be based on the latter. Hence, people sometimes abandon relationships in a quest to find depth and meaning in religious or spiritual pursuits. In our experience, however, this dilemma can be explored and largely resolved in relationships. A relationship can serve as a nurturing and protective garden within which each person is able to grow in self-reliance, finding depth, meaning and connection, while remaining a responsible citizen in the larger society. Relationships can encourage a movement from the limitations of dependency and being cared for towards the more autonomous process of connecting on the level of universal energy. We refer to this latter process as "loving" as distinct from what society calls "love." Both "love" and "loving" are possible in relationships.

Although most people lose their sense of free-flowing connection with universal energy, their inner vibrations do not entirely shut down. Usually, their energy just diminishes in amplitude; as a result people often do not have ready access to their feelings. Fortunately, it is possible to regain a stronger sense of connection with universal energy and hence with one another. This comes about through a process of revelation, which leads to a "thawing" of the previously frozen walls around a person and the phenomenon that we call resonance.

In workshops at The Haven, many people begin the sessions in a state of defensiveness, and are reluctant to share themselves. The walls or boxes they have built around themselves are rigid, brittle, frozen. People experience only a low intensity vibration of energy, and they commonly report feeling tired or depressed. As some of the participants begin to reveal their inner hurts and fears, however, other participants frequently begin to feel their own pain and anxiety in resonance. As the amplitude of these inner stirrings is increased, even the most frozen walls begin to thaw. It is as if the walls around them begin to soften, melt, and become more permeable. There is a sense of emerging spring time after a long winter. In this release, people begin to reconnect with universal energy and more deeply with the other participants as their inner energy grows stronger.

When this happens, people sometimes think that they are feeling the pain of the others. We don't think so; rather, we believe that people are feeling their own pain, which has begun to vibrate or move in resonance with the pain of another. All that is required for this to happen is for the (observing) person to have some willingness to be present and more open. As the resonance increases in amplitude in a group, feelings will tend to spontaneously emerge among the participants, and an increasing feeling of unity and connection develops. Although this resonance often occurs in the process of sharing hidden pains, people do not connect only through pain. Indeed, when people are open with each other, they can resonate with any experience. The thawing can occur through sharing all kinds of feelings, including anger, sadness, fear, grief, and joy.

Restricted breathing is a common habit that inhibits feelings, and thus maintains the frozen state and diminishes resonance. For this reason, workshop participants are frequently encouraged to breathe more fully and are introduced to a range of breathing exercises.

Of course, a group workshop is a learning situation, but not one's usual life. Our goal at The Haven has been to offer programs that assist people in enhancing meaning and personal fulfilment, through openness, sharing and intimacy. We recommend that individuals take what they learn in these programs into their most significant relationships.

The phenomenon of resonance is an important aspect of empathy and intimacy. It can occur between friends and co-workers as well as between spouses and lovers. As people learn to identify and practice resonance through breathing and communicating and connecting, they are able to further the empathy and intimacy they experience in their daily lives.

Resonance connects people to themselves in their deepest nature, and with one another, allowing them to experience true loving. It is thus a vital ingredient in the development of growing self-awareness and communion with others.

4 Intimacy and Communication

A Confusion in Terms

Much confusion exists over the meaning and use of the word "intimacy." Commonly, it is used as a euphemism for sexual relations – which are frequently anything but intimate in the sense we use the word!

For us, intimacy implies closeness and being known to another. The word is derived from the Latin *intimus* meaning "innermost, deepest, most profound, most secret."[1] Intimacy is a state of being wherein the most inner parts of the self are revealed to another, and to oneself, without pretence or defence. Hence, intimacy involves a state of vulnerability and knowing that is achieved through revelation, quite apart from the roles and obligations that frequently exist in interpersonal relationships. With this definition, one person may be intimate – that is, revealed and vulnerable – with someone who might not be intimate in return. In an intimate relationship, such revelation and vulnerability are mutual.

In this book, we will reserve the use of "intimate" to mean closeness and knowing. Hence, intimacy and sexuality are separate phenomena, which can often appear to be in opposition to one another. As we discuss in Chapter 17, however, it is perfectly possible to include sexuality in an intimate relationship.

The Loss of the Feeling of Connection

We assume that in the original state at conception, human beings are at one with universal loving energy. Because they *are* one, they have no need to be known by another or to reveal themselves to one another. However, from infancy, people become separated through conforming and playing roles; by so doing, children learn to make *objects* of one another as well as of themselves. This is a necessary function of socialization. The process of learning for the developing child involves objectification, and language supports this by facilitating the naming of things. As we saw in Chapter 3, the price to be paid for this socialization is the loss of the deepest connection with the universal energy; this connection is replaced by the act of taking care of one another, which is commonly labelled "love." As well as losing contact with the universal vibration, the socialized person loses the ability to know the self. This process of objectifying may continue apace throughout life, and people thus increasingly lose touch with their deeper nature. It's not that objectification is a bad thing; indeed, it is necessary. However, to establish deeper, more intimate contact with others, people must learn to move through and beyond objectification.

The Developing Child

At the beginning, children are not aware of much outside of themselves. The parents or guardians provide for their wants and needs. The infant is dependent, and focused on developing its sensorimotor systems. In this primary narcissism, children experience everything as extensions of themselves. As they achieve some degree of competence with the body and its functions, they gradually become more aware of the world around them, and develop a curiosity in relating to it. In this way, children begin to distinguish self and other, and learn to see themselves in relationship with the rest of the world. They become increasingly social, and interested in others; initially, this seems to be quite self-serving, looking to others to provide sustenance, care and stimulation. As they learn to relate more sensitively to parents, siblings and other people, the early movements of the development of loving are taking place. Having learned to objectify others, they then are challenged to move beyond the objectification into having genuine empathy for the humanness of others.

The development of children involves a movement from dependency and field relatedness into self-reliance and individuation. In the early phases of psychological development, a child's perspective is relatively fixed, based on a black-and-white division of experiences into either good or bad. As children grow, the possibility increases for seeing that other people have concerns, feelings and interests that are different from theirs. As they learn to conceptualize the separateness of others, there is a movement from isolated narcissism into the beginnings of real relationships with other persons. As children progressively learn to recognize the world of others, the possibility opens for the freedom and creativity of being truly autonomous, caring individuals. Such people can accept the differences of others, and thus be in harmony with them. Sensitive and responsible, they can learn to utilize their personal will to act in concert with the desires of the self, other people and the community at large, without being in conflict.

Alone and Separate

We take an existentialist view that the human condition is to be alone and separate; though we are originally connected in universal energy, to live as a human being is to *exist,* that is to "stand out." People live inside their own skins, and one person can never fully know another. Individuals can only know *their experience* of one another. People cope with the separation by social conveniences, and by living in an objectified world; but there is always separation. Intimacy involves acknowledging and accepting this existential separation, and standing in the strength of knowing one's *relatedness* with others. Togetherness comes with sharing aloneness.

Holding this view, we assume that at the core of human experience is a root anxiety, called "existential anxiety" or dread. Most human activity involves attempts to cope with this basic feeling. Generally, people try to bury or deny this feeling, and occupy themselves with diversions to provide the illusion that they can be joined with another.

Indeed, most people seek relationships in order to overcome this root anxiety. Often, they are trying to fulfill a neurotic need to have someone else take care of them and somehow to fill their internal emptiness. Commonly, they want to own their partner as a possession, to have the illusory security of controlling another – in the same way that an infant wants to own the parent, and wants the security of having enough control to be sure that the parent will always return.

The illusions of security and control work against intimacy. As long as people are invested in controlling their image of their objectified partners, their capacity for intimacy and loving will be limited.

Object Constancy: Becoming Separate

Throughout their lifetimes, all persons face the enormous task of moving from the infantile state in which others are "objects" to recognizing them as persons. It is natural to see "mother" as provider and nurturer because of her caretaking functions; it is much harder for children to recognize her as a person in her own right, with her own desires and fears, her own history of life experiences, her own fallible virtues and vices. Too often, children remain mired in the early stage of assessing their parents as either "good" or "bad" without taking the important step of accepting that in their parenting, they have been "good enough."

From the beginning, the child's sense of security is directly related to the quality of caring provided by the parent figures, who at this stage are seen as *objects* that provide – and not as real people. An infant's basic fear of annihilation is assuaged by the loving *presence* of a caretaker, which is primarily assessed by the quality of touch and sight, along with the certainty of being fed and provided with the means for safety and comfort. At the time the child learns to crawl and walk, making voluntary physical separation a real possibility, more importance is attributed to the *visual* presence of the parent. This is evident in the tendency for the newly crawling child to look over the shoulder at mother (making sure that she is still there).

After practicing separation and testing the certainty of the parent's presence over a sufficient period (which varies with each individual), the child will usually reach a stage of comfort over the parent's physical absence. This is accomplished by the youngster having sufficient memories of the constant presence of the parent; it is as though the image of the (object) mother has been taken into the child's inner self where it can provide uninterrupted caring. This process is referred to as *object constancy.*

When a state of object constancy is being established, children have an increasing tolerance of their parents' absence. During that time, youngsters may make use of "transitional objects" such as dolls, teddy bears or some favourite blanket, which provide some substitute comfort and reassurance along the way to becoming separate. The important process of developing object constancy can be interrupted by circumstances and events that the child finds threatening – their parents being anxious or unreliable, family breakup for whatever reasons, violence on television, abusive experiences, unpredictable or frequent absence of the caretaker. When challenged in this way, many children are unable to develop an inner stable image of a caring authority figure whose presence is reliable. Over the ensuing years, they remain *field dependent*, constantly seeking reassurance and security from "objects" (people and things) outside of themselves. They crave attention and tend to control, possess and cling to their partners, feeling insecure when left alone; or they fill their world with adult transitional objects that they can purchase and collect (such as cars, jewelry, electronics – the list is endless).

All of us are in varying ways and to different extents arrested in this course of development. An intimate relationship in which partners discover, express and acknowledge such insecure infantile longings, without being controlled by them, is a place to continue through those stages of development where we are inexperienced or stuck.

The Fear of Intimacy

Becoming intimate and revealed to another can help people to rediscover themselves, by overcoming the objectification. However, people tend to do everything they can to prevent intimacy from flourishing, believing at some level that to do so would be to *lose* the self! Out of the earliest separation experiences emerge the roles we are to play, and thus people learn how to objectify one another. "Mother" becomes a provider and protector; siblings tend to become rivals; fathers become authority figures. These are all *objectified versions* of real people, who may never be known for themselves beyond the objectifications. Children rarely think to ask their parents who they really are, what their hopes and fears are, where their passions lie. Even if they did, not many parents would give them some straight answers! Indeed most parents would probably not know the real answers for themselves. In this way walls are built, roles are established, and lifetime patterns of behaviour are created. Most people identify with their walls, as they lose touch with what is real in their centres!

Unfortunately, because of a lifetime habit of self-preservation, people tend to believe that the revelation of the true self would result in judgment, rejection and abandonment by others. It is difficult to believe that anyone could ever accept the demons of our inner natures – our hurts, angers, pettiness, jealousies, spitefulness, evil desires, and shameful lusts. We don't believe that our own parents would accept these things in us – why then would our partners or close friends, who came into relationship with us thinking we were wonderful and all good! How could we now reveal to them that we have been deceiving them all along? Becoming intimate and revealed would be tantamount to signing our own banishment or death warrant! No! No! Better we should become more perfect partners, try harder to please, repress our own horrible natures all the more. So what if it means that we become more depressed, or more addicted to drugs and alcohol, or develop serious physical illnesses – at least we will not be abandoned, and being a chronic patient is better than becoming abandoned and nothing at all!

Lost and Found

Eventually, after years of identifying with protecting walls, many people begin to feel the stirrings of a desire to know who they truly are. They begin to understand that they are more than their defences, that all such identifications are illusions. This may be the stimulus for a spiritual search for the self, using a wide range of meditative and sometimes, paradoxically, self-denying methods to do so. Unfortunately, many times such attempts result in self-delusions of a new sort, or despair on a deeper level, as they discover that the capacity for self-deception is so subtle and far-reaching.

In a relationship of an intimate nature, people have a greater capability to identify their own walls, acknowledge them and lower them – thus opening the pathway to the revelation of their inner self. If people do not just focus on protecting either themselves or their friends and partners, and commit to share with someone else what they are discovering, then they have a unique and effective way to find themselves. An intimate relationship is a garden in which people can grow!

Roles and Images

From birth, people are expected to become appropriate citizens. Families teach their children how to be socialized through a myriad of expectations and subtle demands, wherein they are rewarded for performance and achievement, and where little notice is given to internal feelings and personal wishes. Thus, from an early age, people learn to play roles, to perform duties and live up to objectified images. Although these roles and images bring some measure of comfort and security, later on they often stand in the way of developing intimacy.

According to Sartre, human beings are not what they are, and are what they are not.[2] By this, he suggested that people live the images of themselves, but they don't know their deeper nature, which is hidden beneath the masks of roles and cultural expectations.

Generally, as we explain in detail in *Being: A Manual for Life*,[3] children adopt an attitude of pursuing achievement and develop an image of an "ideal self" that serves to please others (at first parents, and later others in the world). They learn to be "good" and "appropriate," but they don't know their inner being. Indeed, by the time they reach adulthood, they generally have suppressed so much of their own personal feeling and opinion that they scarcely know their own authentic natures at all. When these people come into relationship, they generally offer one another their achievements, the roles they can play, what they can *do for* each other; however, they cannot come to know themselves or their partners more deeply in this way. Because intimacy involves sharing of the self, these people are limited in their capacity for closeness, in part by their limited awareness of themselves.

Image Projection

People usually don't know one another; they relate instead to the images they project upon each other. This phenomenon, known clinically as "projection" and "transference," and in more popular language as "ghosting," is a normal condition. Children learn to relate to parent objects, much in the way that they learn to relate to stuffed toy objects. That there is a person present beneath the projections of roles and expectations is a fact that slowly dawns, and is part of the developmental process of intimacy.

So, in relationship, people tend to relate to their partners as if they were parents or teachers or other authority figures; they also might relate as if the partner had characteristics of a child, a family pet, or teddy bear. Only by acknowledging and revealing these projections can people move closer to their own feelings and discover a more personal perspective where they take into account the uniqueness of their partners.

Many people are afraid to look beyond their roles and projections because they fear that who they really are will be unacceptable to others; they are afraid that if they are revealed, they face the danger of rejection and abandonment. Indeed, this is the risk of intimacy. Fearing to take this risk, many people opt to remain hidden – playing roles, controlling, projecting and withdrawing. The relationship then becomes less a garden than a playground in which fantasies are enacted but no growth is possible.

Taking Care or Caring About

Taking care of others is different from *caring about* them. (In *Being: A Manual for Life*, we discuss these in the context of a continuum between power and strength.[4]) Both have their uses, but in an intimate relationship, fixation on taking care of one another can cause problems. Caring about or for others often involves leaving them with their feelings, relating to them as fully adult without trying to help or fix them. Generally, however, people are motivated to *caretake* others (take care of them), in effect to infantilize them, in an attempt to relieve their own pain or anxiety. At root, the caretaker is trying to be important to the other person; this pseudo-parenting of another is often a way of coping with the caretaker's root anxiety.

Genuine caring about others doesn't mean trying to take away their feelings or their experience, even if these involve pain or suffering. Caring involves sharing in another's feelings, without trying to take them away. Caretaking minimizes the other person's experience, devaluing and even trying to get rid of their feelings. When people take care of others, they are actually not caring about the others; they are instead defending against their own existential anxiety. Caring about someone involves acceptance of both self and other. To take care of someone involves trying to control the other and the other's experience.

Most people have unresolved childhood issues that are commonly attributed to the "child within." Much passion in life is directly related to satisfying this "inner child" – being taken care of is often seen as one of these needs or desires. (Others might include the wish to be seen as special, being able to act irresponsibly, and even being allowed to throw a temper tantrum.)

An intimate relationship can provide for the possibility of expressing these desires. However, from the outset, they should be acknowledged as related to childhood issues and shared *for a limited time*, thus diminishing the danger of using them for control.

Presence

Presence is a prerequisite for intimacy. In order to relate in an intimate way, it is important that both parties are present for the interaction. By becoming present, it is possible to bridge the gap between oneself and others, providing a means of reciprocal give and take. However, some have found through life experience that the external world is unsafe; this can occur through physical violence or sexual abuse at one end of the scale, or some parental inconsistency or thoughtlessness on the milder end. Whatever the circumstances, most people have learned to withdraw and to become non-present. Originally this was for protection and sometimes even survival; for a helpless child, going non-present may be a self-preserving mechanism to avoid pain. Having learned to become non-present, people can later use this for purposes other than the original ones. For example, when going non-present has some desirable effect upon one's partner (such as arousing concern), it can become a manipulative, controlling device. A person who is fully present will often experience hurt and disappointment when their partner retreats from presence.

In its extreme form, going non-present is a prelude to "splitting off," wherein the self seems to separate from the body. Although such mechanisms can be useful to a helpless child under assault, they become a handicap to a responsible adult attempting to establish an intimate relationship. Such splitting-off – as well as flashbacks (spontaneous regressions, or "time-travelling," to past traumatic experiences) – are stimulated by events in the present that the person is emotionally unprepared (or stubbornly refuses) to deal with in a responsible, mature way. In these reactions, people effectively remain victims to their past. Non-presence, time-travelling and splitting off, which may once have been useful behaviours, now have the effect of interrupting the development of intimacy (and may in part be understood as defenses against the perceived threat of intimacy). Of course, as with all established habits, merely knowing this does not make it easy to quit doing it. But the first step is to begin acknowledging the process to an intimate partner whenever it is happening, thus reducing the possibility of using these mechanisms for the purpose of control.

In an extreme form of splitting off, a person may "leave" too quickly to have time for such acknowledgement. In these instances, people can call their partners back into presence. They may do this by holding their hands and urging them to feel their feet on the ground. They can identify themselves clearly (e.g., "This is Mary") and tell the person they want them to come back to the present situation and that it is safe to do so. Sometimes, a loud authoritative voice is necessary to reach the split-off person. Ultimately, every person is responsible for remaining present, and for returning from splitting off; all parties should be held able and accountable for playing their part in the developing relationship. While being accountable, remember that splitting off is not a symptom of being "bad"; although everyone is responsible, no one is at fault. Becoming non-present, or splitting off, is a weed in the relationship garden that can be dealt with together.

Many people confuse intensity with presence. They believe that they are present when they are highly charged or deeply involved with a person or an activity. Obsessions involve intense participation but not presence. Obsessed people are bound to their *ideas* about the other person, but are not present to be truly engaged with the person who is actually there. In this way, obsessive lovers are more tied to their ideas of love than intimate with the other person; their consciousness has been "captured" by their own concept of romance, thus interfering with their ability to be truly present with the other. In this way, they miss out on possibilities for an intimate relationship, while suffering from intense desires that they might misidentify as love or presence.

Presence is not necessarily conscious awareness; it is possible even in sleep. Throughout the night, sleeping mothers frequently remain present with their babies; even a slight agitation in a child is often sufficient to arouse its mother. People in relationship are able to be fully occupied with other activities, and still remain present with one another. Distances may not matter; even with physical separation and death, people who are intimate with one another continue to feel the partner's presence. Some would argue that this is merely a sign of good "object constancy" in which the image of the other has been internalized and carried within the self as a constant memory. We believe that the development of object constancy is commonly associated with a high level of presence of both parties. In intimate relationships, partners resonate through their continuing presence with each other.

The Communication Model

The model we outline in this chapter is the principal method we have used to develop an intimate relationship for ourselves, the central tool in our own relationship garden. On one level, this model simply describes a process that goes on within each person. On another, it proposes that by revealing that process to another, and being curious about the other's experience, it is possible to build connection, clarity, and intimacy in a relationship. We describe the following aspects to include in communication.

- Context
- Perception
- Interpretations and checking them out (bridging the gap)
- Feelings
- Intention
- Action

For the sake of clarity we describe these elements sequentially, though in reality they will each be foreground at various times for different people. The diagrams on the facing page are intended to show, first, that communication is a repeating cycle of these overlapping elements; and, second, that it takes two to communicate. The key to turning a monologue into a true dialogue is checking out one's interpretations and developing curiosity about the other person. This creates a bridge between two people.

CONTEXT (BACKGROUND)

Each time you enter a new situation, you carry with you a context that is based upon your past experience (both recent and more distant). You do not enter new situations fresh; you colour them in terms of other experiences you have had. For example, if you have been having a bad day and feel irritable, when you meet a new person you will probably begin your interaction in an irritable frame of mind. On the other hand, if you have been feeling buoyant and happy and then enter a difficult situation, you are more likely to begin in a positive frame of mind. To give an example of a context from a more distant past, if as a child you had a frightening experience with a big dog, this may affect your experience of meeting the neighbour's Rottweiler for the first time!

The context is the background or substrate against which immediate situations are viewed. Thus, one can benefit from a periodic checking with one's internal world to see what that context is. One should not take the context for granted, as it can shift and change. A moment of closing your eyes to investigate thoughts and feelings will give you an impression of the

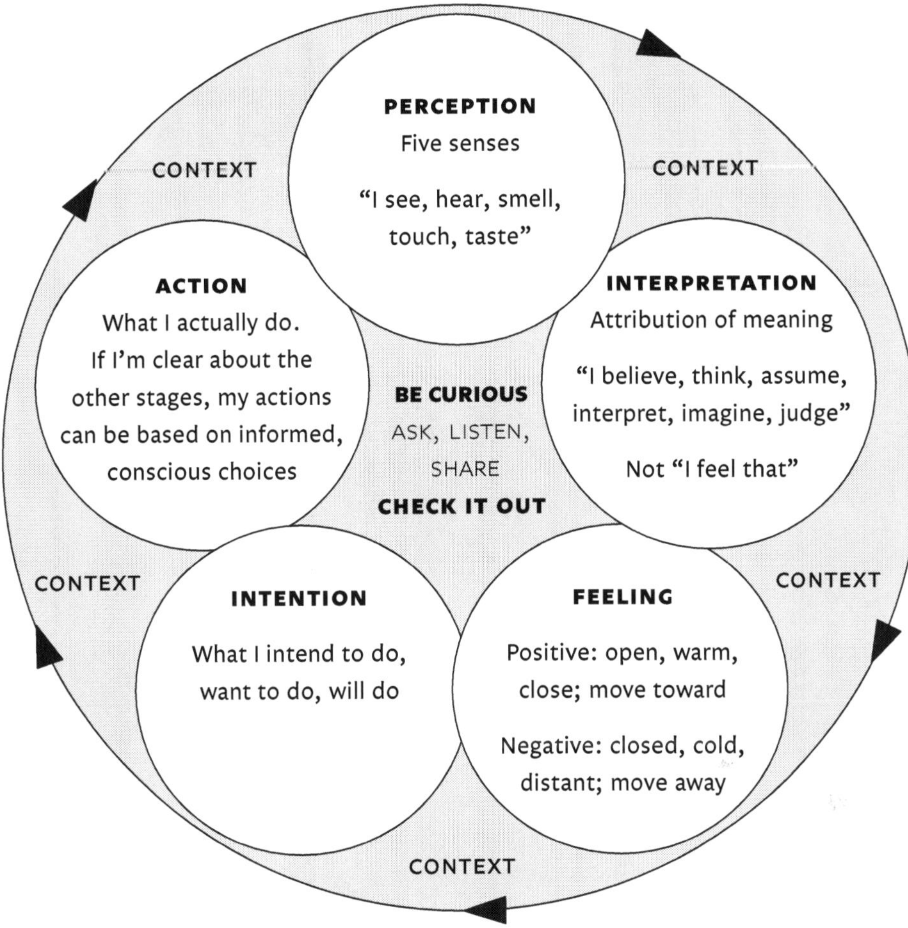

It takes two to communicate, so:

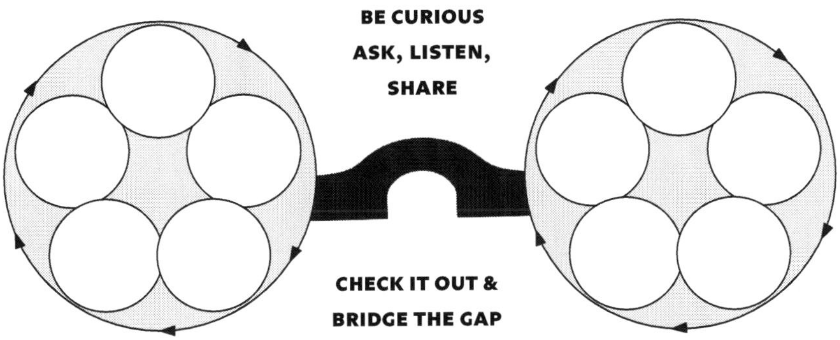

Think of agreeing or disagreeing with one another, rather than being right or wrong. Be curious about each other's realities. Also be clear with one another about your intentions as you communicate.

background you bring in. As you observe your thoughts and note your feelings, you will find what might be seen as trivial experiences – repetitive thoughts, or a vague mood that doesn't seem to have any origin. Note these – they will be colouring the situations you enter. Indeed, the context will even help select, out of the infinite variety of possible perceptions, those that you will notice.

PERCEPTION (THE FIVE SENSES)

As you open your eyes to observe another person, you will begin to absorb information about that person. In a matter of seconds you will take in hundreds, maybe thousands, of items of information through your senses – seeing, hearing, smelling, tasting, and touch. Mostly subconsciously, you quickly take in a vast array of data. What is interesting is that none of these pieces of information means anything in itself – the data are simply the result of stimulation of your nervous system. They are experienced by your brain as raw sensory information – shape, colour, texture, smells, and sounds.

Note that these are often subtle impressions – a fragrance, a sound, a movement on the face of the other. In order to make our world understandable, we go to work subconsciously on each of these pieces of information to make them mean something – that is, we perform the mental operation of interpreting. In the process, we also filter these perceptions to decide which we will bring more foreground in our consciousness; if we didn't do this, we would be overwhelmed by the sheer quantity of data. The perceptions are sensory; interpreting is the mental operation that provides the meaning.

INTERPRETATIONS (ATTRIBUTION OF MEANING) ... AND CHECKING THEM OUT (BRIDGING THE GAP)

As you observe your partner, you will have impressions of the way he or she is sitting; the colour of skin; the position of hands; the colour and type of clothing, jewelry, skin tone, hair style; and countless other features, including their words and tone of voice. From these impressions, you will assemble an overall picture, which you interpret. Now, it is important to realize that your interpretations are neither "right" nor "wrong" – they are best guesses at the meaning of what you are witnessing. These interpretations assist you in making intelligible the huge amount of information that you have received from your senses. They are simply your way of understanding the information you have.

One should always check with the other person, seeking agreement or disagreement relating to each interpretation. Again, it is not a question here of being right or wrong; I can only check to see if my version of you matches your version of yourself, or if my experience of an event matches yours. If you agree with me, I am not right, and if your opinion differs, this doesn't mean I am wrong; we simply agree or disagree. Our experiences are similar or different. When there is a difference in an interpretation, we can become curious about the different viewpoints we have, and learn more about ourselves and each other. This attitude of curiosity with no right or wrong permits an openness to ongoing learning; to become fixated on who is right or wrong brings learning to a halt.

Checking out interpretations, asking and listening with curiosity and an open heart and mind are the crucial steps that allow the transformation of monologue into dialogue. This is how people can "bridge the gap" between them.

Common phrases to express interpretations (and check them out) are:

- I interpret that you are a kind person. (Do you think of yourself that way?)
- I believe that you are being honest. (Are you?)
- I think that you are shy. (Is that your experience?)
- I assume that this is difficult for you. (Is that what is going on for you?)
- I imagine that you are uncomfortable. (Are you?)
- I judge that you are trying very hard to communicate. (Are you?)
- I speculate that you are thinking of something else. (Are you distracted?)
- I have an idea that you are feeling very anxious. (How are you feeling?)

Interpreting is a mental operation that involves thinking. A common mistake is to confuse interpretations with feelings. Thus the phrase "I feel that you are" usually does not introduce a feeling; instead, it is a misrepresentation of "I think that you are..." We think it is very helpful for people to include real feelings (which we discuss below) in their conversation; this can be made more difficult when people are unclear what are their feelings and what are their thoughts.

Many people are afraid to express their interpretations because the idea of judging someone else has taken on negative overtones. Yet judging (interpreting) is merely your way of making sense of information in order for you to more profoundly know another person. Judgment does not necessarily imply a rejection; indeed, pure judgment simply involves drawing distinctions in order to make sense of random data. It is from these interpretations that all your feelings come: how you interpret the data of your senses will determine whether you wish to move toward or away from another person.

FEELINGS

Based on the interpretations you make, you will develop your feelings. Feelings are experiences in the body involving changes in blood flow and energy shifts. There are basically two kinds of feelings, which we label positive (moving towards) and negative (moving away). We do not mean by this that one kind of feeling is good and the other bad. Rather, you might picture the image of a car battery where both poles are necessary if the battery is to work.

Positive feelings involve an opening up of the blood vessels in the body, and are associated with a sensation of warmth and well-being. When you sense this positive feeling, you will be drawn toward the person for whom you have the feeling. You might express a positive feeling in these ways: "I like you," "I am drawn to you," "I am attracted to you," "I feel comfortable with you," "I feel close to you," "I feel warm with you," or "I love you." The overall experience is one of feeling close and comfortable, with a desire to move toward the other person.

Negative feelings involve a contraction of the blood vessels in the body, with an accompanying feeling of tightness, discomfort, coolness and a desire to move back. You might express a negative feeling in any of these ways: "I am uncomfortable with you," "I dislike you," "I feel distant from you," "I am afraid of you," "I hate you," or "I feel like moving away from you." The overall experience is one of feeling distant, cool, wanting to move away. Children are quite willing to express such negative feelings, and let them go. As adults, we are often more reluctant to speak so directly; yet, such expression can facilitate communication.

Note that a negative feeling does not imply that the other person is bad or wrong; it simply reflects a judgment within the person who has the negative feeling, who for some reason experiences a desire to move away. For example, when you chose your outfit this morning, you were negative to all the other clothes in your closet; when you choose chocolate ice cream, you are negative to all the other flavours that you could have chosen. So, negative and positive feelings involve choice and valuing; they do not say anything about the worth of the other person, but rather speak of the valuing process within the person having the feelings.

Also, be aware that the feelings you have are based upon your context and interpretations. The same perceptions can be coloured differently given different contexts and interpretations, and it is possible to feel either positively or negatively about any perception. For example, the sight of a big man with a knife could be interpreted in various ways. If one were to interpret the man as a threatening killer, one would likely have a negative feeling and draw away; if instead one were to interpret him as a chef who is about to carve a roast of beef, one might draw close to get the first piece! The feelings are determined by the interpretations of the perceptions.

For this reason it is useful to tell your partner the feeling that accompanies your interpretations. For example, if you have the interpretation, "I think you are very smart," your feeling may be one of admiration, warmth and drawing close or it may be that you are intimidated and want to move away. Thus, we can revisit a few of the examples we gave a few pages back, this time including feelings:

- I interpret that you are a kind person. I feel relaxed and warm with you. Do you think of yourself as a kind person?
- I believe that you are being honest. I feel scared. What is going on for you?
- I think that you are shy. I feel awkward and rather distant. Are you shy, or is something else going on?

Note too, that in these examples, the speaker takes responsibility for his or her own feelings. When people say, as they very commonly do, "You make me feel relaxed/scared/awkward," their words suggest that the other person is responsible for their feelings. In effect, they are making themselves either dependent on the other person to feel good or, when they feel bad, the other person's victim. We recommend that people pay attention to their language not merely to be "correct," but to highlight for themselves the challenge of taking responsibility for their own feelings. To the extent that people learn to be responsible for their own feelings (and indeed their perceptions and thoughts) they can access their own autonomy and strength to also act responsibly in their daily lives. We discuss this important point in more depth on page 49.

INTENTION

Intention involves the conscious use of the will in translating feelings into action. For each perception/interpretation/feeling complex, it is possible to develop an intention about what you would like to do in response. You do not ever have to follow a feeling; human beings have free will, and can decide to act in opposition to their feelings. For example, you might feel attracted to someone, and decide not to pursue this attraction because of commitment to an established relationship. In a similar manner, you might be afraid of someone and decide to approach that person to talk about your fear, instead of withdrawing and following the feeling. You can always learn about yourself from a situation, whether you follow your feeling or not.

Also, you should be ready in a dialogue to ask of the other, "What is your intention in telling me this?" This question can shift an encounter to the level of the deeper meanings involved in the communication. For example, if someone's intention were to express anger in order to clear the air and become closer to you, you might be interested in staying to face the anger; on the other hand, if that person's intention was simply to try to intimidate or get control of you, you might not want to stay engaged. Clarifying your intentions can allow the communication to proceed to deeper levels.

ACTION

Action proceeds from decisions. Often this is an unconscious process; but, using the Communication Model, it can be brought increasingly into awareness. Once you can reflect on the process, you can make more conscious choices to take actions that are commensurate with your values and wishes. When you are aware of yourself and the other person or people, you are in a better position to make informed decisions about what to do.

The context for all your actions is determined by decisions you make about whether to be open or closed, to be curious or defended, to move towards others or away from them, to connect or disconnect. All of this informs your actions.

We are always making choices, whether we are aware or not. When we are not aware of the choice-making process – which involves our context, perceptions, interpretations and feelings – it can seem as if life just "happens" to us. When we realize that we are able to make conscious choices, our actions can be responsive to our experience of our selves and each other. We take more responsibility for our actions. With this comes extraordinary freedom, and often anxiety.

Once you become clear about your perceptions, interpretations, feelings, and intentions, and become curious about the experience of others too, your decisions to act will be less complicated, more easily understood by others, and more effectively executed. By working with this process, you can develop increasing amounts of self-responsibility, and your inner strength will grow. In this way you can develop considerable ability to respond to each situation in ways that you choose.

You are free to choose, and what actions you freely take shape your life. This opens up enormous possibilities for personal growth, expansion and transformation!

Responsibility for Feelings

As we have already pointed out, it is important in using this model of communication to take the perspective that *no one can make another feel anything.* More often, people tend to think that their feelings are the result of others' behaviours and input. But feelings are the expression of the internal physiology of the individual human organism; they are generated from within. One person does not turn another on or off; nor does that person excite or bore another; one does not make another angry or happy. Individuals turn themselves on and off, excite themselves and bore themselves; people generate their own anger and happiness. Indeed, as a responsive being, each individual is responsible for all of his or her feelings, thoughts, attitudes, and experiences. Although this is usually below the level of consciousness, people nevertheless are responsible at some level for their own experiences.

The same is true of our thoughts and attitudes. Although these can be copied from someone else, the individual internally chooses to copy them. Ultimately, therefore, each individual is responsible for his or her own thoughts, prejudices, attitudes, feelings, responses and desires. It is a malignant social convention that places the responsibility for such things outside of oneself, inviting people to make others responsible for their feelings. Thus, in order to move toward a position of responsibility (and freedom), people have to work through some deeply entrenched attitudes. As they begin to take responsibility for themselves, they are liable to be viewed as unusual in society. Language and culture serve to reinforce the belief that other people pull our marionette strings, and the "normal" position is one of being a victim of others.

For many, a difficult aspect of this responsibility model is the realization that it is impossible for another person to hurt one's feelings. Certainly, people often *intend* to hurt one another's feelings with what they say or do; but in fact, they cannot. The physiological mechanisms of hurt feelings are within the person who hurts, controlled within his or her own brain by their perceptions and their interpretations of what the other is saying or doing. People are in charge of their own perceptions and interpretations; they can use these as weapons to "stab" themselves, to hurt their own feelings. So it is irresponsible to blame another for hurt feelings. But it is possible to share your hurt feelings so that your partner can know what kinds of things you will tend to hurt over. By sharing their hurt feelings, people can stop using them to control their partners. In this vulnerability, they are more revealed; this is how intimacy grows.

No Blame

Although people are responsible for their own feelings, this does not give licence to be insensitive. It is possible to share feelings while remaining considerate of the perspective of another. A gentle introduction such as, "I have something to say that I'm afraid you might hurt over. Are you willing to listen to me?" can demonstrate the sensitivity that invites participation instead of defensiveness. Nevertheless, neither person is to blame for the feelings of the other; neither is responsible for the other; neither is obligated to the other. There is tremendous freedom in this. If people do come together in relationship, it is because they both choose to do so, by their own free wills and desires. When people are genuinely curious about themselves, and about each other, their relationship can flower without either having to feel guilty or blamed for what does or does not transpire. If they don't try to control each other, they can instead have a genuine interest in each other, in which loving and feeling for life can be revealed. When people become caught up in power, control and domination, the possibilities for intimacy and loving are eclipsed.

It is not necessary that partners agree, or have the same perceptions and interpretations. When one partner shares feelings related to different interpretations, the other does not have to abandon his or her position. But it is important that they respect each other's position, and especially refrain from diminishing or belittling one another. Sometimes that leaves people in an uncomfortable state of disagreement that they need to learn to accept and live with. Any relationship benefits from this increasing capacity to accept differences while living with some tension between the parties.

Prejudices (pre-judgments) and interpretations are ways of organizing the world, but they prevent people from knowing one another. Indeed, people only know *their version* of anyone else. By sharing fixed attitudes and preconceptions, people become revealed. In this revelation, the window opens, and intimacy can flourish. The Communication Model presupposes there to be no right or wrong – all that is possible is to agree or disagree. When people are angry because they believe that they have been treated unfairly, that indeed is their reality; but it is never *right!* Indeed, others might even agree with this perspective; but that still does not make it right – it only means that they are in agreement. At the same time, people can disagree, and neither of them would be wrong. Because all feelings are related to interpretations of the perceptual signals being received, it is important that people check their interpretations with each other. It is remarkable how many people suffer in silence over some imagined slight, becoming emotionally distant or angry from someone they love – all because they did not check out their interpretation of an event!

Many relationships head for the rocks because the parties become involved in legalistic battles about who is right or wrong. Usually, it is obvious that they are merely disagreeing, and that neither is right or wrong. When people step beyond this child-like behaviour, they can learn to respect and accept one another's opposing views without giving up their own, and thus can live together in harmony. Instead of becoming defensive, partners can always become curious about themselves and each other, to discover more about how they have arrived at whatever opinions they have. Such an approach provides each person with more information about themselves and each other, hence strengthening their intimacy.

Guilt, Shame and Forgiveness

Much confusion exists concerning guilt and shame. Generally, they are both seen as negative states. We ourselves make a very clear distinction between the two. In our usage, guilt operates against personal development and intimacy; shame can be very useful in personal growth and can enhance intimacy.

Guilt is the painful internal tension generated by the conscience of a person, who has interpreted that their personal thoughts or deeds have broken some law or rule imposed from the external environment. Guilt sees the self as a transgressor, an object that deserves punishment. Guilty people seek forgiveness for having done something that they believe they would not ordinarily do; thus, guilt denies the true nature of the self, by attempting to divorce the self from actions. To be guilty is to be in a position of irresponsibility. A statement of guilt could include: "I'm not the kind of person who does this kind of thing."

On the other hand, shame is a flooding of feelings generated by a *recognition* of the self; no amount of forgiveness can erase the knowledge that a person is indeed the agent of his or her words or deeds. A statement of shame could include an acknowledgement that "I am the kind of person who does this kind of thing." In Buddhist philosophy, shame is seen to be a highly nutritive state of consciousness, in the same degree of importance as faith and empathy.[5] With shame comes revelation and recognition – both key factors in experiencing and expressing one's authentic nature.

Shame should not be confused with guilt, or what is often referred to as "toxic shame" (which we see as another form of guilt, with all its negative consequences). Parents produce confusion when they angrily point an accusing finger with an accompanying "Shame on you!" when what they mean is "Guilt on you!"

With guilt, people make themselves small and worthless. This is accompanied by a physiological closing, with both the physical body and the energy body being tightened and compressed. Shame opens up the energy body, flooding the self with warmth and expansiveness; the person experiences that there is no place to hide. Because guilt results in a shutting down and denial of the self, it works against intimacy. Shame involves a recognition of the self, which allows for true revelation of one to the other – which is the very basis of intimacy.

If while dancing with you, I step on your foot, I might automatically say "I'm sorry," begging your forgiveness so that I will not have to feel guilty. In effect, I am proposing that I am not normally the kind of person that steps on feet, so this time was perhaps an accident. However, when I view this event in a responsible way, I cannot deny that, indeed, I am the kind of person that steps on people's feet, because I just did so! Recognizing this, I am flooded with shame (and embarrassment, which is a particular form of shame), knowing that you cannot forgive me for being who I really am; I am caught, revealed as the klutz I am. To dance with me is to take the risk of being stepped on! Knowing this, I cannot any longer ask for your forgiveness; I can only ask for your recognition and acceptance. This attitude of acceptance of shame brings me closer to you (and myself), while the guilt approach further separates us through power dynamics.

People generally think of forgiveness in moral terms. In this way of seeing, I judge you for having done something wrong, and I banish you, moving you away from me. When I forgive you, I permit you to come near again. This involves a hierarchical, one-up/one-down view, where one person is in the right and is a *victim* of the transgressor's behaviour.

A more responsible way to view forgiveness is to recognize that *neither person is wrong*. When I do not like what you have done, I may feel hurt, become angry, and withdraw from you. My act of forgiveness is my letting go of my anger to return to be present with you. In forgiving, I do not permit you to come back to me (you might not have gone anywhere); as *I have moved away*, so I choose to return.

Familiarity Is Not Intimacy

Familiarity arises from having much information about one another. For example, a spy knows his adversary, and a boxer knows his opponent well; in war, generals know how enemies are likely to act, and the soldier in the trenches is hypervigilant to the activities of his counterpart across the battlefield. People who live together for a long time know one another's predictable habits. In all of these examples, the people have much information about one another, establishing a high level of familiarity, but not necessarily very much intimacy. To become more intimate would require the addition of more vulnerability and a greater access to one another's feelings.

When people do not share their inner feelings with each other, they are not intimate, and hence do not feel close. Whether they stay together for security, convenience or any number of other reasons, such people can live a satisfactory life together. However, their relationship will likely lack passion, caring or personal growth. For those experiences to occur requires the addition of the sharing of feelings, especially those of caring and loving. For a full relationship, the darker and more negative feelings must also be surfaced and shared.

This movement from familiarity to intimacy is movingly illustrated in the play *Shadowlands*, in which C.S. Lewis is depicted as discovering about intimacy and loving in his later years. In the following scene, Lewis' wife Joy already knows that she is dying of cancer.[6]

JOY: *We'll have journeys.*

LEWIS: *And little by little I shall dwindle into a husband.*

JOY: *And I shall fatten into a wife. I know your footsteps. I can tell it's you long before you reach the house. I know it's you coming up the road.*

LEWIS: *I never thought I could be so happy, so late in life. Every day when I come home, there you are.*

JOY: *The first words you speak, I know what kind of a mood you're in. Just from the sound of your voice. Even if you don't speak, I still know, from the lines on your face. I watch you when you're working at your desk. I study you. I learn you.*

LEWIS: *Every day when I come home, there you are. I can't get used to that. Every day it surprises me. There you are. It's the sheer availability of the happiness that takes my breath away. I reach out and there you are. I hold you in my arms. I kiss you. All I have to do is reach out, and there you are. You've made the world kind to me. You've made me so grateful. Grateful for all the ordinary domestic pleasures.*

Levels of Intimacy

It is not possible to be equally intimate with large numbers of people. Because time is limited, there is little possibility of sharing a great deal of personal information with more than just a few others. People have a different location and perspective in each of their relationships. In families, all persons have a particular place in each other's lives; some relationships are more intimate than others, while some are merely different in nature. For example, the kind of intimacy that exists between parents is likely different from the closeness shared with children. What is shared with each child may be different, even if the intimacy is of the same degree.

The levels of intimacy for each person form concentric circles of increasing distance. Closest to the centre is the person (or persons) with whom you are establishing a *primary relationship*, with whom you are willing to share the most about yourself, and from whom you can expect the greatest amount of feedback. Such relationships are developed and maintained by a commitment to openness and honesty. Here you will feel the most vulnerable, discover your deepest feelings, and stimulate the greatest growth and connection.

In the next closest concentric ring of intimacy will be a variable number of different people – perhaps your children, your friends, other family members. Each individual locates these people in different places; there is no right way to do this. When children are involved, we recommend that parents locate their primary relationship solidly with one another. Parents who depend upon their children for their primary relationship can contribute towards the children developing feelings of obligation for the parents' health and happiness, along with increasing amounts of guilt and resentment. Furthermore, such children tend to develop unrealistic feelings of entitlement, which may hobble their future initiatives in emotional and vocational endeavours.

Even though each person has concentric rings of decreasing intimacy, the nurture generated within the garden of the primary relationship can be used at all the other levels. The co-creating style established by the process of mutual revelation will be inspirational to people at all the other levels within the sphere of influence of that relationship. What benefits one will benefit all.

5 Sharing Feelings and Emotions

In this chapter we look at ways of sharing feelings such as anger, sadness and hurt as part of a growing intimate relationship. We start with some ideas we think are helpful for the many people who say that they, or their partners, have no feelings or are unemotional. This can be a cause of considerable strain in relationships. For example, one partner might think he's showing his feelings by chopping a cord of wood and taking care of home repairs, and is puzzled when his partner doesn't realize that he is expressing his loving, albeit not in a tearful emotional expression she might recognize more readily.

It can be very useful in such circumstances to distinguish between emotions and feelings. Although sometimes not very aware of them, everybody has feelings. Whether or not we express these feelings *emotionally* is another matter.

Feelings are parameters of the internal environment, just as temperature is one of the measures of the external environment. Some heat fluctuation is necessary in order to experience the temperature for what it is; the change allows for comparison. The same applies to feelings. Just as a person living in a constant temperature will lose heat sense, so it is with one whose internal feelings do not vary greatly. The feelings are there; the problem is that if the feelings do not change much, one tends not to notice them at all. A person who is experienced by others as "cool and controlled" likely has feelings but does not register them.

Emotions are the vehicle through which feelings can be expressed. Emotions are feelings that move out from the internal environment to find expression on the surface in the external world. Thus, a person might feel sad inside, revealing that as emotion through weeping or becoming withdrawn. Many people who say they are afraid of feelings are actually afraid of the external manifestations, the emotions. When this distinction is clarified, they can devote more attention to becoming familiar with their internal environment rather than spending so much energy trying to control what might be revealed. Being afraid of having emotions generally means being afraid of losing control or becoming too vulnerable. Consequently people often develop a pattern of "moving into their heads," becoming rational and distant for the sake of security. Proposing that they allow some emotion is like suggesting a safari into a deep jungle without either provisions or weapons – a terrifying proposition!

Much understanding and encouragement is needed for unemotional people to engage in emotional relationships. Unemotional people are not wrong or abnormal, and any suggestion that they are will tend, understandably, to meet with defensiveness. Embarking upon a project of sharing feelings can be a mutually beneficial adventure in which everyone can learn. The intention of sharing feelings should be discussed and clarified; when it is for the deepening of the relationship, perhaps even a frightened person might be willing to try. Issues of control, intimacy and trust must be addressed; the unemotional person must know that the environment is safe and accepting. Many find it valuable to review the past from the vantage point of discovering the situations that fostered the lack of safety for emotional expression. It can be very useful to identify the catastrophic consequences that people sometimes imagine might occur if they were to express emotion in the present, based on their experiences in the past. In an intimate relationship, people can learn to find ways in the present of expressing and sharing their feelings.

To do this people need to breathe. A regular practice of deep breathing such as we recommend in *A Book about Health and Happiness*[1] can help people who, for whatever reasons, have "lost touch" with their feelings to recognize them once again and share them with their partners. People express their feelings in all sorts of different ways and styles; some are loud and demonstrative, others are quieter and more contained. In an intimate relationship, people can explore their feelings and emotions with one another and contribute to a growing closeness.

Sometimes people experience feelings but have difficulty in articulating what they are. Because they are unable to name the feelings, or explain the causes for the feeling, they may believe that they are not having any at all. We suggest they should learn how to express whatever interior climate they are experiencing – a tightness inside the gut, a tension in the chest, an increased pulse rate, a choking sensation in the throat, a desire to move away, and so on. As people examine and interpret these sensations, they will often come to identify and find names for the feelings, and in this way more clearly understand, and help others understand, their experience.

When feelings move to the surface, they are expressed as emotions. The reasons for becoming emotional are varied. For example, crying may be either a manipulative strategy or an expression of a genuine feelings, ranging from sadness to anger, joy, or nervousness. In intimate relationships, it is important to keep one another informed about the feelings underlying the expressed emotion (and the deeper context and meaning connected to the feeling if it is known), so that they are not misinterpreted. More important, sharing the reasons for the feelings makes for deeper intimacy and knowing of one another; expressing the emotions deepens the way in which energy is shared, providing for a greater sense of connection.

Responsibility for Feelings and the Choice to Share

Feelings are the inner subjective climates related to outer objective experience that help to direct our choices in life. As we saw in our discussion of the Communication Model (Chapter 4), there are basically two broad categories of feelings – the "positive" that tend to urge us towards others and the "negative" that motivate us to move away. Painful feelings such as hurt and anxiety tend to motivate us to withdraw and protect ourselves from others, while the more positive feelings of attraction, closeness, warmth, pleasure and joy motivate us to move closer to others.

Here are some examples of how the words we use to describe feelings might fit in these two categories.

POSITIVE FEELINGS	NEGATIVE FEELINGS
excited	anxious
moved	repulsed
relaxed, comfortable	upset, uncomfortable
joyful, open	tight, closed
energetic, engaged	tired, withdrawn
appreciative	jealous, envious

The generation of these feelings, and the responsibility for them, always originates within the self, never in the object or other. For example, as a parent, I could feel a sense of warmth and pleasure over my children being engaged in a game of cops and robbers; but if I suddenly began to think that they were becoming too serious and real about the game, then I may begin to feel uncomfortable, and become concerned and worried. The difference need not be how they are actually playing; the difference lies more in my ability to interpret their behaviour in a variety of ways!

In relationship, one person might begin to feel anxious when the partner begins to show signs of being secretive. After doing some sleuthing, she discovers that he is busy planning a surprise birthday party for her; as the interpretation changes, her concern fades and she feels a sense of loving warmth for him, even though he continues to be secretive and furtive. Some people would say that his secretive behaviour caused her to be anxious, thus making her a helpless victim to his activities. It is more responsible to understand all our feelings as entirely our own, generated by ourselves through our interpretations of what we perceive. Consequently, it is an option, before becoming distraught, or acting on any particular feeling, to check out with one's partner the interpretations that underlie the feeling.

This is a crucial choice that comes with the realization that all feelings are self-generated over our interpretations. We can decide to share our feelings with the other person, or keep them to ourselves. If we share them, our own energy is released, we establish a greater sense of intimacy because we are better known and can thus feel closer. If we choose to withhold feelings, our energy body closes down; then we feel more distant and unknown to the other, and we forego the opportunity to know the other better – consequently, there is less intimacy. This happens especially frequently with negative feelings; if we do not acknowledge our feelings of repulsion, anger, jealousy or sadness, we become more distant from our partners in the withholding.

If I am uncomfortable with someone because of something that I find unlikable, I am probably afraid to tell her about the discomfort, for fear of hurting her feelings. But I cannot hurt her feelings; she can only hurt her own. Often I am more concerned that she will not like me for feeling the way I do and that she might reject me. If I withhold my feelings, I am less known by her and we are less intimate. If I want to share such feelings, it is important to ask permission before I do so. The more I accept responsibility for my feelings, the more I can share them with her in a non-blaming way that does not demand that she change. The negative judgments then can be received as information that can be either useful or discardable. If I find that I am disappointed or resentful over the outcome, then I know that to that extent my sharing came with an expectation, and was probably controlling, thus endangering our intimacy. Of course, sharing my awareness of a wish to control can itself foster intimacy!

Sharing Anger

Most people are afraid of anger. As children, most of our experience has been with anger that is accompanied by violence (our definition of "violence" is any act that crosses a known boundary). It is important to understand that anger and violence are not the same! We believe the feeling of anger is not primary – it usually is a reaction to some hurt. How we express this natural feeling makes all the difference. When people learn to share anger responsibly, with permission and agreed upon boundaries – that is, non-violently – it can enhance intimacy and closeness. Too often, however, anger is expressed with the intention of being intimidating, controlling and vindictive, all of which will serve to destroy a relationship. When the elements of safety and respect for one another are included, the expression of that same anger can create a greater knowing, understanding and closeness between partners and within families.

The usefulness of anger as a feeling is that it motivates toward action; whether we act violently or non-violently is crucial. This is of special importance in situations in which the person has withdrawn or regressed to a chronic state of helplessness in the face of a threatening or unmanageable power or authority, or after the loss of a loved one through rejection, death or any form of separation. Frequently, such withdrawal is accompanied by a denial or repression of feelings. When repressed anger is expressed, it can provide the energy to move out of this static, blocked state.

The sharing of anger in safe, non-violent, responsible ways can be accomplished through the use of such techniques as "fair fighting" that were first proposed by George Bach in his book *The Intimate Enemy*.[2] In the "Vesuvius technique" described by Bach, the angry person receives the consent of the rest of the family to blow out his feelings in front of them, after carefully setting the limits of safety and time. It is worth noting that in the expression of anger, some unfair blame and name-calling can creep in; this can be allowed with the provision that at the end of the Vesuvius, it will be acknowledged and "cleaned up" by the angry person taking full ownership for his or her feelings. Committing to, and following through on, the "clean up" time after the anger has been expressed is essential to the success of the Vesuvius process. This reconnection time, in which both partners share, reinforces the intent of intimacy.

Other safe ways of expressing anger include using punching bags, pounding pillows or mattresses, tearing up old telephone books or catalogues, kneading bread, or chopping wood. With children, safe situations for expressing anger can be created through play, throwing rocks into the ocean, punching air bags, kicking mattresses, and hollering loudly. Keep in mind that the expression of anger should be boundaried and safe, always emphasizing the difference between sharing anger (which is encouraged) and sharing violence (which is not).

Many times, people are afraid to express anger to or about people they love or depend upon, for fear of hurting those people's feelings. To deepen in intimacy, it is important to reassure them that nobody can hurt another's feelings, that each of us is responsible for our own feelings, and that it is safe to share them. Sometimes, at first, such people need to learn to express anger with the object of the anger being physically absent from the situation. Hopefully, they later can find the courage to share the anger in person; generally, it is advisable to explain the purpose first to the persons who are objects of the anger, to help them to understand the intention of this process, and to receive their permission to continue.

We write more about this important topic in *Being: A Manual for Life* and highly recommend Joann Peterson's *A Book about Anger, Boundaries and Safety* to anyone who wishes to explore this further.[3]

Sharing Jealousy

Jealousy is another feeling that people in relationship have difficulty in handling. This is because such feelings have mostly been used to control one another's behaviour – because I am hurting over what you are doing, you should stop doing it! Actually, as with all feelings, jealousy is self-generated. It stems from early childhood feelings of insecurity, fears of being not good enough, and fears of abandonment. In jealousy, one has made the other person more important than oneself, moving one's centre from within, and placing it in the other person. On the positive side, this kind of projection is a symptom of greatly valuing the other; on the negative side, the hurt and jealousy could be used to control and own the other. If jealousy is used for control, it can destroy any relationship. If jealousy is shared, rather than used for control, it can be viewed from a positive light; both members of the partnership can rejoice in how important they are to one another *so long as they agree not to allow those feelings to govern what they do!* People can hurt with their jealousies and share them, without any demands that their partners change their behaviour. When the partner responds to these fearful hurt feelings with sensitivity, understanding and acceptance, the result can be a high level of intimacy and caring. In a close relationship with an atmosphere of acceptance, people can feel safe enough to address past issues and to heal old wounds of unresolved hurt and rejection from childhood.

Sharing Sadness and Hurt

Most people believe that when they are sad or hurt in any way, others tend to see them in a negative light. Another common belief is that sadness should not be shared, as those who love us deserve to have enjoyable, rather than depressing, experiences. People who think that suffering should be felt in silence or isolation tend to repress all such hurts. This contraction of feelings results in a restriction of life energy; the feelings tend to leak out in a minimal fashion over a prolonged time. This attitude has generally been learned in childhood from parents who say such things as "Stop your crying before I give you something to *really* cry about!" or "Go to your room! Nobody likes to see your long face!"

In this environment, children soon learn that their sad feelings are not respected; still, they frequently work to produce guilt in their parents so that they can get their own way. This is seen in the common mechanism of "feeling sorry for yourself." With hurt feelings, there is no better salve than self-pity; yet, too often this self-soothing has been abused and overused as a control mechanism to get one's own way. The pout, the extended lower lip, the whine and groan are all part of that process. As with jealousy, when self-pity is expressed freely without controlling the other, the experience can be truly healing. Because self-pity is too often linked to controlling, a productive solution is to remove yourself from the company of the other when you feel a good self-pity attack coming on, and give full vent to those delicious feelings in private. If you have an intimate partner, this event could be shared (with an agreed time limit!); or you can describe the feelings to your partner *after* the self-pity party!

Boredom and Apathy

There are some important differences between boredom and apathy, though both reflect an existential loss of the sense of purpose. The apathetic person has disengaged from real contact with the world and has settled into a low energy state with little interest or caring. In his book *Love and Will*, Rollo May describes apathy as "the withdrawal of love and will,"[4] and, as such, the opposite of love. Such an individual is indifferent, lacking in passion and emotion, uninvolved, detached and unrelated, with little will to do anything about it. The energy body is so contracted that it is unreachable and ineffective. In relationship, such a person no longer cares to fight or even engage in any way; both meaning and hope are lost and there is no motivation to change. In an apathetic relationship, partners may go about their daily routines in an effective way, but utterly without passion. Because they do not fight, others tend to see their relationship as ideal. The way to get through and past apathy is to mobilize the fixated energy. We encourage partners in apathy to engage in some energetic activity such as a rousing card game or a tennis match. Breathing together can accomplish this too; so a brisk walk together, or a time of joint exercising in some way can help to get things moving again, physically and emotionally.

On the other hand, a person experiencing boredom is filled with energy, with a restlessness and a desire to change. Although there may be little interest in other people or the task at hand, the self has a strong urge to find something or somebody in which to develop an interest. Too often, bored people blame something or someone else for the feeling of boredom ("they are boring" or "it is boring"), thus keeping themselves as victims in a state of helplessness. In our view, it is those people themselves that produce the boredom by not engaging their interest.

To take ownership of the feeling of boredom means assuming the responsibility to do something about it, using one's will, initiative, courage and creativity to make necessary changes. In relationships, revealing feelings of boredom to one another is important, as the problem is a shared one that requires shared solutions; when one person is bored, both partners are challenged. At this point a review of the Communication Model would be helpful, stressing ownership of one's feelings and ruling out all blame. Remember the dictum that *there are no boring people – there are only bored people!*

Most people assume that boredom arises from a lack of interest in the subject or person. Many times this is so, in which case it would be useful to pursue an investigation as to why so little energy is being invested there. When facing boredom in a relationship, people might consider attempting a "trial interest" for a limited time in order to discover what is going on in themselves and to actively engage their capacity to be curious about the other. In some instances, boredom is actually an active defence against becoming involved. In intimate relationships, it is worthwhile to consider the possibility that boredom is masking a fear about intimacy; the greater the emotional charge related to that boredom, the greater is the possibility that it may be a defence.

The Interior Landscape

Within each person, all of the feelings exist as in a huge landscape – here is a cool valley of tranquillity, there a desert of despair, while in this area are the expansive fields of openness, over here the mountains of exhilaration and joy, close by the frightening cliffs of risk-taking, over there the gentle rains of sadness, here the steamy jungles of desire. While in the midst of any of these areas of your inner geography, you will tend to believe that that's all there is. You will tend to forget that you have merely brought into the foreground that particular feeling with which you are now in touch. All of the other feelings – the other aspects of your landscape – are still present, even though they are currently in the background. You can be sure that you will move on to the other areas at another time. Remembering this will provide you with some perspective when you feel irretrievably stuck in a part of your inner landscape of feelings. Remember the peaks when you are stuck in the swamps. While you are visiting your joyful mountaintops, keep in mind that your deserts are not far away, so that when you slide down into them, you need not despair. Keep your compass and your perspective!

6 From Object to Person

Objectification

The human capacity to objectify one another – that is, to understand and treat one another more as things or objects that are of potential use to us than as living individuals with their own thoughts, desires and feelings – is remarkable. In our work, we have sought to understand this phenomenon principally through the lens of object relations theory.

According to this view, the early human experience is largely one of objectification. Infants are physiological beings capable of physical survival only through being taken care of by another – any caretaker who is prepared to feed them, clean them up and keep them warm. Humans at birth have only the potential of a personal self; thus, early experiences are as one impersonal object to another – as child to parent, not as person to person. In this primary paradigm, no person is necessary; at the beginning, babies merely need beings that are prepared to play the roles of provider and protector. For this, "parents" are ideally suited. Motivated by some primordial urge to procreate and care for their young – an urge that is contained in the genetic code and mediated by a complicated system of endocrine and biochemical imperatives – parents respond to this task with relish. Neither the child nor the parent, however, has any idea who this other person really is; nor does it matter at this beginning stage. It is an object-object ("objectified") relationship of great importance to the human race – but one in which neither party is privileged to see the real person behind the object.

This condition has a complex set of parameters that operate to ensure the safety and health of the developing child-being whose "self" has yet to be born. Roles, expectations, a sense of entitlement, obligations, morality and taboos, guilt and pride all are a part of this objectifying experience. With ever-growing consciousness, the self of the child is finally "hatched," with the potential of developing into a whole person. Only after this hatching occurs does the possibility exist of having some person-to-person interaction. Unfortunately, since the objectifying experience has become so deeply ingrained both in individuals and in the operation of society at large, for most people, person-to-person contact will be a rare occurrence!

We have found this frame of thinking about objectification extremely useful. Nevertheless, it does not tell the whole story; indeed some people question its basic premises. Object relations theorists maintain that the birth of the self is somewhere toward the end of the third year of life; and until that time, they assert, the young person has been mostly living in an objectified world. Others disagree. Daniel Stern, for example, says that the self is present from the beginning, as a "prestructured emergent entity."[1] Current research provides good evidence that children are empathetic and interactive much earlier than the object relations approach would allow; in this view there is much less emphasis on the role of objectification in the early stages of life.

This disagreement has given rise in psychological theory to what Morris Berman refers to as "murky territory."[2] We ourselves see merit in both approaches. We like Stern's idea of the self as a preconfigured potential, and at the same time we see the value in directly addressing the many issues of objectification which inevitably arise in a developing life. So, in our own thinking, we utilize both viewpoints. To us, infants seem relatively little capable of recognizing the concerns and interests of those around them; and until about three years of age, children are good at following rules, but not adept at being considerate of the feelings and experience of others. Yet, this is not as clear cut as some object relations theorists have tended to think. So, our position at present is that the self as personal is only a possibility at birth, and develops in interaction with other humans. At the same time, we do believe that a distinct *being*, full of potential both to objectify and become personal, is present from the beginning, the seed of an individual personality.[3]

Whatever the genesis of the self and its capacity to objectify and be personal, it seems clear to us that most children are raised by a process of training rather than one that encourages personal development. They are taught appropriate behaviour, they learn whom they can depend on, they learn how to distinguish right from wrong, they know what it means to be grateful and guilty. Thus they learn to operate in a world of roles and objects; but they are not provided with much education in relating to others as persons or becoming a person themselves. They do the best they can, struggling to become perfect as successful objects playing socially acceptable roles (that is, they become "good" children, then later "good" students, husbands, wives, citizens, business people, and so on). Such striving may be quite effective for most of their lives, providing them with a meaning for their existence, especially if they succeed. However, at some stage (even if they succeed) many begin to wonder what it all has been for. Feeling some lack of fulfilment, they may come to realize that they do not know themselves or others as persons. All they know well are their roles – their objectified self!

Mirroring

Developing the self as a person rather than as an object is a complex process, in which *mirroring* and exercising the use of *boundaries* play important roles. As the child-as-object is being cared for, the infant looks searchingly into the caretakers' eyes for reflected messages about who the child is. Because most parents see their children as possessions and objects to be trained, *that* is what is contained in the reflected message. As we discuss in more detail in Chapter 18, most parents serve as *distorted* mirrors – either magnifying their children's importance (convex mirroring) or diminishing it (concave mirroring); rarely do parents see their children as the *persons* they actually are (*direct* mirroring). Thus, most children develop their self-concept through their roles, and see their parents in the same way. This parent-child relationship is mainly an object-to-object one, rather than person-to-person. To become more personal, the parties of the relationship must provide direct mirroring for one another. Because children have little experience or authority to do so with parental figures, such a process must begin with the parents. Parents themselves have had little practice with their own parents, so they likely will learn it with peers. This is one of the main functions of intimate relationships.

Boundaries and Walls

A boundary is the felt interface between self and other; it is flexible and in constant motion, moving outward to reach for experience, and contracting to protect the self from experience. Contact at this boundary stimulates an excitation within the self, motivating movement toward contact or away from it; these directional excitations are the feelings of interpersonal communication. An individual's feelings depend upon that person's interpretations of the quality of contact.

Roles are useful for protecting the self from vulnerable contact. In taking on roles, the self builds walls to contain itself and control others. Unlike boundaries, walls are inflexible and unchanging, characterized by "shoulds" and rules, and have little ability to adapt to changing conditions. Within these walls are the major defence mechanisms that are used to maintain distance from others. They also contain all of the social training that provides people with social acceptance and financial reward. Because walls are thick and impermeable, they are unresponsive, and have little sensitivity to those outside of them. Walls are like grand castles that have been erected for looks and defence – impressive and useful for keeping out enemies, but cold and difficult to live within.

Walls can only be changed from the inside. In intimate relationships, a person can lower the moat, and open the doors and windows to reveal what is going on inside. Taking your partner on a tour of the walls is to acknowledge where, how and why you are defensive and controlling, providing information about your inner world and offering a vulnerable state of intimacy. When you are secure enough with your partner's visits into your inner world, then you can begin to dismantle your walls and *replace them with boundaries.* Many people who have had walls for a long time get too enthusiastic about getting rid of them when they find an appropriate partner – they tend to want to *merge* with the other, which is another way of losing the self. "Give thyself, but give thyself not away."[4]

Boundaries are established by first recognizing that you are fully responsible only for yourself, your own feelings, and your own behaviour; there are no grounds for blaming others. Then you can see all of the options that are open to you; in choosing any of these options, be prepared to accept the consequences of that choice. The choices that are made at the interface between the self and others create the boundary; remember that the choice can be a "yes" as well as a "no." With boundaries, you can change your mind so long as you keep others informed of such changes. In this way, boundaries remain flexible and are in less danger of solidifying into walls again. To become more boundaried is to become more fully human. *Persons* can live fully with boundaries between them in intimate relationships; *objects* (i.e., objectified persons) are separated by walls and are only capable of familiarity at best.

To encourage the development of the person in their offspring, parents must always acknowledge the perspective of the child. "It's your bedtime, go to bed now!" expresses a rule without regard for the person. How different it would be if the parent could say, "I know it must be difficult to stop your current activity [acknowledging the person], but to get enough rest for tomorrow's activities [consequences], you'll have to get some sleep now [boundaries]." Rules are shortcuts to control behaviour, but they have the unfortunate consequence of building walls and making objects; boundaries, on the other hand, strengthen the development of the person. Permissiveness is an abandonment of both walls and boundaries that arrests development of the person; often, children will interpret permissiveness as lack of caring (which it often is!).

Political and Personal

We define "political" as being related to power; generally, the political is involved with domination and submission. "Personal" has to do with the unfolding development of the human being, without any reference to power or domination or submission. From the vantage of the political, the person is not valued; in the personal, humanness is of concern. As people acquire power, they lose touch with their authentic nature; they become powerful, but out of touch. When people become more authentic, they manifest "strength" in being in touch with themselves and others; although they might have little power, they are present in themselves.

Most educational systems are authoritarian in nature, promoting objectifying behaviour that may ultimately lead to socioeconomic security. Usually, people are taught to develop *power* over others; in this way, education tends to become *political*, and its concern is in dealing with the other objectified beings in the external environment. Fortunately, some schools and teachers do attempt to reach and teach the person to grow with an inner *strength*. Nevertheless, most people have experienced a great deal of this politicized education at home and at school, "for their own good." When they enter into relationship, they usually do so with an objectifying ("political") attitude, concerned with the power to control or to be controlled, to own or be owned.

The Garden: From the Political to the Personal

For a relationship to serve as a garden that promotes growth, we recommend that partners agree to weed out political interpersonal behaviour by identifying it when it emerges. A basic principle is to reveal and acknowledge all the ways in which each person attempts to control the other. Once political behaviour is identified, the focus should then shift to sharing the feelings underlying that political behaviour – is there some hurt or fear in that person? When the relationship remains political, the atmosphere is like a police station or courtroom, with partners trying to determine who hurt whom, or who really said what, or who really is to blame for the mess that has been created. When a relationship becomes personal, both parties stand revealed and vulnerable; they both acknowledge responsibility for their own feelings, and are willing to share them. In such an atmosphere both individuals can grow in strength.

Objectification can serve us very well; it is worthy of being honoured rather than reviled. In order to create an intimate relationship, however, people must learn new skills that go beyond objectification. With an understanding partner, these skills can be learned and developed.

Incorporating Objectification into Intimacy

In intimate relationships, much passion can be created by objectifying the other and playing power games. Such is the nature of sexual excitement; such is the pleasure of dependency. Most sentimentality is based on objectification; our most popular love songs announce "I can't live without you" (i.e., I have shifted my centre into you), "You hurt me when you left" (i.e., you are to blame for my pain), and "Nobody knows the trouble I've seen" (i.e., a full attack of objectifying self-pity). Life without these objectifying experiences would certainly be dull! In intimate relationships there can be some agreement for partners to feel and express those feelings to one another, *so long as they do not control one another!* A productive agreement would allow partners to play with those feelings, expressing them for limited times and in designated places. Then these potentially destructive elements become more like movie theatre experiences – they can be enjoyed thoroughly for the moment, without controlling the direction of the relationship. We summarize it this way: *Feel, but ultimately get real!*

The Reward for Being Personal

Even though it may be risky, the act of moving outside the walls and defences of an object position has many potential rewards. It is an opportunity finally to learn how to become a person – beyond depersonalizing rules, obligations and expectations!

Through the development of the intimacy of a relationship garden, people can discover themselves beyond the limitations and encumbrances of their objectified roles.

> *The basic word I-You can be spoken only with one's whole being. The concentration and fusion into a whole being can never be accomplished by me, can never be accomplished without me. I require a You to become; becoming I, I say You. All actual life is encounter.* – Martin Buber[5]

PART II

The Stages of Relationship

7 The Relationship Cycle

The bird a nest, the spider a web, man friendship. – William Blake[1]

People seek relationships in order to satisfy deep motivations; there seems to be a basic drive to associate and establish ongoing ties with other people. Often, people seek others to compensate for their own limitations and to overcome fears first experienced in infancy. Frequently, people select partners in an attempt to mitigate their inner feelings of emptiness (angst or existential anxiety) and loneliness.

Commonly, people also use their partners to justify themselves. They either crave the agreement of a like mind, in order to feel more secure; or they want a scapegoat to blame for their troubles. At first glance, this seems a useful way of making life dependable; if people dedicate energy to being "right," whether with or in opposition to a partner, there is little time left to feel basic anxieties and insecurities. However, they also feel much less of themselves, and can become walled off from their partners.

As we have already seen, it is also possible to become vulnerable and revealed to one's partner. This may be risky but can open up new possibilities in relationship, including learning about self and other through intimate dialogue.

In this part of the book we present a cycle of stages that are possible in relationship. Sadly, many people's experience is more or less limited to the first two stages we describe, Romance and Power Struggle. However, any two people who have good will, intention and endurance can experience all the stages of relationship and deepen their awareness and acceptance of themselves and each other in the process. This applies in male-female and same-sex adult relationships and also in parent-child relationships, friendships, and work relationships.

The Five Stages of Relationship

The five stages of relationship we present in this book were first proposed by Susan Campbell in *A Couple's Journey*.[2] Her work has provided a basis for our own, although we have made some significant changes.

Firstly, because the term "Stability" seems to imply some kind of static condition, in this book we have used the word "Integration" in its place. Thus, our five stages are Romance, Power Struggle, Integration, Commitment and Co-creativity. Secondly, although the stages were originally enunciated in a vertical list, we believe this process is better represented by a circle, a repeating and evolving cycle, which we diagram on the facing page. There is remarkable similarity between the process of relationships and the dynamic energy states of the Chinese Five Stages of Change, and the gestalt cycle that we detail in our book *The Illuminated Heart*.[3]

Every turn of the wheel involves a return with more experience and more degrees of freedom. Hence, if we could make our diagram three dimensional it would show that the movement from Co-creativity to Romance is not a return to the original Romance, but extends into the space outside or above the previous Romance phase, indicating the opening of a spiral. Life, energy and relationships evolve in ever widening spirals.

In a relationship garden, the overall movement is from objectification to subjective knowing of the self and other. The early stages (Romance and Power Struggle) are characterized by much chaotic energy (passion, obsession, sexual excitement, and anger), whereas the energy in the later stages is more calm, coherent and fulfilling. In the earlier stages, partners have very little knowing of each other. A developing closeness is characterized by increases in knowing of self and other. As this increases, so also the possibility for intimacy grows; with revelation, vulnerability, curiosity and commitment, a mature and enduring relationship can be established.

The Process of the Relationship Cycle

These stages can be experienced in all relationships – husband/wife, lovers, parent/child, siblings, other family relationships, business partnerships, and friends. All people can potentially go through these phases of relationship. The progress through the stages is from imagination with little experience of the other in Romance, to the turmoil of the Power Struggle, to getting to know one another in Integration, to mutual willed activities in Commitment, to creativity in the Co-creative phase. People can learn the principles of the process in any kind of relationship; what they have learned in one relationship is applicable to all of their other relationships.

Power, control, entitlement and isolation tend to diminish as people move through the stages. At the same time, humanness, knowledge, and self-awareness grow. There is also steady development of responsibility and strength. A sense of aloneness increases, though not loneliness; in fact, the sense of aloneness is accompanied by a sense of being connected to others and to life.[4] Strength, passion and humility increase. One's capacity for intimate contact steadily grows. There is less caretaking and more being in touch with the other person. The earlier stages of Romance and Power

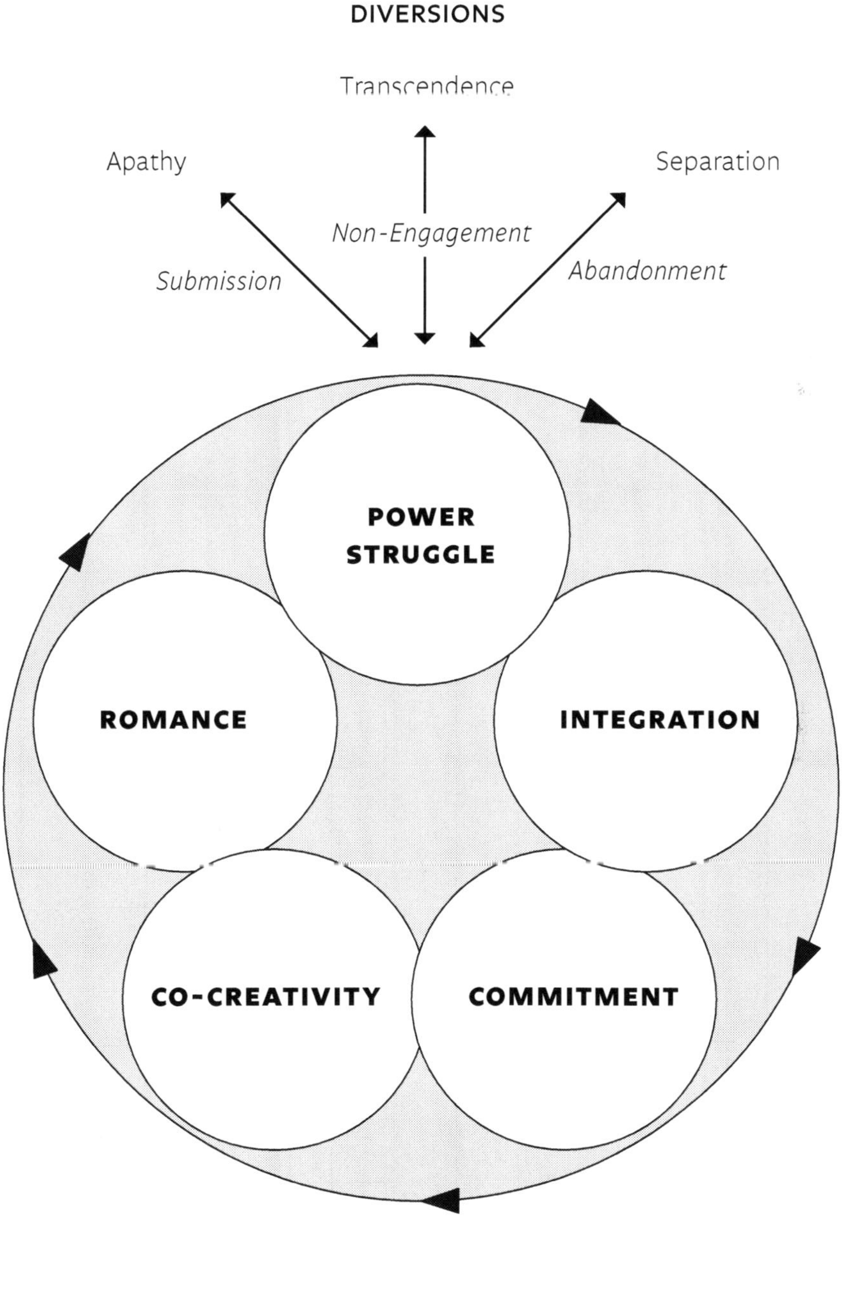

The Relationship Cycle

Struggle are characterized by high energy and excitement. In Integration and the phases that can ensue, people experience much more fulfilment, with less of the frantic drivenness of the earlier phases.

In the following chapters, we will go into detail about the unfolding stages and their characteristics. We also offer suggestions for working through these stages in order to keep the cycle moving.

Being in Different Stages in Different Phases of Life

It is possible to be at different stages in different phases of one's life. For example, an individual might be predominantly in Romance with her newborn infant, while she is frequently in Power Struggle with her spouse, and in a state of Integration with her older children; she might experience Commitment with her community work, and Co-creativity in her art projects.

Two different people can be at different stages in the same relationship. The wife might be in Integration with the husband, because she accepts him for who he is; meanwhile, he may be in Romance with her, because he refuses to see her beyond his image projections. This does not mean the relationship has to end! Indeed, in most relationships, there are frequently periods where the partners are at different stages. When they learn to acknowledge these differences without defence and to appreciate each other's viewpoint, the relationship can continue to grow. When couples use this difference in phases to blame and criticize, the whole endeavour is threatened.

The Diversions from the Cycle

The states of Apathy, Transcendence and Separation are not stages in the developmental cycle, but occur when people divert from engagement, and thus step off the circle. We discuss these side paths more thoroughly in Chapter 9. The process of the Relationship Cycle is dynamic, moving, energetic. Often when people move into the diversions, the result is an interruption in the flow of the cycle, involving fixation and limitation in engagement.

Stages within Stages

Just as in the Chinese Five Stages of Change, where every stage contains the others, every stage of the relationship cycle contains every other stage. So, there is a Commitment in every stage; there is a kind of Power Struggle at every stage (for example, the struggle to create together or to share ideas); there is a Romance (a dream) that fuels every stage; every stage has its own capacity for Integration; a Co-creative possibility exists in every stage (for example, there can be a Co-creativity of sharing romantic fantasies).

Partners are rarely in one stage to the exclusion of the others. Commonly, a couple who is largely in Integration Stage can readily revert to a Power Struggle in times of stress. Certain situations will provide a trigger for the re-entry of earlier stage behaviour; for example, when he buys her a special gift at Christmas, she might well re-enter the Romance Stage with him for a time.

Some Images

For those of you who like visual metaphors, the following images might stimulate some associations.

ROMANCE	a movie theatre
POWER STRUGGLE	a battlefield
INTEGRATION	a lush garden
APATHY	a desert
SEPARATION	a single figure under a street lamp
TRANSCENDENCE	an echoing cathedral
COMMITMENT	a drawn bow with stored, constrained potential energy
CO-CREATIVITY	the artist's workshop

Intentions in Relationship

In each of the five stages, the following are useful questions:

What do I want?
What do you want?
What do we want?
What do we choose to do?

Another useful question is "What is this all for?" The answer could be "for happiness," "for excellence," or "for security." The answer people give determines how they will proceed through the various stages of relationship. If they are seeking vulnerability and intimacy, their relationship will have a very different texture than if they are after security, or power, or sex, or some other aspiration. These queries involve the notion of will and intentionality; in our Communication Model, this is the aspect of intention, through which people decide what actions they will take.

People define their position first through their attitudes, and then through their efforts. In living in relationship, partners can come to know themselves more fully, and thus they can move increasingly in harmony with self and other. People pass through the various stages by a mutual interaction and sharing. They tend the garden of the relationship through the various seasons; their success in dealing with the contingencies of each phase is dependent upon how much mutuality and sharing they are willing to have together.

8 Romance

Q. What do most people do on a first date?
A. On the first date, they just tell each other lies, and that usually gets them interested enough to go for a second date. – Martin (age 10)
A. Many daters just eat pork chops and french fries and talk about love. – Craig (age 9)[1]

The first phase of any relationship is based upon the imagination; in this "Romance," very little is known about the other. The relationship is a dream, a story, involving hopes and expectations; the partners have little experience of each other. Because they do not know each other, they first relate to their mutual image projections – their objectifications of each other. This is not limited to the traditional male-female Romances of "falling in love." Indeed, the first phase of any relationship is a Romance, in that the parties do not know each other; this is equally the case with budding friendships, having a new child, or in a fledgling business enterprise. Hopes and dreams are strong, and the sobering influence of experience has not had the opportunity to modulate feelings.

Thrilling, but Not True Closeness

The period of Romance is a most stimulating time in any relationship. The world seems brighter, and people in love feel more energetic, with more sense of purpose and zest for life. They are willing to consider unusual things, and every moment seems fresh. Indeed, Romance is the spice of life!

In the Romance stage, and in the objectification of sexual charge, people tend to feel important and close to each other. Yet, on closer examination, we can see that they are actually only obsessed with each other's image. What they feel is a simulacrum of true closeness; in their objectification, they are disconnected from the universal energy, and thus are actually separate, even though their experience is one of being close and connected. They are excited, but they are not resonating. They have a charge, but they are not intimate.

This excitement and strong interest in each other also occurs in the early stages of nonsexual relationships. At the beginning, people generally do not relate to each other as persons; instead, they relate to each other's images.

Romance with Children

New parents usually have a Romance with the new infant in the household. They are full of excitement for buying baby clothes and planning the future for this little being. The dreams, the imaginings, are very stimulating, and provide an energy of engagement that is nourishing to both the child and the parents alike.

Romance in Friendship

At the beginning of a friendship, people are enthusiastic about their new-found ally. They have energy to talk together, to discover areas of common interest, and they often pursue many stimulating activities together. They are in the Romance phase, as they don't really know each other yet.

Romance in Business

The beginning of business ventures is also a Romance. Initially, the whole project is a dream, undampened by experience. The fervour at the beginning is similar to the beginning of a courtship. In both cases, the individuals are eager to get together, to talk, to plan, to dream. The air crackles with excitement as they imagine what will be in their future together. Whether they are talking about how wonderful it would be to have a little cottage together with children and pets, or a giant factory pouring out gadgets to the world, the state of enthusiasm – the Romance – is the same.

The Root of Romance: Infantile Insecurity

The first Romance occurs in infancy with parents or protectors. To infants, parents seem larger than life, wise, strong and ever capable. This is the fabric of the child-parent Romance: children have an unrealistic view that their parents are all-powerful and can protect the child at all times. For the infant, this objectification and inflation of parental potency helps them to cope with their insecurities; yet it constitutes a denial of their basic state of anxiety. This dependency upon an external object to provide protection and security becomes the paradigm for all subsequent relationships – a search for "someone out there" who will make everything all right.

The Pattern of Being Pleasing

Children establish relationships of pleasing their parents, in order to avoid being abandoned. In the infantile logic, if they are pleasing, the parents will want to stay with them, and thus their protection will continue. This theme is adopted as a basic pattern, and is carried on throughout life. In later relationships, people continue to try to please others, in order to establish the security of a relationship (someone to help and protect them), to help deny their basic existential aloneness.[2]

Following upon the relationship with their parents, children seek to please friends and teachers; as adults, they have romances with partners and spouses. Then, later in life, people pursue romance with their own offspring, and even later with grandchildren. This theme of wanting to please others continues in these later relationships. Ultimately, it is based upon a denial of basic insecurities, and involves a desperate dependency upon someone else.

Objects, not Persons

Q. What exactly is marriage?
A. Marriage is when you get to keep your girl and don't have to give her back to her parents. – Eric (age 6)[3]

In Romance, the other is not a person so much as an object that has the function of taking care of one's anxiety and needs. This perspective is rooted in the objectifying experiences of early childhood. For infants, this objectification is normal; they learn to relate to the outside world by objectifying it, dividing it up into "objects" and learning to interact with these objects in their field. The early relationship objects (generally the parents and other siblings) are seen as protectors and caregivers. This becomes the prototype for later objects of choice for relationships.

In parent-child relationships, this objectification occurs equally on both sides. Parents do not know their children at first. The children are little objects, projections of parental imaginations and desires. Indeed, infants have scarcely developed, and there is little of a "personal" nature to know. Also, the child does not know the actual personhood of the parent; the parent is largely an object to the child, necessary to fulfil desires, to protect, and to minister to needs. Many people do not outgrow this romantic view of their parents, and later in life, when some parents want to establish a more interpersonal relationship, it is often the children who resist, for example by refusing to shift from calling the parents "Mom" or "Dad" into using their given names.

Many people do not move far beyond this state of objectification in relationship, even as adults. They continue to relate to objects, rather than people, by operating within roles, and expecting others to do the same.

Obviously, the relationship at this stage of objectification (the Romance phase) is not personal, as neither individual knows the other. Because there is little knowing, there cannot be any true acceptance of the personhood of the other.

The Perfect Partner

Q. What is the proper age to get married?
A. Once I'm done with kindergarten, I'm going to find me a wife. – Bert (age 5)[4]

In the Romance phase, people project their concept of the perfect partner onto the current individual of choice. Children do this with their parents to cope with insecurity; parents do this with their children to have an object of meaning; dating couples do this with each other; and the same process of projection occurs in business relationships as well.

People select someone for relationship who has specific attributes, consistent with an internal image. In short, people have a codified notion of who will be a perfect partner, and they are attracted to someone who fits this image. They believe that if they can make a relationship work with this ideal person, then the shortcomings and insecurities of their life will be solved. The problem is that in looking for someone else to fulfil their romantic wishes, people place their centre outside themselves; hence they remain weak, unknown to themselves, and incapable of caring dialogue with others. In relationship, their partners are objects to possess, not persons.

The Microdot

Robert Stoller, in his book *Sexual Excitement*, describes the concept of the "microdot."[5] This is a term that was used in World War II by experts in espionage. Vital information was photographed and the picture was reduced repeatedly in size, until all the information was contained in a small dot (the microdot), the size of a period at the end of a sentence in a book. Then, a period was punched from a designated page in a book, and replaced with the microdot – the encoded reduced information. Someone could then carry the book across a dangerous border, delivering it safely into the hands of collaborators, who simply had to turn to the proper page, and have the microdot blown up, to see all the information. In a similar fashion, the attributes of the "perfect partner" are condensed and encoded; when people meet someone, they can subconsciously check off that individual's attributes against the checklist of the internal microdot. This explains the specificity of the sexual charge, as we explore further in Chapter 17. It also explains the very exact elements that determine who is deemed attractive for all sorts of relationship.

To the child, whose world is insecure, the idealized parent figure has many features of the "saviour," who will make life safe and meaningful. At the beginning, the elements of the saviour are quite vague and generalized. As people grow and gain experience, they commonly stay with the infantile theme of looking for a parent or saviour figure to take away their pain and insecurity. As they develop relationships, they continue to look for the microdot saviour, who has the qualities that will overcome their internal struggles and discomforts. The underlying theme in Romance is that *someone out there is going to protect me, help me, save me.* The romantic story becomes increasingly elaborate, and the characters in the story begin to fill out, and have very definite characteristics. These characteristics might include a certain tone of voice, particular mannerisms, a predilection for certain authors or subjects of interest. These elements that are part of people's Romance are encoded in their personal microdot (the detailed romantic image of who will save them).

Desperateness in Romance

Romance is an attempt to deal with fear of non-being; hence, underlying Romance is a desperateness. Romance actually involves a great deal of control, aimed at reducing the insecurities of life. In D.H. Lawrence's novel *Women in Love*, a young man tries to save his girlfriend from drowning; she pulls him down in her attempt to cling to him, and they both perish.[6] This is allegorical of how people's Romance tends to drown the selfness of both parties in their desperate clinging attempts to avoid reality. In a relationship at the Romance stage, it can be as though two unconscious robots are in operation, with no actual persons visible. Sometimes, there is an eerie, deathlike quality lurking under the fervour of Romance – the desire for it is so strong, it is so unreal, and the people seem so lost and desperate in their obsessions with each other.

Hope, Disappointment and Faith

In the Romance phase, hope is a common underlying theme. Dissatisfied with their basic insecurities, people commonly hope that a newfound romantic partner will solve their problems, and that life will become better. Hope involves a basic lack of acceptance of self and other. Indeed, in the

Romance stage, awareness of self and other are so clouded by the romantic dreams and projections that people have insufficient information to actually accept anyone or anything with any validity.

Hope and faith are different. Whereas hope involves a dissatisfaction with self and present circumstance, and is dependent upon external events or people to provide change, faith is self-affirming and accepting of life as it is.[7] In Romance, people hope that life will be different, or better, or fuller; their hoping involves a lack of acceptance and a thrust toward change.

Disappointment is the other face of hope; like hope, disappointment is based in a discontent with the present. The Romance phase is generally destined for disappointment, because the things people are trying to change probably will not alter at all; once they emerge from the swoon of Romance, they are once again faced with their basic insecurities, and their hoping flips into disappointment.

Romance is Exciting

The stage of Romance is an exciting time. There is some degree of romance in any relationship. Because people do not know each other at the beginning, they have to depend upon their intuition and their past experiences with other people, which they project upon their new partner. In the Romance, they imagine what could be.

There is nothing wrong with Romance. Indeed, this is a very energetic phase. Imagination is high, little is known for certain, and much is possible. There usually is much enthusiasm and vitality in this stage.

In Romance, the world can change. When we imagine, and then try to realize the romance, we are recreating the world afresh. This is the projected possible. Although the purpose of the original infant's Romance was to overcome pain and uncertainty, later in life, Romance can be for excitement – the stimulation of doing something new.

9 Power Struggle

Q. When is it OK to kiss someone?
A. You should never kiss a girl unless you have enough bucks to buy her a ring and her own VCR, 'cause she'll want to have videos of the wedding. – Allan (age 10)[1]

Romance Fades: Enter the Power Struggle

The Romance phase persists by limiting information; in these circumstances the images partners project onto one another can be maintained by low lights and sensual diversions. When couples are dating and can go home to their separate abodes to dream about each other, the Romance is maintained. When they move in with each other, they find it more difficult to maintain the projections of their romantic images of each other. As partners become more familiar, they gradually accumulate evidence of each other's true nature and behaviour. There is nothing like seeing one's partner's personal habits on an ongoing basis to have reality insistently begin to impinge. In such a state, one might say, "This is not my handsome prince (or my beautiful princess) after all! This is a person who has qualities that I find quite objectionable! However, all is not lost! I can devote my efforts to changing my partner into the perfect being that he (or she) could be." This marks the entry into the next phase of relationship – the Power Struggle stage.

This dawning of awareness of the true nature of the other occurs in all relationships, given time and experience together. The Romance of finding a perfect partner fades into a realization that one is living with someone with particular foibles, desires and habits. Similarly, the Romance of having a baby is eclipsed by the weariness that comes with night-after-night experiences of a crying infant. The Romance of a new job soon gives way to the recognition that this occupation is not going to fulfil all one's dreams.

Gentle Beginnings

Generally, the manoeuvres of the Power Struggle stage begin with quiet admonition, urging the other to change slightly. "Dear, you would look so much more handsome if you were to comb your hair like this" actually means "You would more perfectly fit my ideal man microdot if you were to alter your appearance." People buy each other gifts of clothing to wear and encourage behaviours that suit their image projections. Of course, their partners never fully get the message, and they insist upon remaining the persons they are. Thus, people are thwarted in their desire to turn their partners into the perfect object of their romantic desire, the saviour who will take away all discomfort and cravings.

This Power Struggle goes on in every relationship, regardless of its nature (husband/wife, parent/child, siblings, business associations). The Romance fades with the recognition of the limitations and specifics of the other; when this happens, people usually try to control their partners into conforming to the image of what they believe the partner could be. Partners become dissatisfied and try to change each other, to satisfy hidden security needs. They often think that their motivation is for the benefit of the other: "You are not fully the person you could be, but I can help you; it's for your own good!"

The Gloves Are Off!

The subtle, "nice" hints gradually give way to more overt forms of control and conflict. Subtle reminders become repetitious chiding; sweet requests become whining demands. People want their partners to change, and they are desperate to accomplish this mission. They are driven in this project, in order to hide from themselves. People don't actually want to know who their partners really are; rather, they want their partners to conform to images they are projecting. They want partners to fit into their script, which they began to develop in childhood. If people actually could succeed in changing their partners into the perfect object of their romantic image, they would then be relieved of so much discomfort – they would have a saviour! The lurking anxiety and discomfort of existence would be relieved if people could gain full control of a perfect object.

Motive for the Power Struggle

Many times, people are trying to undo unhappy experiences from their pasts. For example, if someone were beaten or abused as a child, she might be seeking someone to protect her; she thus continually attempts to control her spouse's outbursts of frustration or anger (for fear that he might become like her abusive father). Her motive for control is to find some security for herself; she is trying to control the present because of past experiences. However, this is quite illusory and fraught with trouble. In trying to control her spouse, she has objectified him, and relates to him as if he were actually her abusive father. There can be no security in such a situation; of course she cannot really control her father from the past, and she does not relate personally to the actual person who is married to her. Such objectification often lurks beneath the surface of people's attempts to control one another in relationship. Notably, it also is involved in the control of oneself in order to impress or otherwise influence the other.

War Is Declared

As partners remain together, the subtle forms of control are replaced by repetitious patterns of conflict. Sometimes all-out war is declared. Rather than accept the uniqueness of their partners, people often persist in their efforts to have them conform to the image that they think will satisfy their inner insecurity. They blame and complain, and try to move the partner into the role they have designed. In the Power Struggle stage, partners actually know more about each other than in Romance; however, because they are not willing to accept what they know, they persist with attempts to control rather than face the possibilities for intimacy that could occur with acceptance. The partner is still being used as an objectified image; this is the same process that children use with parents in an attempt to overcome basic insecurity. Instead of the dialogue that could occur, partners in Power Struggle are invested in the clashes of attack and defence. While defences are high, intimacy is impossible. At this stage, partners retreat behind roles and obligations, and fuel the conflict with guilt and blame and defensive behaviours.

Expectations

The Power Struggle involves expectations of the other and of oneself. If partners adopt a moral stance, then their expectations are mixed with righteous allegations. There is nothing wrong or destructive about expectations in themselves; indeed, relationships can grow very solid through mutually agreed-upon expectations. The problem occurs when one partner tries to control or dominate the other with expectations.

The Power Struggle Is Exciting

Most couples do not experience much beyond the Power Struggle stage. Still, they can find much stimulation in the back-and-forth conflicts and mutual controls; they can persist for years in blame, withdrawal and game-playing. Indeed, for some this is a satisfactory existence. In the play *Who's Afraid of Virginia Woolf,*[2] George and Martha, a middle-aged couple, talk with each other after an evening of intense, alcoholic fireworks and conflict; in apparent friendship and in conspiratorial tones, one talks to the other tenderly. The young couple who had witnessed the earlier fighting had gone home in dismay at the intensity, the cruelty, and the relentlessness of the games that their hosts had displayed to them. What the young couple did not understand was that the bickering, sarcasm, shouting, and abusive behaviour were all part of a well-executed script that the two had worked out over years of Power Struggle stage together. They were willing combatants, and actually enjoyed the fight!

Sexuality and the Power Struggle

As we will further discuss in Chapter 17, sexual charge is often rooted in infantile insecurities; the theme of domination and submission in charged sexual fantasies can be an attempt to overcome earlier inadequacies, to feel power through sexual activity. Thus, within highly charged sexual interaction – and within highly charged power and control issues – often lurks a history of insecurity and unresolved childhood inadequacies. People attempt to dominate their partners in the present (either sexually or in other forms of conflict) in an attempt to bolster themselves up, to prove themselves powerful; all this is to make up for a time when they felt powerless.

The motif in the Power Struggle stage involves domination and submission and control. When disagreements are sexualized, there can be a high degree of excitement and charge. With conflict comes tension, and the release can take the form of explosive sexuality. Fighting and making up typically precede sex play in this stage. The misery of conflict is balanced by the sexual charge that is maintained.

Guilt and Blame

The Power Struggle is maintained by a moral stance. In this attitude, there are definite rights and wrongs. When people blame their partners, they are saying "You are wrong, and you should change." Similarly, guilt also involves a moral process; instead of saying "You are wrong," the guilty partner is saying "I am wrong." The result is the same. Guilt and blame are the coinage of interaction of the Power Struggle.

The Power Struggle stage is inevitable. There is nothing wrong with it. Indeed, it can be exciting; to struggle with another can be a stimulating experience, one that encourages strength. In the Power Struggle, partners can begin to see the differences between themselves; they just don't like or accept these differences at this stage. During this period, partners prefer the security of roles and walls, rather than the insecurity of authenticity and self-reliance, through which personal boundaries could be created.

In the Power Struggle, partners are caught up with idealized images of themselves and others. Guilt and blame are attempts to create and maintain these images. With blame, one is trying to mould the partner into an idealized image; in guilt, one is trying to conform oneself into an image of perfection. In this way, intimacy is limited; partners are fixated in objectification, both of themselves and each other.

Symptoms and Illnesses in Power Struggle

In the Power Struggle stage, people often experience physical and emotional symptoms. Headaches, back pain, depression, and other psychophysiological complaints commonly accompany the frustrations of trying to control oneself or one's partner. This stage is highly charged and volatile, with much tension and anxiety; frequently, partners succumb to illnesses that express the turbulence of this period.

Turbulence Precedes New Order

We recommend that partners in Power Struggle commit to stay in for the conflict, rather than withdraw, abandon, or attempt to overpower the other. In conflict, new information can emerge, and each can learn a great deal. The fights seem so disruptive; however, if couples do not fixate in repetitive control struggles, they can learn more about themselves and each other. Struggles such as these can be a stimulus to challenge fixed ideas of self and other. Indeed, without some disruption, fixations of attitude and activity tend to persist. In chemistry, no molecular change occurs without disturbance; much work has been done in science in the area of "dissipative structures" – the orderliness in which disruption occurs.[3] In chaos theory, turbulence involves hidden patterns of order that can unfold into unforeseen possibilities. In the turbulence of interpersonal conflict, there can be revelation of self and the other. Joseph Ford wrote that "Evolution is chaos with feedback."[4]

Indeed, when partners are willing to face the new information that emerges, they can use this to proceed to the next stages, where more intimacy is possible. Because the Power Struggle is so universal, and has so much energy involved in it, we recommend that couples really come to know their Power Struggle, and find a field of activity to share conflict that is mutually agreeable, as well as safe and respectful. Instead of throwing china and hurling insults, partners can engage in energetic competitive sports, card and board games, or intellectual thrust and parry. Instead of avoiding or denying the strife, partners can come to actually enjoy it and to learn about themselves and each other. These periods calls for presence on the part of both partners; when people succumb to non-presence, they enter the deviation of Apathy, which we will describe below.

Entitlement

To repeat, there is nothing problematic or wrong about the Power Struggle itself; difficulties arise when one or both parties remain stuck and fixated in moralistic, combative positions. One common factor in remaining stuck is the phenomenon of entitlement. When partners believe they have a "right" to specific behaviour from the other, they become fixated in blame, guilt, and control. Once people face and deal with their feelings of entitlement, they are able to unfixate, and they can open themselves to the curiosity that will help carry them into further stages where intimacy and authentic sharing are possible. When partners relinquish the position of entitlement, they also become free of the prison of being invested in the Power Struggle. At this point, they can leave the battle, acknowledging their disagreements and their attempts to control; the path is then open to move beyond righteousness into further and deeper dialogue. In this way the relationship cycle can begin to move again. However, there are other common ways of reacting to the power struggle, which we refer to as diversions. These diversions, all of which involve stepping out of the relationship cycle, are Apathy, Transcendence, and Separation.

Diversion One: Apathy

If one gives up the power struggle by submitting to the will of the other, one can enter a state that looks quite peaceful compared to the turbulence of previous conflict. Suddenly, one is calm, and there is less turmoil. This is Apathy, in which people step off the relationship cycle, and enter a lifeless state.

Apathy can be mistaken for Integration: superficially they might look the same. However, Integration involves much vitality and acceptance, whereas Apathy is lifeless and resigned. In Apathy, one simply decides that the fight is not worth the trouble, and closes off. There is no longer any argument; the apathetic person gives up, moving away from the life dynamic. Apathetic individuals have less passion; calmly, but lifelessly, they conform to the forms of relating, without any actual investment or enthusiasm.

Some couples spend many years like this, and then just separate; others remain under the same roof, and live their days in a semblance of togetherness, but without love and passion. Socially, these couples don't make any bother and look good together (albeit somewhat dispirited). Often people are very approving of them, and even hold them up as models to emulate. These people play the role of relationship, and live and work together – but without intensity!

Apathy is the withdrawal of will and love, a statement that one's partner, or one's relationship, or oneself "doesn't matter." It is a suspension of commitment.[5] Apathy involves numbing of feelings to avoid the turmoil of Power Struggle; apathetic people are walled off, out of touch with themselves and others. Often they are depressed, remote from their feelings for themselves and others. Or they might become addicted to drugs or alcohol, in an attempt to maintain a semblance of quiet. Sometimes, people who are addicted to work or other activities, who appear so vital and energetic during the day, sink to a quiet resignation in the evenings at home with their partners; their driven activity is an addiction, to fill the emptiness of the Apathy. These people laugh rarely; or when they do, the laugh can have a hollow ring. Often a symptom of Apathy is the loss of a sense of humour.

With Apathy can come psychophysiological illnesses, depression, and other symptoms of being closed off. People with allergies sometimes have submitted, and have not defined their own boundaries; hence they acquire an illness to make defensive walls instead of making life-defining boundaries. Other signs and symptoms of Apathy can include compulsions, weakness, tiredness, boredom, ennui, and chronic fatigue syndrome. These states involve numbing of the self.

Because people in Apathy don't make trouble, they don't bring much attention to themselves. Others may believe that they have an "ideal relationship," as no one ever sees them in disagreement. Often people are shocked when a couple suddenly separates after many years of marriage; they seemed to be such an "ideal couple," but they were walled off from each other. This ideal couple had been in a state of peace; but they have not had the mutual respect and acceptance that occurs in harmony. Sometimes people discover their Apathy after the early demands of relationships are satisfied. When couples have young children, their time can be filled, and they don't have to face the distance between them. Then years later, when the children all leave home, they are alone together in the home, with the dawning realization that they don't know one another and don't have much feeling at all for one another!

The way out of the death-in-life of Apathy is to re-enter the Power Struggle. Because apathetic people are not present, they need to come back to presence. Often in rekindling a Power Struggle, people rediscover a degree of presence that is lacking in the Apathy state.

Diversion Two: Transcendence

Rather than simply submit to others, one can leave the field of endeavour altogether, and become interested in nonphysical planes of being. In Transcendence, people rise above the day-to-day concerns of relationship, and attempt to become uninvested in interpersonal interactions. Some spiritual teachers advise rising above the behaviour of oneself and one's partner, to "disidentify"; such leaders teach "You are not your body" and "You are not your behaviour."

The partner who remains is often frustrated with the superior, condescending, "holier than thou" attitude of the transcendental one. The transcending one can become quite defensive and righteous, albeit in the "higher" language of spiritual truths; yet, hidden within this dismissive attitude is non-acceptance of the other, and a devaluing of the life process in relationship. In short, in transcending, the individual has risen above the concerns of the personal relationships.

To us, this is neither human nor personal nor spiritual. In the guise of a spiritual rise, the person has abandoned the field of relationship to pursue investments on other planes. For us, true spirituality involves finding meaning in daily activity, high or lowly. Transcendence converts spirituality into a religious dogma of superiority and condescension, where the physical, day-to-day struggles of humans are devalued or reviled.

Certainly, transcending is an attractive life choice for some. However, there is little possibility in it for an ongoing interpersonal engagement, where partners can grow authentically in genuine dialogue. The transcending one prohibits interpersonal deepening, valuing the spiritual practice more than the relationship itself. Often people can experience peace in transcendence; the tragedy is that this peace is accomplished by denial of the physical being, the relationship, and the partner.

After all the years of our relationship project, we have continued to value interpersonal processing. One of us (Jock) certainly did his best to explore the realms of transcendence.[6] Now, for us, our spiritual practice is the Communication Model. We are interested in *transformation* (working through all the issues that arise in dialogue, and growing through progressively and repeatedly accepting these issues).

> *As we become transparent, revealed for exactly who we are and not who we wish to be, then the mystery of human life as a whole glistens momentarily in a flash of incarnation. Spirituality emanates from the ordinariness of this human life made transparent by lifelong tending to its nature and fate.* – Thomas Moore[7]

Diversion Three: Separation

Often, partners give up and walk away from the Power Struggle and the relationship. Wishing to avoid further fighting and disagreement and disappointment, they abandon their partners (and themselves) and break off the relationship. Generally, they find themselves searching for a new Romance, and enter the cycle of expectation again, with rekindled hope that someone outside will provide the solution to their life difficulties. Sometimes partners separate and come to new Romance with the same person; others separate from one person and find a Romance with another one. In separating, people are often showing their field dependence, searching for solutions to their problems outside of themselves.

Certainly, in an abusive relationship, where a partner continually crosses stated boundaries (for example, with violence or repeated addictive behaviours), separation is sometimes the only solution. When separation is accomplished without resentment or rancour, people can find more of themselves in the process, and then can approach a new relationship with deeper self-awareness, rather than blindly seeking a new Romance to ease their pain.

If partners do choose to separate, we advise them to stay long enough to process through the pain, grief, guilt, anger, and resentment, so that they can leave the relationship peacefully, and not carry the conflicts into the next one. If people are going to separate, at least they can learn from what they have done, so that they don't recreate similar fixations and destructive behaviour in the next relationship.

Getting Back on Track

If partners are willing to stay in and work with Power Struggle, it is possible to experience the other stages of the relationship cycle. Later in this book (Chapters 14 and 15), we revisit the elements of Power Struggle and suggest constructive ways to engage in it. When people experience times of apathy, transcendence, and even separation, it is possible to return to the deepening of the relationship. If they take the risk of revealing to one another what is happening, they create the possibility of moving into the stage of Integration.

10 Integration

Q. Is it better to be single or married?
A. It's better for girls to be single, but not for boys. Boys need somebody to clean up after them. – Anita (age 9)
A. It gives me a headache to think about that stuff. I'm just a kid. I don't need that kind of trouble. – Will (age 7)[1]

After an extended period of Power Struggle, couples tend to come to some new ground with regard to their differences. Often they stop fighting, or have more of a sense of humour about going through the same old routines over and over. But when the turmoil of the Power Struggle settles, couples frequently enter a period of calm that many find disturbing. When they are no longer fighting, they find that the excitement they expect seems to have gone. In this phase, couples who are in a sexual relationship often find that their sexual charge has diminished. This is characteristic of what is sometimes referred to as the "seven-year-itch." Many times couples separate at this time, thinking that something is wrong. Often, something is actually very right!

The so-called "seven-year itch" reflects the tendency for Power Struggle to quiet down. As their relationship calms, people invested in having a constant charge with their partner will tend to look elsewhere for stimulation, believing that the relationship has gone dead. Commonly, this is not so. The partners might have achieved a level of awareness of themselves and each other, and might have diminished their investment in proving the other to be in the wrong. However, if people think that a charge is the only measure of vitality, they might begin to look for an affair, or for a brand new relationship to find the stimulation of a charge again. This seeking of a new Romance may lead to the diversion of Separation mentioned previously.

However, after the illusions and disorientation of Romance, and the storms of a long period of Power Struggle, couples often emerge with a solid relationship that has flexibility and endurance. Having arrived at some stable knowledge of each other, they are capable of embarking upon a new adventure – the journey into a deepening intimacy. For them, the preliminary phases of Romance and Power Struggle were tests and proving grounds, in which they worked through and past many blocks, in order to be able to witness each other with more receptive eyes and hearts. They are ready to enter the other phases of relationship, beyond illusions and defences, beginning with the phase of Integration.

Couples who accept this, and begin to share with each other, often find that they are in fact feeling very warm and close with each other, now that the charge has diminished. They are actually beginning to become intimate!

Beginning to Learn Together

In the Power Struggle, both parties are invested in being right; thus, they stay remote from themselves and each other in the charge of conflict and defence and blame. They don't come to know each other more deeply, because they keep themselves and each other objectified in the conflict. They don't know the personhood of their partner, who is more the object of defensiveness and blame.

With a shift in attitude, partners become less invested in control, change and blame. Instead, they begin to listen, with genuine interest and curiosity. In Power Struggle, partners have had the information to come to know the other; however, they generally have used this information in order to keep distant in conflict. In the Integration stage, they become curious to know each other; with this attitude, they begin to listen and question rather than defend. The relationship deepens, and the partners come to know each other and themselves. As they come to accept what they discover instead of resisting it, the flower of intimacy opens.

Curiosity, Communication and the Five A's

Curiosity is the catalyst to proceed from Power Struggle to Integration. By using the Communication Model we describe in Chapter 4, people can become more compassionate and curious about themselves and each other. As part of this, we recommend a process that we call "The Five A's" (Awareness, Acknowledgement, Acceptance, Action, and Appreciation). People can choose to become more *aware* of what they are doing, thinking or feeling in any situation. By *acknowledging* this to their partner they can move to a growing *acceptance* of themselves. This acceptance does not require that people *like* what they have done or the attitude they have taken, or that they resign themselves to always acting in the same way – only that they recognize honestly and compassionately *what is,* without excuses or denial. In this process, they begin to know themselves and their partners more fully; rather than being defended and unaware, they are learning with each other.

This awareness can be translated into *action*, where further self-development and relationship enhancement can take place. This may involve a choice to act differently in the present situation, without denying or erasing what has already taken place. In this, partners can *appreciate* themselves and each other. Since this whole process is energized by breathing, we have an acronym for it, BAAAAA: Breath, Awareness, Acknowledgment, Acceptance, Action, Appreciation.

Here's an example of how this might go: "I am *aware* that I tend to blame you when you are late, and I *acknowledge* that I just did it again. I *accept* that I tend to do this (though I don't like the fact that I do). I'm also curious about your experience. Will you tell me more of what has been happening for you? My *action* is to sit down and talk with you about this, rather than just storm out in a rage and break off communication! And I can *appreciate* myself for doing something different here ... and you for being willing to talk with me."

Weeding the Garden

Just as an established garden requires maintenance and regular care, the Integration stage involves work to deepen the relationship. We recommend that partners devote a period of time each day to sharing their perceptions, thoughts, feelings and experiences, to keep up to date with each other's world. In this way, they can gradually come to know themselves and each other beyond the limited viewpoints of their idealizations and objectifications. Each time the partners acknowledge a moralistic fixed belief about the way things are, they have an opportunity to move through the limitation into a process where they can gain increasing awareness of themselves and each other.

Partners Can Disagree

In Integration, partners can disagree without fighting; they are not invested in being right, they can accept differences, and they can stay together with someone who has quite different viewpoints. This process involves progressive acceptance of both self and other. With this growing acceptance, intimacy deepens. Partners find more self-awareness and more awareness of each other. The relationship garden now is in a rapid stage of growth; the partners (the plants in the garden) are maturing and ripening in their development as individuals together.

People gain strength in recognizing themselves and their partners for who they are, without any necessity to change. They are visibly more calm, secure, and stable in other phases of their life, too. They are moving past being dependent upon someone else for the security of their existence into becoming more self-reliant. They don't need their partners to be a certain way in order to solve their existential dilemma. They might say, "I am OK and you are OK, and we can each be together, accepting our separateness, and our differences. And we can love each other."

In Integration, couples are *not at peace*, which occurs in the diversion of Apathy we noted in Chapter 9. Rather they share in a *harmony* of differences. They each can sing their own note, without having to move to the melody of the other; in this mutual acceptance and acknowledgment, their melodies will harmonize with growing intimacy and depth of interaction.

Finally They Are Personal!

In the Integration stage, both partners are for the first time truly personal; in previous stages, both were primarily objects in objectified roles. Now in Integration, each person is valued, accepted, and acknowledged. With the sharing and witnessing of each other, they both are revealed. As partners open to themselves and to each other, they become more substantial as individuated persons and as participants in relationship.

What begins as an interpersonal sharing moves into deeper, more spiritual domains. Partners come to know each other more substantially, and witness the life process revealed in each of them. This is the opening of true dialogue; in terms introduced by Martin Buber, the relationship moves beyond "I-It" to "I-You."[2]

The Courageous Life

This stage of Integration rarely occurs to much degree. More often people remain mired in the conflicts of the Power Struggle, and the heady illusions of Romance, and do not fully enter the domain of Integration. When partners do find harmony between them, they can still have power struggles and romance; but they acknowledge them for what they are and don't take them too seriously. In short, in Integration, people have moved their centre from outside of themselves into the centre of their own beings; they are now increasingly self-reliant, and hence more sensitive and aware of both themselves and each other. They are no longer attempting to overcome their existential condition through the mirages and facades of romance and objectification; increasingly, they possess the ready certainty of individuals who are growing strong in their own autonomy and self-directed purpose, while remaining sensitive to their partners.

The emptiness and meaninglessness that lurks at the centre of existence provides a challenge for people to grow and develop and become stronger in themselves. By being in relation with another, people can courageously face the dread of non-being without succumbing to the illusory objectifications and images of Romance and Power Struggle. When they face their insecurities and share them, they can accept themselves and their partners as they are; they then know themselves to be alone, without a definite meaning provided for them.

Although meaning is not given, it can be created; emptiness can be filled with one's own actions, consistent with one's own values. People who have experienced the Integration stage are in a position to create their own personal meaning and fill the emptiness by courageous acts of intimate sharing and openness with themselves, and with their partners. In relationship, the project of self-becoming is enhanced through the mirroring of dialogue. Partners gain both knowledge of themselves and each other; as they open, revealed to each other, they also become open and revealed to themselves.

Integration and Anxiety

For people in the Integration phase, neurotic anxiety diminishes as they progressively accept their own separateness. When they do experience deeper levels of angst, they are likely to rise to the occasion with a further confirmation of faith. Such people acknowledge their own despair and face the challenge with a further acceptance of even the darkest aspects of their beings:

> *The acceptance of despair is in itself faith and on the boundary line of the courage to be.* – Paul Tillich[3]

With experience of Integration, people can go through their dark periods without closing off, or abandoning themselves or others; they continue to operate in courageous dialogue with their partners, and with life itself. Their spirituality is grounded in a profound acceptance of themselves and their partners; in so doing, they embrace life, with ever-growing feelings of participation and reverence.

People in Integration are more able accept the existential condition of aloneness and separateness. In so doing, they are open to experience the fulfillment that comes with sharing with another separate being. They come to celebrate themselves, their relationship, and their interactions with all of life, with courage, strength and dedication.

Humour

Humour and lightheartedness are characteristic of the phase of Integration. The intensity and seriousness of righteousness, guilt and blame give way to spirited teasing and self-aware laughter. What previously were heavy subjects now are simply more things to face, with equanimity and with pleasure. Partners begin to celebrate their everyday life together, with all its challenges, tribulations and joy.

Honesty and Responsibility

Honesty is of paramount importance; it is a required tool to deepen interchange. By the time partners have reached some Integration, they have come to recognize that one person cannot hurt another's feelings; indeed, their attitude is that one person cannot make anyone else feel anything, as we discussed in Chapter 4. The attitude that one person can hurt another leads to protection, defensiveness, secrecy, and diminished intimacy. When partners acknowledge that each is responsible for his or her own feelings, a sense of openness and freedom arises; no subject is taboo, and they can face any situation, willing to communicate and learn together.

Sharing

In the Integration stage, people are prepared to share more and more of themselves, in dialogue with each other. Anything shared can enhance the intimacy that comes in the unfolding honesty of the Integration phase. Indeed, when the elements of the Power Struggle (jealousy, guilt, anger, blame, etc.) are shared, they become useful information for the Integration phase. When partners accept these elements in themselves without trying to use them for control, they become interesting items of curiosity, useful for the growth and enhancement of the relationship. When they are shared, previously disruptive elements become the ground substance for the stable relationship.

Sexuality in the Integration Stage

Although the sexual charge tends to diminish in Integration, it can be rekindled if people want, by coming to a deeper understanding of how the charge is generated. In couples who are willing to share sexual fantasies, the possibility exists to find new levels of sexual charge through playing with objectification. This sharing requires mature stability from each partner, to avoid the guilt or blame that might be generated in the Power Struggle stage. We discuss this in detail in Chapter 17.

Flow

Whereas people tend to become stuck in repetitious righteous fighting in the Power Struggle stage, partners experience movement and flow in the Integration stage. They are becoming persons, beyond the objectifications that they have experienced from themselves and from others. They come to know themselves and each other. In this movement, they enter the flow of life, and experience greater degrees of freedom. They readily shoulder the increased responsibility that accompanies this freedom.

Mihaly Csikszentmihalyi has described the qualities of people in the "flow experience."[4] These people tend to have clear goals, to act decisively, and to be single-minded, capable of focus and concentration, possessing a sense of being in charge in their lives; they tend to experience loss of self-consciousness and a feeling of participation in something greater than themselves. For them time passes faster, and they find enjoyment of experiences for their own sake. Partners in the Integration stage often show the characteristics of the "flow experience." They are involved and present, with themselves and each other; hence, they experience themselves as participating in life, and they find they have a sense of belonging to something greater than themselves.

Continual Renewal

Couples can maintain the dynamism of Integration in their relationship through continual renewal. They cannot rest on their laurels and expect the relationship to take care of itself; indeed, the relationship is the vehicle through which they continue to grow and develop, together and separately. In order to continue to grow together, they need to find new things to share. The following are some key factors in maintaining an ongoing Integration, and prevent a slide into self-satisfaction or boredom.

1 *Frequent dependable contact* keeps the partners aware of each other and the life process. Having coffee together as a routine, or sharing a favourite television program together, brings an ongoing natural awareness of each other.
2 *Daily clearing* time is important, in order to keep informed and aware of one another's thoughts, feelings and experiences, both positive and negative. This might be in the early morning, before the day begins, or later in the evening, to recap events of the day.
3 *An ongoing project of mutual interest* brings a focus to the relationship. This can be tending a garden together, or researching some topic, or collaborating in business. Partners who have projects together have a natural inclination to interact with each other.

4 *Reporting of individual interests* keeps both partners informed and involved in each other's lives. For example, when one partner is interested in jogging, and the other one likes to stay at home to read, they should ask each other how the individual experiences of the solitary activities were for each of them. This way, independent interests can be shared, to avoid them becoming elements that introduce distance.

5 *Novelty and experimentation* help to keep a relationship bright and vital. Trips together to unknown places or experiencing new foods or artistic performances together can provide fresh subjects for discussion and sharing. As the experiences accumulate, the partners discover an ongoing sense of challenge and enjoyment within themselves and with each other.

6 *Learning together* brings new dimension to the relationship. Whether couples decide to informally research a topic together, study ballroom dancing, or attend a class at a community college, the act of learning together helps to deepen their interaction.

7 *Renewal of romance* through affectionate gestures and rituals brings a feeling of warmth and specialness to the relationship. Couples can have their own private jokes and signals, which mean that they are special to each other.

Loving

In the relationship garden, loving blossoms in the Integration phase. Partners begin to know each other; there is more reality and less fantasy. Perhaps the period of Integration is not as exciting as the tumultuous periods of Romance and Power Struggle; but, for the first time, these people are able to experience true fulfilment, with themselves and each other.

Individuals in this stage are very responsible. They tend not to blame their partners; nor do they indulge in the self-blame of guilt and regret. In the Integration phase, partners have moved beyond the limitations of morality; instead of seeing situations in terms of right and wrong, guilt and blame, they are more likely to see possibilities for curiosity and learning.

They accept themselves, and in the process, begin to forge an authentic relationship with each other. The process of dialogue enhances the growth and development of both persons, at the same time as the relationship is deepening.

> *For one human being to love another human being: that is perhaps the most difficult task that has been entrusted to us, the ultimate task, the final test and proof, the work for which all other work is merely preparation.*
> – Rainer Maria Rilke[5]

11 Commitment

Once partners achieve a degree of Integration in their relationship, they are engaged in active meaningful dialogue. Each is a person, not merely an objectified role. Their knowledge of themselves and each other deepens, and they become stronger, both in themselves and in the relationship. There is no requirement for anyone to change, which is just as well, since this is fundamentally impossible![1] Instead, they are progressively more aware and accepting of themselves and each other. Once this process of Integration is well-established, the partners are ready to enter the next stage, Commitment.

The Commitment Stage

In the Commitment stage, partners know each other very well – both in their authenticity and in the games and power plays that each can play. They communicate their thoughts and feelings readily, and in this way continue to deepen their awareness of themselves and each other. They are more and more engaged with life, with each other, and with themselves. Now they are ready to make an informed commitment, with real knowledge of themselves, and the other with whom they are committing.

Because partners know each other well at this stage, they do not commit out of the illusions of Romance or the obligations of the Power Struggle. Instead, with awareness, they commit with free choice.

They do not commit to each other; indeed, they affirm their commitment to life and to themselves. In this process, they are willing to make agreements to share a commitment, to embark upon projects together with mutual expectations and decisions.

Having Children in the Commitment Stage

This is the best stage at which to have a baby. More often, couples become pregnant in the Romance stage, without knowing themselves or their partners adequately. Also, many children are conceived in the context of Power Struggle, when the partners may believe that bringing another life into the relationship will help to ease the tension and struggles that occur as a consequence of their projected objectifications of each other. Children born in the early stages are faced with parents who have little awareness of themselves and whose energies are invested in struggling with each other. More stable parents will be aware of themselves, each other, and their motivations and desires; such individuals will naturally be aware of their children, and can be clear in setting boundaries with their partners and their children. In this environment, youngsters can have the experience of a strong relationship matrix in which to grow and develop into authentic personhood.

The Evolution of Commitment

Commitment matures and changes as the partners change. There actually is a commitment required at each stage of relationship. At the Romance stage, commitment is to a dream, an ideal; when people marry at this stage they frequently promise to "love, honour and obey" someone they don't yet know. We suggest that at the Romance stage, couples should commit to staying together long enough to get to know each other. In the Power Struggle stage, partners can commit to being present with each other, in order to work through the conflict; more often at this stage they have an unconscious commitment to win or to overpower the other (which obviously works against developing of intimacy). Most commitments in Power Struggle or Romance are ultimately life restricting; such inclinations tend to limit the relationship, or even terminate it. This need not be so.

After partners achieve some degree of Integration, they are more capable of a solid, informed mutual commitment. Having developed honest, dependable communication and curiosity in the Integration stage, partners can put plans and imaginings into action. Such commitments are not whimsical or naive; they proceed naturally from informed knowledge of both self and other in the Integration stage. By now, partners are individuating, unique and strong within themselves. With knowledge of themselves, they are able to commit with assurance, and dedicate their wills to whatever they choose. In relationship, when these partners commit together, they can depend upon themselves and each other. At this stage, partners can embark upon a solid commitment, for life, both separate and together. They do not need each other; but they have the assurance that they can depend upon themselves and each other.

Will and Willfulness

The Commitment stage involves the use of the will. Note that *willfulness* is a characteristic of Power Struggle, and generally involves objectification and defence; clear expression of the *will*, on the other hand, is an aspect of a mature personality, and is important in developing integrative abilities such as dedication, dependability, industry, responsibility, and purposeful, responsive action. The will is used to work *for* a purpose; willfulness operates *against* growth and thus often leads to fixation. Willfulness serves the purposes of pride, righteousness, security, and walls – thus interfering with intimacy. Clean use of the will supports the growth functions of the relationship garden, while willfulness tends to grow like a weed, suffocating tender new growth.

Care and Maintenance of a Relationship

With a commitment to deal with any situation that comes up with sharing, honesty, and openness, a relationship can be kept in a healthy state. Just as a garden constantly needs weeding, watering, and fertilizing, a relationship needs the constant care and maintenance that mutual commitments can bring. Where there is genuine care and curiosity for the other, and sharing of the self, there is revelation of both partners; this revelation brings renewal to a relationship through time.

In the relationship garden, committed people are like deeply rooted plants. Knowing themselves, they can remain in place, and dedicate themselves to the life of the garden without requiring special attention or excessive care. They reach deep into the soil, and nourish themselves to the centre of their beings, in harmony with nature and their surroundings. They are strong enough to endure temporary hardships and challenges, and can grow in harmony with the other strong plants in their garden.

Commitment Is to Oneself

Commitment in this stage is not so much to another as to oneself, as both partners dedicate their lives to specific activities or purposes. Each person's growth is enhanced, and develops with the discipline and restraint of commitment. Instead of impulsiveness, where one cause or position is abandoned for the next whim, partners in the Commitment stage can weather storms together and continue to grow, develop and deepen through time. With commitment, focus becomes possible, and the partners are increasingly capable of managing large projects, and growing with increasing challenges. The use of the will in Commitment permits the evolution of strong, mature, individuated selves. When such selves commit together in relationship, they each grow, and the relationship grows.

Commitment Together

I do not commit to you; I commit myself to whatever I choose. In relationship, my commitment involves what I offer to the relationship. When you offer to commit as well, we are able to be together in relationship with expectations that are not demands, but mutual agreements. The more I value you, the more I will commit myself with you, and the more expectations we can have with each other. This is the root of dependability; when people are dependable, their roots grow deep and strong, and the changing winds of events cannot disrupt their lives. When partners learn dependability together, they and their relationship can grow to become strong and sturdy.

Limited Commitments

Many people who are commitment phobic can dedicate themselves for a limited period of time. If people are afraid of the immensity of commitment, they can probably accept a limited one – for example a month-by-month commitment, or a three-month period. When they agree to the time, they can devote themselves without worrying about it being forever. As they learn that they can live through a short period of commitment, a longer one does not seem so impossible. We recommend that people who are reluctant to commit make short-term commitments and gradually build up their capacity to hang in.

In our own case, Jock cured his phobia about commitment when he found that he could save money on an extended subscription to a magazine; he elected to stay with Ben for the longer period to economize – his Scottish blood won out over his fear when he could save a few dollars![2] In the same manner, by committing together to a financial responsibility, people can learn that they indeed can last through the vicissitudes of circumstances, and feel stronger in themselves for it. For some, buying a house together can be a very fulfilling proposition.

Teaching Children about Commitment

The ability to commit is a developed skill, and grows by diligent repetition – just as athletic practice develops the muscles and the endurance that accompany increasing prowess. A child learns self-discipline by committing to small projects. Children's self-acceptance and self-esteem grow as they learn that they can commit themselves to something and follow through, sticking to what they set out to do. Children become more secure in themselves as they learn that they can depend upon themselves to do what they intend.

In this way, children can learn to depend upon themselves and become self-reliant. For example, by learning to budget their money, spending only a little of their allowance and saving some for later, young people can learn how to maintain their resources. Thus, children can very early develop good financial sense, and grow in the knowledge that they can increasingly manage their own affairs.

Commitments for Different Relationships

In relationships of different types, different commitments are needed. For example, business partners need perhaps only a few minutes each day to keep their business enterprise on track. For friends, a commitment to spending an evening once a week together permits them to develop the relationship adequately. For partners in a primary relationship, we recommend a minimum of a half hour per day devoted to sharing, clearing (see page 149), and focusing on feelings and thoughts with each other.

For long-standing relationships, we recommend that couples re-evaluate their commitment from time to time; often, they discover that they have acquired a taste for commitment, and like the strength that longer commitments afford.

In our own relationship, we summarize our commitment as follows:

> *Our commitment is for life. The commitment could end tomorrow, if the life went out of the relationship. This is not a time-based commitment; rather, it is a life-based commitment. But then, we are also committed to work through all the details of ending a relationship before we would separate; so, we likely would not leave each other, since we likely would find new life in the stimulation of finding out about the issues of separation. Both parties are free to choose to stay in or leave. We stay because we continue to find life together.*

Commitment Is the Basis of Life

In Commitment lies the key to a great secret, the secret of manifestation.[3] When partners direct their wills in creative, life-enhancing pursuits, they participate and contribute beneficially to the larger social context, bringing forth life and newness. The brilliance of life is materialized through their cooperative interplay and effort.

> *Until one is committed, there is hesitancy, the chance to draw back, always ineffectiveness, concerning all acts of initiative (and creation). There is one elementary truth the ignorance of which kills countless ideas and splendid plans: that the moment one definitely commits oneself, then Providence moves too. All sorts of things occur to help one that would never otherwise have occurred. A whole stream of events issues from the decision, raising in one's favour all manner of unforeseen incidents and meetings and material assistance which no man could have dreamed would have come his way. Whatever you can do or dream you can, begin it. Boldness has genius, power and magic in it. Begin it now.* – Goethe[4]

12 Co-Creativity

When partners have experience of Integration and Commitment, they proceed with knowledge of each other and themselves. They know their strengths, their weaknesses, their desires, and their dreams. Being dependable in their commitments, they can join in the mutuality of genuine collaboration. When they are together, any task they choose becomes a creative endeavour. There seems to be a field of originality and vitality around such pairings. When they dedicate themselves together, whatever they touch seems to become infused with life and light, and is inspiring to others around them. The creative partnerships in the world of the theatre illustrate the fine-tuned sensitivity and great work that emerges from such interaction – the musical collaboration of Rodgers and Hammerstein is a good example.

In this Co-creativity, partners' efforts harmonize with each other. There is a flow that seems tangible when they are together. Whether they are joined in a pas de deux, or are just washing the dishes together, their movements and interchanges are fluid and possess a simple grace. Their very interaction serves as an inspiration to those around them.

When partners have moved beyond the moralizing of the Power Struggle, have achieved awareness of self and other in the Integration stage, and have learned to team up with their wills in the Commitment stage, they find a multitude of possibilities opening up before them. Some report an aura of life and love around such people; even their most mundane pursuits have a spiritual life to them. They manifest the Zen spirit of life in every moment – together, yet distinct, separate, individuated, and authentic. They show a vitality in body, mind and spirit, which expresses itself in their creative work. They are fully incarnating.

With their capacity to acknowledge and share all aspects of their beings, cocreative partners can make use of what were earlier seen to be negative or destructive aspects in the relationship. They can convert differences into creative challenges rather than fighting over legalistic points. One partner's negative aspects can be used positively: the stingy partner can be the one who does the bookkeeping, and the partner invested in control can do the scheduling and planning. Elements in their personalities that were originally developed for defence can be used creatively in the service of the relationship and in projects together. By acknowledging and accepting character traits, nothing needs to be seen as inherently negative.

The Cycle Regenerates

Freedom abounds, and life is full of possibilities; in this phase, people are strong, with full capacity to actually manifest their dreams and desires. Because there is less fixedness, these people are ready to entertain new ideas and imagine novel approaches to situations. In short, they are open, and ready for entering the next phase, which is a return to the domain of Romance.

Because these people now have the accumulated experience from the learning of the previous stages, this is a *more informed* Romance. Thus the relationship cycle spirals and opens, expanding into life and further creativity. The imagination reopens into a new Romance; people enter new territory they do not know, with much anticipation of what is possible. With this enhanced view, people can see further ranges of life, love and relationship, which they can pursue. Soon, the partners enter into further learning, with new Power Struggles; now they are capable of moving more quickly through to new Integration, with ever-increasing awareness of themselves and each other. And so on they go, through further Commitment and more Co-creativity. This is indeed the cycle of life, lived out in relationship.

When Fritz Perls wrote his famous poem in the 1960s ("I am not in this world to live up to your expectations, and you are not in this world to live up to mine"), many people believed that the way to grow was on one's own, and that relationships were counterproductive to growth. The following answer to Perls provides a relationships perspective:

BEYOND PERLS

If I just do my thing
And you do yours
We stand in danger
Of losing each other
And ourselves.
I am not in this world
To live up to your expectations,
But I am in this world
To confirm you as a unique human being
And to be confirmed by you.
We are fully ourselves
Only in relation to each other;
The I detached from a Thou disintegrates.

I do not find you by chance;
I find you by an active life of reaching out.
Rather than passively letting things happen to me
I can act intentionally
To make them happen.
I must begin with my Self, true;
But I must not end with my Self:
The truth begins with two.

– Walter Tubbs[1]

PART III

Moving through the Cycle

13 Chaos and Relationships

Chaos theory proposes a still state referred to as *equilibrium* in which energy is in its lowest state of activity and is largely predictable. On the other extreme of a continuum is *turbulence*; in turbulence – or chaos – energy is organized but its patterns are unpredictable.[1]

Consider a stone that is rolled uphill. The farther away from equilibrium it is moved, the more unstable it becomes; it stores more energy and is increasingly more precarious, ready to roll back to its state of equilibrium. Hence, the greater the distance from equilibrium, the greater is the possibility of turbulence, or unpredictable behaviour.

Viewing human life and individual development from this perspective, people move a certain distance from equilibrium as they face the demands of living. If that distance from equilibrium is small, people's lives will be predictable but relatively static and unalive; if the distance is greater, the person is more anxious and uncertain, but also more alive. Maximum growth is possible in what we refer to as the Zone of Optimal Integration (ZOI), a kind of plateau beyond which turbulence (experienced as anxiety) becomes too great for a person to handle. The more turbulence a person can manage, the greater the distance from equilibrium that person can move. With increasing distance from equilibrium, the opportunities are greater to discover and experience more of life.

As a growing and developing person handles new situations, the Zone of Optimal Integration expands; when that person is at rest, or retreating in face of threats (real or imagined), the ZOI contracts. This pulsatile process of expansion and contraction is characteristic of healthy, live organisms (including humans!) – the greater the range of pulsation, the greater the flexibility of movement and the fuller the experiencing of life.

Chaos is not random disorder; rather, it is patterned but unpredictable complexity. The farther from equilibrium that a person moves, the more turbulence and complexity is encountered. In such chaotic situations, it is common for individuals to contract in fixed ways, narrowing their range of experiencing by drawing in their boundaries and walling themselves off from contact. This is a *neurotic* solution to turbulence. When people do this, they not only diminish the size of their Zone of Optimal Integration, but they also rigidify their boundaries into thick, defensive walls that prevent them from feeling alive, fulfilled and whole. The more that this rigidification happens, the more the ZOI tends to shift toward equilibrium. The stillness of this equilibrium is what existentialism might identify as "death-in-life."

Neurosis is a narrowing and fixation of the life process as a means of controlling the uncertainty of chaos. Anxiety occurs with a threatened loss of that control. People are afraid that in loss of control, disastrous things will occur; in the extreme, they fear that the loss of control can result in either criminal or psychotic behaviour. People who fear experiencing the expansion of life with all its complexity and chaos often develop an interest in power and control, which provides some semblance of security; by controlling themselves and taking power over others, they hope to avoid the perils of chaotic expression.

The Self in Context

The diagram "The Self in Context" on the facing page illustrates the relationship between equilibrium and chaos as it applies to human beings. At the centre is *equilibrium* (stillness), where there is no movement, no growth, no change; events here are predictable and certain. The farther from the centre, the greater the tendency to unpredictability and chaos (turbulence). The movement from equilibrium into chaos occurs in three zones: the *spiritual*, the *training camp*, and the *relationship garden*. In the training camp, chaos is controlled and resisted through socialized repetitive behaviours and attitudes. In the relationship garden, chaos is transformed through dynamic acceptance of it. In the zone of the spiritual, meaning is given to chaos. As we will explain, there are also "interface regions" (responsibility, religion, laws) between these three zones.

The Training Camp

In life, people gradually encounter increasing amounts of chaos, and learn to deal with it. Most early training and schooling involves learning standard approaches and tools to deal with unpredictability. Indeed, language, roles and rules of conduct embody the conventions that help society to keep order in the midst of unpredictable chaos. The more successful the training, the more predictable and socialized a person is; unfortunately, this training also involves fixation of life-force energy, so that the individual's creativity and sense of vitality are often stifled. In order to fit into the constraints of the social order, one must suppress one's authentic life-force energy. This is the project of the training camp.

Children learn to adopt the behaviours and concerns of their parents and,

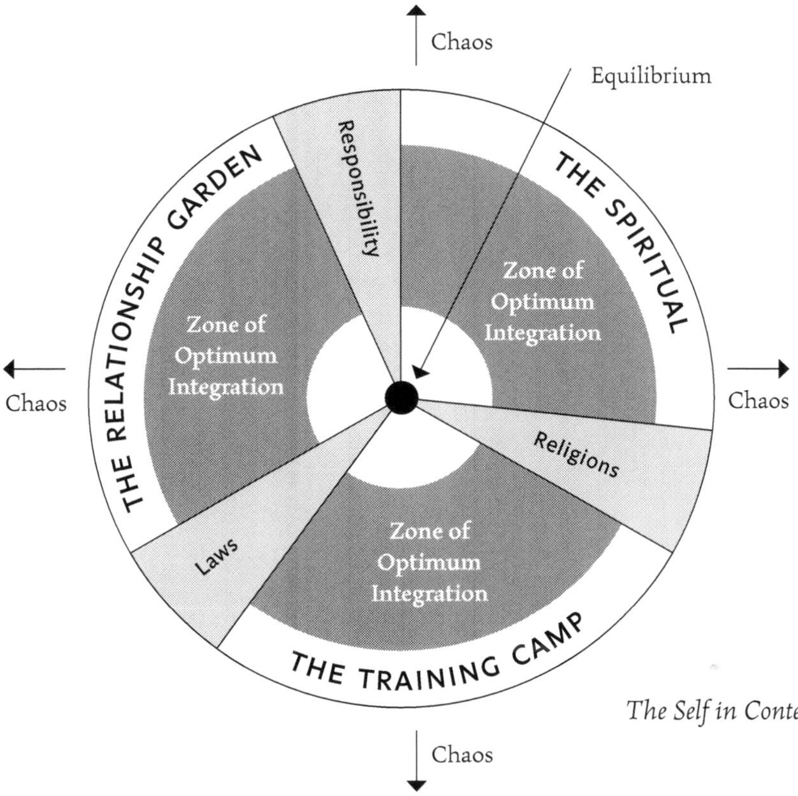

The Self in Context

through mimicry, to become more socialized. The parents give approval as their youngsters become more trained into their ways. The children feel more comfort as they fit in; they are less anxious, but, at the same time, their spontaneous enjoyment of life is constrained. By a process of externalization, children learn to redirect the focus of their attention from within, to seek instead the approval and attention of outside referents ("authorities"). At first these outside referents are people (teachers, parents, siblings); later, they are more abstract rewards from the culture at large (reputation, titles, etc.). Thus, the training camp teaches control of impulses that are deemed inappropriate; in the process, people lose touch with their authentic self in pursuit of an ideal self;[2] this results in an objectifying, depersonalizing externalization of energy.

The Relationship Garden

The attitude in the relationship garden is one of accepting chaos and working with it. Instead of trying to control and suppress chaos, the individuals in a relationship garden will welcome the unpredictable events as sources of newness and creativity. When unanticipated events occur between them, they will tend to share their anxiety rather than try to diminish or ignore it. Hence, the energy of turbulence becomes available for interaction, communion, and personal growth.

In this process of intimacy, sharing, and acceptance, both parties become more fully themselves and more fully engaged with the authentic personhood of the partner. With the revelation of their internal process, they come to know both themselves and each other better. Thus, they can experience growth and increasing autonomy. Whereas in the training camp the participants *react* from fixed attitudes and patterns, in the relationship garden they *respond* to each other as sensitive persons. In the training camp, participants are *objects*, relating on an "It-It" basis; in the relationship garden, they become *people* with an "I-You" orientation.[3] The training camp is characterized by roled individuals who emphasize morality and erect walls; the relationship garden involves responsible people who develop boundaries with interpersonal sensitivity, and who thus can apply their personal ethics to each novel situation.

Thus, the relationship garden fosters freedom of expression, while remaining sensitive to self and other. This facilitates the ongoing discovery of one's authentic personhood. People in the relationship garden are less ideal, but they are more responsive, more vital, and more personal.

The Spiritual

We define the spiritual in a similar way to Paul Tillich and others, as having to do with *meaning*. The existentialist position is that life has no definite meaning, and meaning comes with individual decison-making, responsibility and action. In this way, each person creates or manifests his or her own meaning based on his or her own value system, and arrives at decisions and actions in keeping with this value system. When people adopt this viewpoint they will experience anxiety. Many are reluctant to face the enormity and the uncertainty of this attitude and the chaos that is inherent in it; they would rather play safe, staying closer to equilibrium by holding to established meaning and behaviours. As a result, they have less felt experience of life, but also less anxiety (chaos). This security seeking is involved in identifying with a particular group; one accepts the directives of the group in exchange for the security that comes with belonging.

Chaos provides a challenge to find meaning. The spiritual is the domain where this occurs. By facing the emptiness and unpredictability of chaos, people can learn to contend with these factors to discover their own meaning.

The Interface Regions

There is an interface between each domain, represented in our diagram by the narrow segments in between them.

Religions are developed in the interface between the spiritual and the training camp. The training camp is involved in rules and regulations and expectations that maintain the social order. Children are trained to be appropriate, to fit in to the family expectations, and by extension, to the requirements of the culture at large. As we mentioned, the spiritual is characterized by having no set meaning separate from the lived life and experience of the individuals. Religions function to link the individual's meaning (spirituality) to the culture.

Responsibility occurs between the relationship garden and the spiritual. This involves the capacity to be sensitive and aware of one's partner, family members and others in the environment, and be respectful and responsive with them. In the spiritual, there is nothing beyond the individual's felt meaning. But for the relationship garden to grow, there is necessarily a dynamic between one individual and another, which occurs through the agency of responsibility. Responsibility thus links the spiritual to the relationship garden.

Laws (structured social directives) occur between the training camp and the relationship garden; this is where social rules, obligations, roles, and conventions reside. The laws are the linking that organizes the rules of the society with the novelty and possibilities of the relationship garden. Laws in this way are the short form of social conveniences, agreed-upon conventions that provide a scaffolding for one's civic duties in balance with one's relationship concerns.

The Zone of Optimal Integration

The Zone of Optimal Integration (ZOI) is where integration of chaos is possible without unbearable strain. This is indicated by the band that runs through each of the relationship garden, the spiritual, and the training camp. It is a region that is not so close to the centre that there is no movement or flexibility or change possible, and at the same time not so far from equilibrium that the anxiety of chaos could be overwhelming. In terms of ego dynamics, the ZOI involves the integrative functions of the ego, balancing the raw force of the id (chaos) and the restraining forces of the superego (equilibrium).[4]

There is an area of the ZOI in each of the three regions. In the ZOI of the spiritual, the individual is not overwhelmed by emptiness, and yet has the pleasure and creativity that comes with being at some distance from equilibrium. In the ZOI of the training camp, conventions and rules are not so strong as to overwhelm the life force entirely, and life activities have room for spontaneity within the guidelines of social propriety. In the ZOI of the relationship garden, individualism will be balanced with sensitivity and awareness of self and other.

Being in Sync

The greater the distance from equilibrium, the more important is the relatedness to context.[5] When people move into greater chaos, they need to be more related to the context in order to maintain themselves, while remaining sensitive to others. This *phase locking* (also called "slaving") at a distance from equilibrium occurs in a jazz group, when the musicians progress farther and farther from conventional melody lines; the drummer sets the context through the rhythm, and the other musicians become increasingly dependent upon the drummer's context. Although the other musicians are very dependent upon the drummer's rhythms, they have great freedom within these constraints. They become "in sync" or "in the groove" with each other (in our terms, they are "in harmony" or "in resonance").

This relatedness to context occurs in each of the three domains (the spiritual, the relationship garden, and the training camp). Being in sync need not be unduly limiting; rather, it occurs when people are in harmony, responsively relating to each other. It involves being self-reliant, not dependent upon externals and yet remaining sensitive to one's environment. This appropriateness arises from autonomous inner sensitivity, rather than obligatory behaviour dictated by rules from without. When people learn to respond to their context without ignoring or resisting it, they can come to know more deeply their unique place in resonant harmony.

Freedom and Chaos

People lose their freedom by externalizing, becoming field dependent. In the training camp, people learn to fit in, in order to limit chaos; in this trade for security, they lose their freedom. In the training camp, when people obey the dictates of an authoritarian figure, they lose their autonomy. In the spiritual, people might be tempted to follow a guru in a training camp manner, and hence lose themselves in adopting their meaning from the external. When partners lose contact with themselves or each other, they become isolated, lose their place, and hence are not free.

Boundaries and Walls

Boundaries are related to the relationship garden, because there is acceptance and sensitivity to self and other that embraces unpredictability and turbulence. In the training camp, *walls* are erected to maintain defensive controls over self and other. In the spiritual domain, there are no walls or boundaries; there are only universals.

Peace and Harmony

Peace involves tolerance, rather than true acceptance; people learn to negotiate temporary peace in the rules and structuring of the training camp. Thus, the Romance and Power Struggle stages of the relationship cycle involve peace and conflict (which is lack of peace). The diversions of Apathy, Transcendence or Separation occur with the restrictions of peace, or when the failure of peace breaks into battles.

Harmony involves acceptance, and occurs in the relationship garden. Couples manifest harmony in the stage of Integration; they can accept themselves and each other, even in face of disagreement. Whereas peace involves tolerance and requires agreement, harmony can embrace differences without undue strain.

The spiritual involves oneness; hence there is neither agreement nor disagreement. The human experience can encompass all three zones.

> *In order to find one's place in the infinity of being, one must be able both to separate and to unite. – Yi Jing*[6]

Romance and Chaos

In the Romance phase of relationship, the imagination of possibilities breaks through the rigid confines of each person's neurotic walls, resulting in the heady release of pent-up chaotic energy called "being in love." This condition is usually valued as a positive experience, even though it is similar in many ways to a temporary psychotic state; the *excitement* of Romance is deemed to be desirable, even though in other circumstances the same feelings might be called *anxiety* and would be negatively valued.

The surrendering of control that is so much the experience of Romance becomes possible because the imagination provides an illusion of safety and security, with the belief that the loved one either will be possessed or wishes to possess. Hence, walls and boundaries are dissolved in the promises of mutual concern and control, and the persons feel glad even in the midst of much turbulence. In this phase, which is akin to a neurosis, the relationship narrows all consideration of the problems and turbulence that exist outside of the relationship. At this time, there is very little intimacy (by our definition of really *knowing* one another); however, there is a great deal of discovery of one another's world of imagination (which is no small feat in itself!).

Power Struggle and Chaos

When couples begin to know one another past their romantic versions, their protective bubble bursts to reveal the threats of harsh reality. This heralds the expression of each person's typical patterns of control – of one another as well as of the relationship – to handle the hitherto denied turbulence. Most people become possessive, attempting to narrow their world to manageable proportions, walling themselves off from the rest of their social contacts. Bribery, jealousy, caretaking, guilt, placating, and blackmail are all too common symptoms of this process. If the controls are successful, the relationship may appear stable; nevertheless, under the surface the relationship becomes rigid and suffocating. The relationship's Zone of Optimal Integration ceases to pulsate, losing its vitality to all of its walls and regulations, and begins to slide toward equilibrium, carrying both parties with it. Inside the relationship, each person's own Zone of Optimal Integration also narrows, rigidifies, becomes walled and less pulsatile, contributing toward both parties becoming bored and apathetic, even while they remain secure. Personal growth becomes greatly restricted as each manages to contain turbulence within the walls and controls; creativity and learning both suffer. The spiritual sense of aliveness is replaced by a strict adherence to moral judgments and righteousness. Such a relationship ceases to be a garden for growth and becomes more a prison for security. However, as we outline in the next two chapters, it is possible to deal with Power Struggle in such a way as to make growth possible and allow for an increasing experience of Integration.

Integration

If Power Struggle is handled with sensitivity, care, understanding, and acceptance, the relationship can enter periods of Integration that progressively move farther from equilibrium. The relationship garden expands to promote the growth of each of the individuals (which may include children) within it. Dealing with the turbulence of new ideas, novel experiences, travel to distant places and cultures, and deeper questions about spirituality and religion has a kind of fertilizing effect on all of the inhabitants within the garden, as well as on friends and any others operating within this couple's sphere of influence. By integrating new insights into their everyday life, these kinds of relationships continue to expand the boundaries of each individual so that increasing amounts of turbulence can be encompassed.

Although control is frequently used to manage the chaos and differences in Power Struggle, turbulence and diversity are welcomed in Integration. Being responsible for their own feelings allows partners a wider expression of who each person is. Instead of the limitations of compromise, each seeks to expand the range of understanding and acceptance, even though it may mean having to face jealousy, hurt, and insecurity. In this way, the Zone of Optimal Integration incorporates new life and greater growth.

The mind operates within the context of a body, which lives in an environment; the mind "couples" or associates experiences in these realms. For example, children that have been physically abused by parents would likely experience fear inside their bodies in the presence of authority figures. The mind has "coupled" the traumatic parental experience within the body; the body becomes set in this attitude, and is preconditioned to have similar reactions in similar contexts in the future. The very same process operates within all of those persons' encounters, sometimes having profound effects in their most intimate relationships.

The revelations of these coupled, often walled-off, experiences can sometimes become the central issue in the relationship garden, which affords a unique opportunity for healing and growth. In an atmosphere of understanding and acceptance, old coupling patterns can be challenged, unearthed, examined and tested in this nutritive, safe context that offers the possibility of a new contextual coupling. This is what therapy attempts to do with patients. In the same way, couples can learn in the dialogue of intimacy to uncouple their old habitual patterns of relating, and embrace new styles of interaction and mutuality.

A relationship that moves farther from equilibrium creates an environment of exploration and creativity. In this kind of "garden," each person supports the other(s) in uncovering old habits and discovering new things about themselves. When partners enter this zone of increased intimacy, many find it helpful to make a commitment to remain in relationship through what may become very difficult revelations. Couples can reach a plateau of comfort where they are able to accept much turbulence; this becomes an exciting milieu for sharing growth.

14 From Power Struggle to Integration, Part I

Understanding can permit shifts in perspective that allow people to move beyond the limitations of fixed attitudes and beliefs. As we discussed in the previous chapter, exploring relationship in the Integration phase often challenges people to *uncouple* their previous beliefs and assumptions and learn fresh viewpoints. Besides the practical tools we describe in this book, people often find much use in concepts that can help them to understand and clarify their relationship issues. This chapter and the next include a range of ideas that many have found important in understanding and working through Power Struggle issues into a deeper experience of Integration.

Any Two Bozos

We take it as a dictum that *any two bozos can create an intimate relationship.* As a corollary, we maintain that it is easier to do this with some people than with others. As long as both parties are willing to reveal themselves to each other, to be honest, and to dedicate themselves to ongoing mirroring and feedback, their intimacy can deepen. This can involve people of the same or different sex, and applies to people of the same or different age. The important factor is that both people want to explore and be honest with each other, so they can work through the issues of Power Struggle.

Why Exchange Charge for Intimacy?

Often sexuality interferes with intimacy. Usually, people find intimacy easier with a friend who is not a sexual partner. Although it is perfectly possible to develop intimacy with a sexual partner, it is often not so easily accomplished. Usually, the sexual charge remains most intense with people whose intimacy is limited, while people who explore intimacy find that their sexual charge diminishes as the closeness increases. We discuss this dilemma further in Chapter 17 and offer some ideas for couples who wish to explore intimacy and maintain a fulfilling sexual relationship.

Many people think something is wrong when the sexual charge diminishes, when it can in fact be evidence of deepening intimacy. As our cultural ideals have emphasized the importance of charge, why would someone want to move away from an exciting relationship into a more stable one? Why not look for hedonistic satisfaction, more sexual excitement, or another obsession somewhere else, instead of trying to move into a growing intimacy? Our answer is that sensual pleasure, sexual excitement, and the charge of romance are time-limited and tend naturally to diminish. The sensual pleasure of having someone minister to us has a short half-life; after a time of pampering, we want to get on with something else. So it is with the excitement of sexuality or obsession; they too have a half-life, and to maintain the level of excitement takes increasing demands on time and personal resources.

A growing intimacy does not decline in this way – it builds on itself, like a self-seeding perennial flower. Partners experience feelings of strength, security and an ever-expanding sense of fulfillment with the growing knowledge of one another. Excitement is a phenomenon that is doomed to decline; intimacy tends to grow to ever greater levels of order and satisfaction.

The satisfaction of intimacy is different from that which arises from the satisfaction of a power drive. Capturing another person, either in a romantic endeavour or by a sexual conquest, provides a sudden flush of achievement that does not last. Almost immediately, the uncertainty begins to creep in, and people try to maintain control of the other. In sexual games, one has to prove oneself over and over again. In romance, more and more gifts seem required to provide the assurance that the beloved will not lose interest. And of course there is a natural tendency for partners in such games to lose interest over time and drift into the pursuit of some other person or activity. In sexual games and in romantic pursuits, people want to "capture the other's consciousness"; as Sartre wrote, this is doomed to failure from the beginning.[1]

Sliding toward Intimacy

It has sometimes been theorized that the basic human condition is separation, and that people naturally default to isolation. We ourselves believe that both to separate and to unite are vital aspects of our human task. Nevertheless, we see and experience a natural inclination toward closeness. By being together, people tend to slide to intimacy, as if they were at the top of a slippery hill. If they let go, they will inevitably move by gravity toward becoming closer.

Most of us carry unconscious fears of intimacy ("I'm afraid if you know me, you'll leave me" or "If we get close, I might dissolve, or lose my sense of myself" or "If I let you get close, you might smother me"). Out of this fear, people generally offer resistance in the form of walls and defences, to prevent the slide toward intimacy. Ironically, these blocks, which people think serve to preserve them, are what prevent them from becoming whole, fully developed, and authentic.

Good Will versus Legalism

People's basic intent sets the tone for all their interactions. This applies to all relationships – family, friends, lovers, spouses, and business partners. Many people would rather be right (legalistic) than happy (vulnerable and intimate). In being legalistic, people are trying to trap their partners into a Power Struggle rather than sharing in the vulnerability of a revealing intimacy. With good will, people can take ownership of their own experience and, hence, avoid inflicting blame or guilt; they can share with honesty and curiosity, to develop an intimacy.

This involves the *spirit* of an interchange, rather than the content. If the basic intention is to be legalistic, people will become snarled in a Power Struggle; if they intend to work through to Integration by way of vulnerability and sharing, they can say the same things, and the end result is quite different!

Staking a Claim

We make a distinction between trying to control one's partner and staking a claim. The latter situation involves a declaration that one has made the partner important and is committing oneself to this particular relationship. When prospectors stake a claim on a particular mine, they dedicate their efforts to mining in that location, and remove their focus from other potential sites. Staking a claim in relationship is tantamount to saying, "I will dedicate my time to you, and I am requesting that you dedicate your time to me." In so doing, people establish a primary location in their relationship. They *claim their position* with their partner; they do not claim the partner's life.

When I do this, I am indicating that I will maintain the garden of our relationship; I will put my efforts toward building ongoing interaction between us. I am not saying I own you; I am saying that I dedicate myself to living with you and growing with you. I claim a particular position with you.

Coffin Nails

Any time a conflict in the Romance or Power Struggle stages is left unattended, the intimacy is threatened; a little of the life goes out of the relationship each time partners fail to communicate. When people choose to hold back, their energy becomes fixated; their life vibration is dampened, and they become less present. Increasing non-presence accompanies the progress towards apathy or separation.

These fixations are like little deaths, and a relationship can withstand only so many of them before it dies altogether. Each unresolved issue is like a coffin nail that further limits the relationship. Because it is impossible to know how many coffin nails are needed to completely take the life from the relationship, wise partners deal with each issue as it comes up, no matter how painful it is to do so. This prevents the threat that could come with untold secrets or holding back information.

Prejudices and Fixed Beliefs Limit Intimacy

Prejudices (literally "pre-judgments") are simply interpretations that are determined ahead of time. They are not true, nor do they accurately represent each specific situation; they are simply short-form instruments of prediction that are constructed by codifying past experience. They offer a convenient way for an insecure or immature person to understand the world, but they prevent knowing another as a person. Prejudices are guesses, approximations, which people can use to roughly align themselves with someone; they designate the thoughts and feelings that the judging person will have with that particular individual. However, if people accept their prejudices as true, they will never come to know the genuine human nature of the other. Rather than simply maintaining prejudices, people can share them with each other, and invite the perspective of the other; when this is done, dialogue re-opens. When people share that they are operating from feelings that represent their prejudices, they become revealed, open to new possibilities with themselves and others; this opens the gate to growth and intimacy in the relationship garden.

Ghosting

Closely related to the notion of prejudice is the concept of "ghosting." People do not know each other; they know their impressions of one another, which they generate within themselves, based upon interpretations of their sensory input, and synthesized with their memory of past experiences. The feelings one has for another are based on feelings for people previously known who have similar qualities. Often, one partner will relate as if the other were a parent figure, or a person from the past. So, when people are being defensive or argumentative, or trying to control, maybe it is not their partner that they are actually trying to dominate; often, they are trying to compensate for experiences with people in their past. For example, when one partner is afraid of sexual activity because of painful past experiences, that partner may be "ghosting" a previous assailant upon the present partner. In this process, the other is objectified, and the relationship becomes fixated in the political struggles against the ghosts of the past.

If people are unwilling to acknowledge ghosting, the relationship is likely to remain stuck in Romance or Power Struggle. When this occurs, people maintain the image projection, and remain unaware of further possibilities of knowing themselves and their partners. They turn themselves into helpless victims of circumstance.

To move beyond this ghosting requires courage, dedication and honesty. When people acknowledge the ghosting, they are beginning to move past the limitation of the objectification; often both parties will have feelings to process. The person doing the ghosting often will feel resentful, then afraid, then guilty, then embarrassed and ashamed, as the acknowledgment steadily deepens. The person who has been objectified might feel hurt, enraged, indignant, sad, or compassionate. In the sharing of the feelings that accompany the objectification, both have the opportunity to know themselves and their partners more fully. Once again, this is a theme that is common in working through Power Struggle – to share objectifications affords the possibility of opening into new vulnerability and interpersonal dialogue.

Doomed to Repeat

People are attracted to enter relationships to work out unresolved issues from childhood, and tend to project patterns and impressions from earlier times. The stages of Romance and Power Struggle are characterized by this projection of past experiences upon the partner. People are drawn to relate to a specific type of person, to fulfil cravings, desires and unmet needs. When people abandon Power Struggle and go into Apathy, Transcendence or Separation, they are often just avoiding the lessons they could learn by sharing the underlying patterns and tendencies with their partners. Separation never solves the problem, because the unexamined patterns will simply show up in the attraction to the next partner. So people might as well work out their issues with the current partner; if they leave one relationship, the tendency is strong for them to simply find someone else of the same type again.

People are doomed to repeat their repetitive compulsion patterns in subsequent relationships until they know themselves and their choice of partners better. Only then are they free to relate with someone of a different type, or to choose the same type of partner with a more open-eyed interest in learning. What they don't learn in this relationship is still there to be addressed in the next one. That said, there are certainly circumstances, such as in abusive relationships, when separation may be the only responsible action.

Afraid to Love

Some people say they are afraid to love, because they fear losing the person. They are afraid of the pain and grieving they may experience if or when the loved one leaves. So they don't open, remain paralyzed, and don't experience their caring feelings. Then they feel empty, because they have closed off to what they want. Loving involves risk and daring. If you don't dare to open the window, the breeze cannot enter. When people become more certain of their own autonomous loving, they are more free to feel for themselves, without the concern that the love object might be lost. Indeed, they could never have possessed the love object in the first place. You cannot keep the ones you love, but you can keep your loving.

> *The deepest lesson you can ever learn in relationship is that you can't possess anyone.*[2]

Alone is Different from Lonely

As people become more individuated, they become more aware of being alone in their own skin. In relationships, the closer one person gets to another, the more this separateness is apparent. People can share this aloneness as part of a genuine dialogue of intimacy. When people do not accept being separate, they feel lonely. The feelings that accompany aloneness involve self-acceptance; the feelings associated with loneliness arise from non-acceptance of self and life, with a yearning for circumstances to be different from what they are.

Some people are afraid of intimacy because they fear facing aloneness; they involve themselves in power games (such as sexual promiscuity) or become dependent, as a means of avoiding themselves and their aloneness. Many of the issues of Romance and Power Struggle result from a desire to avoid aloneness; amidst the illusions that characterize these stages, people often still feel quite lonely. In trying to fulfil an image of being joined to others through enmeshment and dependency, people feel isolated, because they are out of touch with themselves and their partners.

Guilt as Control

In guilt, people do not look at themselves honestly. Instead, they objectify themselves as bad, and they punish themselves with guilt. No self-awareness comes this way. In addition, the guilty person is often trying to control the partner ("How can you be angry with me when I'm feeling so bad?"). Guilt can be used as a ploy to diminish the other's expectations. Self-recrimination is a convenient substitute for self-investigation, self-awareness and sharing.

In this way, guilt works against intimacy – *unless it is shared.* Sharing anything can enhance intimacy. A person could say, "I'm feeling insecure, and I recognize I'm afraid to look at myself. I'm busy feeling guilty instead of looking at my actions clearly. I'm telling you this, because I don't want you to get wrapped up in trying to appease my guilt. My guilt is an attempt to manipulate you, and to prevent myself from looking at myself." Guilt shared in this way can be clarifying for the partner, and can re-open a door to intimacy and self-awareness.

Possessiveness and Non-Possessiveness

In Romance and Power Struggle, people attempt to hold on to each other as possessions. The other becomes "my boyfriend" or "my child" and so on. In possessiveness, people maintain an objectification of the other. As people become more self-reliant, they are more willing to see others as separate persons. They can acknowledge the desire to hang on and own the other, and can share this as a way of letting go of possessiveness. As people become more stable in their relationships, they tend to celebrate their interaction with their partners, without having to possess them. One of the characteristics of people in the Integration stage is that they tend to prize each other's freedom.

Becoming non-possessive can look like not caring. However, we believe the most profound caring occurs when partners relinquish their ownership of each other and enjoy a relationship in which each is autonomous. They are then free of obligation or demand, and can choose to be together or not; this is the basis of the stage of Commitment.

Attachment and Letting Go

People can make one another significant and special, and thus develop a consistent, ongoing relationship; when people do not make the other important, they remain isolated and their potential is not challenged. At the same time as making another important, people also have the capacity to become autonomous, and learn to let go of dependency on others; this letting go is especially poignant when a loved one dies, or in divorce.

In growing and maturing relationships, people need to learn both to attach (to bond, and make another important) and to let go (to relinquish infantile dependency and grow into increasing autonomy).

Expectations

In the humanistic movement of the late 1960s, expectations got a bad name.

By the ethic of those days, people followed Fritz Perls' gestalt prayer[3] ("I am not in this world to live up to your expectations, and you are not in this world to live up to mine"). The "free spirits" who followed this ethic did not develop ongoing relationships; instead, they moved from one person to the next. The Perls poem was sometimes interpreted in a selfish and childish fashion: it was taken by many to mean that they did not have to consider anyone else, and could proceed on their own solitary, uncaring way. This attitude is still maintained by some today.

For a relationship to endure and deepen, expectations become important. People can gauge their distance or closeness by how many expectations they have. It is easy to love all the world and have no particular expectations of specific individuals. When people become closer and want to live in harmony, they find they tend to develop expectations of each other. Sometimes, expectations are the currency of intimacy. The closer people are, the more expectations they are likely to have of each other. Certainly, to use expectations as controls is very limiting; however, it is realistic to expect more of people who are the closest. Ultimately, after making a person important in your life and having acknowledged expectations, you must be prepared to feel emotional pain.

There is no justification for blame, or inviting guilt from the other, when an expectation is not met. People have expectations because they choose them, not because they have an inherent right to them. People should be responsible for their expectations, recognizing that they generate them themselves. Partners can agree to meet each other's expectations; but this still does not give them the right to have them fulfilled. Expectations involve a contractual arrangement, not a right.

Resentments are rooted in expectations. If people had no expectations, they would not resent anything; an easy way to reduce resentments is to lower expectations. Whenever people find they are resenting another, they could simply lower their expectations; however, with intimate partners or family members, this might become problematic, because the lowering of the expectations can produce a greater distance.

The degree of expectations is related to how intimate a person is with someone; the more that is expected, the more special that person becomes. To have very high and very detailed expectations is a way to set a relationship apart from other acquaintances. The closer people are, the higher will be their expectations of each other. Often, pain and disappointment occur in both parties when an expectation is not met. The one with the unmet expectation may experience abandonment, while the other may experience remorse. One possibility when expectations are not met is for one or both to re-evaluate the agreement. Many times they choose to continue with the expectation, which represents a challenge for both to grow and develop.

Expectations can be negotiated. In a relationship, the fact that one partner continually fails to meet expectations that have been agreed upon is not a cause to resent or blame. This is a time to re-evaluate the expectations, and decide if both still want them. Perhaps one person wants to lower expectations, and thus potentially have more distance (since the other becomes more like everyone else). This has a consequence: in lowering expectations, the specialness that comes in being able to depend upon each other is lessened. Perhaps the person who has not been meeting the expectations decides to make more effort to do so, in order to maintain the level of closeness that expectations bring. Such issues are ongoing in the dialogue of intimacy.

Investment

Investment is a concept related to expectation. Investment is a dedication of one's life energy. By investing in their partners, people dedicate interest and time to the relationship with that person. The investment represents how important they have made the other – the less investment with someone, the less importance that has been assigned to them. This can be a tricky shoal to navigate. If people have no investments, they don't care very deeply; if they invest heavily, they will be prone continually to enter Power Struggle.

Expectations arise out of investment. In relationship, the level of expectations indicates the degree of investment people assign to another. With people to whom little importance is assigned, it is easy to have little expectation. If a casual acquaintance does not live up to an agreement, one can let this pass with very little concern. However, if a primary partner does not live up to even a small agreement, the other is likely to become quite upset, because of the degree of importance assigned to that person.

When people care, they invest; when they invest, they experience pain when hopes and expectations are not met. There is nothing wrong with investment; problems arise when people are not willing to face the discomfort that sometimes accompanies investments.

In the Romance and Power Struggle stages of relationship, people tend to complain over unmet expectations. Later, with more experience and maturity, they come to see that investment is a natural correlate of caring about someone else. In an intimate relationship, people can share disappointments without blame; blame limits intimacy, while sharing increases the feeling of closeness.

Trust

To trust someone else fosters field dependency and maintains the impotence that lies beneath the Romance and Power Struggle stages. Instead, people can learn to trust their own evaluation of others. If someone else wants to trust you, ask for a definition; if you are being trusted to do something you can't do, don't agree to it. Many problems in relationships could be averted if couples did not *trust* each other but, rather, clarified their expectations of each other.

In place of trust, couples can clarify their expectations of one another, define their boundaries and bottom lines, and enunciate the consequences that would result from any breaking of the agreements. Trust in the other is unnecessary. However, in exploring intimacy, each person must be prepared to experience the consequences of broken promises and generally to accept any accompanying pain without blame.

React or Respond

A reaction is a fixed behaviour pattern that expresses a closed attitudinal position. Hence, a reaction likely indicates what we term a political stance (see page 67). When partners are stuck in Power Struggle, they tend to react in knee-jerk fashion, not to the person, but to an objectified other.

A response, on the other hand, is a process of involvement that is personal. In responding, one is curious and considerate of both self and other. With response, one listens with interest, considers, ponders, attempts to see the merits in opposing views, and tries to learn in the situation, rather than simply "dealing with it."

Often, fixed reactions are habits from early life. Many times, especially in the beginning years of a relationship, partners find themselves reacting to each other from old prejudices and attitudes. As they become aware of this, they can share these patterns; in being curious, they become more intimate with each other. In time, the reaction patterns become known, and one or the other can note that a reaction has just taken place, and invite a dialogue into the responses that humanize the interchange.

For example, if a husband arrived home late for a dinner his wife had prepared, her reaction might be to flare in anger, blaming him. Her response, on the other hand, might be to become curious at how important she had made his coming home at a particular time, and search for the underlying meaning. As she probed, she might discover that she was feeling insecure and housebound, and she was afraid that his being late means that he might be less interested in her, and might be considering leaving her. So, in sharing her fear, she might feel sad and embarrassed. If the husband is not defensive, he can then appreciate the vulnerability that she is offering. Similarly, he could consider and share his own expectations and reactions in this situation.

Reactions maintain the Power Struggle. Responses are the royal road to personal interchange and growth through increasing Integration.

Pride

Pride limits intimacy. Whenever people become invested in their pride, they are more concerned for their image than in sharing themselves. They would rather be "right" than happy. Pride tends to feed a Power Struggle. In become vulnerable, people relinquish their pride and become more revealed as their genuine selves.

Contempt and Arrogance

Contempt involves devaluing the other in disdain. In contempt, one objectifies, devaluing the other person and life itself. Indeed, in this process, people also devalue themselves and their feelings; to be contemptuous, people step back from life and are out of touch with themselves as well as others. Contempt is usually a defensive posture that masks underlying feelings such as insecurity, fear, or pain. Hence, contempt is often a self-protective posturing. When people want to become closer, they can share their contemptuous feelings, and search for the underlying meaning that maintains the objectification.

Unlike contempt, which devalues the other, arrogance overvalues the self in relationship to the other; the word is related to "arrogate," which means "to claim to oneself unduly" (from the Latin *arrogare* – to appropriate to oneself). An arrogant person claims superior consideration or privileges, much as a child would. The positive aspect of arrogance is that it can be a step toward the establishment of healthy self-esteem when a proper perspective is learned in relationship to others. Although arrogance is often seen to accompany contempt, the consequences of each in relationship are very different; contempt always involves negative energy, but arrogance can further growth.

Indulgence

Indulgence involves an excessive involvement with a particular activity or thought or experience. To indulge in an activity means that the activity takes precedence over other people and situations; in this process, the person is often compulsively stuck in repetitious behaviour. This interferes with a relationship, because the indulgence takes precedence over interaction, and curiosity for the other is lost.

Most experiences are worth having for a limited period. However, when a person indulges in something, it occupies more and more time, and the person becomes less present. Obsessions, jealousy, grieving, sexuality, work, food, self-hate, guilt – these are all delicious morsels that are attractive for indulging. Whenever self-hate, for example, is expressed for more than two minutes, be alert to the possibility that you are indulging!

Hope and Faith

To be in a state of *hope* interferes with intimacy. Hope anticipates a better circumstance in the future; hence, it is rooted in a dissatisfaction and non-acceptance of the present situation. In relationships, to hope for something different is to fail to contend with the situation as it is. By contrast, *faith* involves a profound acceptance of how things are. In faith, people acknowledge and accept themselves and their partners, and are open to interchange.

When relationships reach an impasse, as they frequently do, people who rely upon hope will focus on the future when things will be different. Too often, such people become passive and helpless, tending to freeze action while waiting for a favourable turn of events. On the other hand, when people in relationship have faith, they stay present to address themselves to the issues at hand with the assumption that they can make some positive adjustments; they have confidence in their capabilities to handle all difficulties.

Sulking and Pouting

People hurt when an expectation is not met. One can be responsible for one's own hurt, realizing that it comes from one's expectations. In so doing a person would be vulnerable, and the hurt would be something to share.

By contrast, a person may *react* to such an experience by sulking or pouting. To sulk is to hang one's head in dejection; to pout is to thrust one's lower lip in defiant displeasure. Sulking and pouting are self-pitying posturings that are used for control; often a sulk or a pout is a reaction to a hurt that the person does not want to feel. Besides the self-pity, the sulk or pout is often heavily laced with blame toward the partner for not providing what is expected. To move from Power Struggle to Integration, people can acknowledge when they are sulking or pouting, and become vulnerable by opening to share the hurt that the posturing is covering, without any investment in getting what they want.

Self-Centred Is Not Selfish

We use the term self-centred in a particular way. For us, to be self-centred is to have one's centre within oneself, rather than outside; this is a necessary condition for self-awareness and personal development in the individuation project. In being self-centred, people can remain aware of their own feelings while being sensitive to their partners; hence, they are responsive and open for contact.

Many people confuse self-centredness (which facilitates intimacy and Integration) with selfishness, which is a closed, power position. Selfishness is shortsighted. In selfishness, people are related to the image of themselves, and are out of touch with genuine feelings for self and other. Pride and indulgence are phenomena of selfishness, not self-centredness.

Selfish people move their centre from within themselves to place it in the other; the focus then becomes what the other person can provide, because selfish people, lacking a centre, cannot do things for themselves. Relationships then become mired in objectifying control for personal gain.

Self-centredness is not selfishness. Selfish people indulge in their own self-importance and fail to establish dialogue; self-centred, autonomous persons can be quite sensitive and responsive to others. Selfishness is objectifying; self-centredness permits intimacy. "Selfish" is a moral word; "self-centred" is a location word. They are not the same.

Field Dependence and Self-Reliance

In field dependence, the centre of focus is outside of the self, in "the field." Children are taught to pay attention and obey their parents; they generally do, out of insecurity. This pattern of external dependency, watching for pleasure and displeasure in the field, becomes the prototype for later interactions. People learn not to pay attention to themselves; instead, they become increasingly concerned with whether or not others are pleased with them. In relationships, when people are caught up in their partner's approval and disapproval, they are not self-directed, and remain inwardly weak, infantile, and undeveloped. This attitude of field dependence underlies the Romance and Power Struggle stages in relationships.

To become self-reliant means to acknowledge one's externalization and field dependence when they occur, and to take responsibility for them. In this process, people can shift their centre back into themselves, becoming self-centred (but not selfish!). They are field-aware or field-sensitive, but not field-dependent. Thus they are in Integration with themselves, and capable of engaging in intimate contact with another.

Dependence, Independence, Interdependence

Independence and dependence are flip sides of the same coin; they both involve having one's centre outside of oneself. Interdependence occurs when two autonomous people share without leaning on each other. Our own development around this issue has been most important to both of us:

> *In our relationship, we started out as two ferociously independent people, afraid of clinging, or depending upon anyone else. As we opened to each other, we found we had unfulfilled desires to cling and be clung to (an early stage of loving, from the early childhood experience). Thus, we explored dependence. Not wanting to regress to mutually limiting forms, we agreed upon short-term excursions into dependency. As we became more comfortable with our dependence, we found we could share both our independence and dependence; hence, we entered a phase we call interdependence. In this, we are both autonomous, but willing to be vulnerable and share our own thoughts and feelings, while being open to appreciate those of the other.*

Big Deal

What is a big deal for one partner isn't necessarily a big deal for the other, and vice versa. Both should remember that what one finds very threatening or challenging might seem very small to the other. For example, if one person is afraid of heights, the partner might not understand his reluctance to go somewhere that she finds so easy. In the development of empathy, one learns to see the world as the other sees it. Often a wife expects her husband to be soft, warm and affectionate (a big deal to him because of his violent non-touching family history, but no big deal to her, based on her touching family background). The same husband expects the wife to be compliant sexually (no big deal to him, but a huge effort for her, because of her history of trauma and abuse). To get past such difficulties, people need curiosity, compassion, empathy, and a willingness to see beyond their own entitlement and fixed perspectives. If people fail to see each other, they remain in the Power Struggle; in acknowledging each other's differences, they can move into Integration.

Humour and Intimacy

The early life struggles to achieve success are serious indeed. In striving for perfection, people grit their teeth, and have little room to enjoy the process. Indeed, under the strong thrust for achievement lurks self-hatred and self-doubt. In this driven pursuit, people do not open to themselves or others. Such people remain objects to themselves, and play roles to satisfy their intense striving. Hence, intimacy and self-awareness are both restricted.

As people gradually relinquish the goal of perfection in exchange for the increasing ease of self-compassion, they relax internally. They begin to enjoy the process of increasingly knowing themselves, drawing ever closer to their authentic nature. These people become more available to be known, and hence are more capable of forming loving intimate relationships.

When people become more comfortable with being revealed to themselves and to their partners, the seriousness of the goal striving is replaced by a hearty humour. As partners advance into growing Integration, Commitment and Co-creativity, they find more humour and an increasing sense of play in life, loving, and relationships. The whole ridiculous affair is fun! Perhaps this is what the fabled Zen monks of old were laughing at, as they went about their daily existence with full hearts.

Grieving, Sadness and Depression

Grieving and sadness occur as part of a relationship when there is a loss – through divorce, or death, or when a beloved friend moves to another location. In both grieving and sadness, one is letting go of investment in the other. The greater the investment, the more extensive will be the sadness when that person is lost. Grieving is more complicated, as it involves incomplete feelings (such as anger, resentment and love) that have been unexpressed in the relationship.

You do not grieve the person; you grieve your image of the person. What you are relating to in grieving is the store of held memories related to the experiences you have shared with that person. Partners who share and work through disappointments and disillusionments as they proceed in relationship will experience sadness and "missing" feelings, but relatively little grieving, when the person is actually gone, physically or emotionally. If one does not face up to one's investments at the time, they will have to be faced when the relationship ends. When people do not acknowledge their investments as they proceed, they remain tied to their partner after the person is gone. Partners who are responsible for their feelings and investments throughout the relationship are more likely to experience sadness as they proceed, rather than storing feelings to grieve later.

In grieving, there is a mixture of anger, hurt, love, and sadness. The anger that people experience emanates from infantile attachments to the other as a possession – inevitable in any relationship of depth. In the grieving process, people are expressing blame of the departed one for leaving. So, grieving fully, with vocalized expression of emotions, is important in order to let go of the departed one. This proceeds more easily if the individual will acknowledge the resentment, disappointment, love, anger, and hatred directed to the departed. The feelings associated with grieving will wax and wane. Often people are angry at the other for having left, and angry at themselves for having entered into the relationship in which they have ultimately been left.

Unexpressed feelings can become stuck in a chronic state of contraction that is experienced as depression. Thus, incomplete and fixated grieving underlies some depressions. The person's emotional energy remains tied to the inner image of the other – consequently, there is less available for investing in other relationships.

Grieving can also be sentimentalized; public ritualized forms of grieving sometimes interfere with the genuine expression of grief and loss, which is personal and often private. In personal grieving, people often find deeper resources in themselves, and open themselves to new levels of loving, even after their partner has gone. We explore the distinction between sentimentality and more genuine feeling in *Being: A Manual for Life* (Chapter 3).

The price for a meaningful relationship is pain; there is no free trip. This inner pain cuts new channels into the bedrock of the soul; the person who will invest meaning in the other can mature and deepen. Paul Zweig has said that people reach a level of maturity, and can embrace the art of living, when they reach the age of pain.[4]

15 From Power Struggle to Integration, Part II

The Jerk

Often, people will try to limit intimacy by defensive behaviours. In relationships, each party holds a trump card. When all else fails, they pull out this card – *the jerk*. Everyone has a particular jerk. For some, it is an offensive jerk, who drives people away by churlish behaviour. Others use an addictive jerk; still others have a violent jerk. The range of possible jerks is rich and varied: the pick-a-fight-and-then-leave-indignantly jerk; the victim jerk; the "I'll get sick" jerk; the blamer jerk; the guilt tripper jerk; the super-reasonable jerk; the leave-and-go-on-a-trip jerk; the go-into-alternate-realities crazy jerk; the "I'm too tired" jerk; and so on.

To develop a relationship, it is helpful to know which jerk(s) you have available, so that you can see what your defences against intimacy are. If partners can have good humour and are willing to share these defences with each other, they can facilitate their movement toward intimacy.

Secrecy Opposes Intimacy

Often partners are unwilling to share information, because they are afraid of the consequences – that the other might not accept the information, or that they could be ridiculed. When partners keep secrets from each other, they also keep hidden from themselves; intimacy is limited, and there is a much stronger tendency to objectify.

Intimacy flowers in the light and degenerates in the dark. For a relationship to deepen in intimacy, information must be shared. Many people maintain that a relationship will not tolerate all this honesty. They believe they have to hold back hurtful information to protect the partner. But when information is held back, there is an accompanying distance. Indeed, the entire attitude is objectifying, displaying a belief that the "weak partner" could not take such information.

We reject the view that people should keep some things back for fear of hurting one another. Being honest involves a respect for the capability of both partners. Furthermore, as we explained in Chapter 4, we believe that it is impossible for one person to hurt another's feelings; people's hurt is an expression of their own self-generated tightness, based on their own context and their interpretations of events.

Having said that, we also believe that the motive for sharing is important. Some people provide information in order to try to hurt the other in retribution; even though this is impossible to do, people still might have the intent to hurt their partner. This is quite different than sharing the same information with the intention of having it in the open, so that the intimacy can deepen.

The price of such honesty is frequently pain; however, the reward is the growing intimacy that comes with having all the information available.

Resolve It Now

Any impasse in relationship is an expression of fixation of energy. Often a similar impasse has been reached previously with nuclear family members, and the same pattern is being replicated with the current partner. An intimate relationship is a unique opportunity to resolve issues from the past, so that people can become free from the tyranny of their fixations. If parents clear up issues in their primary relationship, then they will be free to raise their children without unconsciously passing on the same fixed patterns. What the parents don't resolve themselves is more likely to be passed on down through the generations.

We recommend that people stay in dialogue to resolve issues, even if they are ultimately going to separate. Thus, they can become aware of their patterns of fixation, so that they will not get snarled up again in the next relationship. If they choose to stay together, they can become increasingly familiar with the limiting patterns, and can share their awareness about them, rather than blaming the other, and staying stuck.

Updating the Past

Many people have had trauma in the past and are now afraid to open to new experiences, because they think the old pains will be reproduced. They carry prejudices from the past experiences, and do not come fresh to the present. In one workshop we conducted, a middle-aged woman became stiff and frozen when she was invited to do an exercise with her beloved partner, which involved him tenderly opening her physical position from tightness into a relaxed open stance. Although she knew that he was a loving, sensitive soul, she had a flashback of a previous husband who had violently torn her open in the mornings to have sex against her will. When she embarked upon the exercise, she flashed back to her violent abusive husband, and went into the body memory associated with her fears of previous events. She was not responsive to her sensitive, loving partner. By succumbing to her body memory, she treated the new partner as if he were the old one. She knew her new partner was different, but reacted as if he were her previous husband, because she had a fixed association to the activity of opening.

This is one of the tasks of relationship – to update bodily and emotional reactions to others.[1] With a developing intimacy, people can become aware of fixed reaction patterns and can acknowledge them, rather than unconsciously succumb to them. Thus, even though people might be afraid of touch because they had unhappy experiences with touch in the past, they could acknowledge that fear, and accept the touch in the present, recognizing that the motivations of the current person are different from those of people in the past. Many times, a fearful person will need a code word and a definite agreement that the partner will stop an activity if the body memory becomes too much. When the partner demonstrates dependability, people can overcome even the most intense associations to the past and learn to enjoy experiences in the present.[2]

Clinging to Romance Prevents Growth

People can so easily lose themselves in an unrealistic pursuit of someone else, hoping to relieve anxiety, pain and loneliness. Although the fairy tale stories of the handsome prince rescuing the beautiful maiden are virtually impossible to realize, people are desperate to live out such fantasies. In Romance, people yearn to find someone special, who will relieve all the disappointments and discomforts in life.

In relationship, people are reluctant to give up their dream of a perfect Romance; instead, they impose all their (often unconscious) unmet hopes and desires onto the partner, and expect that the relationship will solve all problems. People are often miserable when they do not have a Romance; and, when in relationship, they continue to be miserable when they discover that their partner is not living up to previous hopes.

Such people will continue to be unhappy until they accept that they are responsible for their own lives, and that no one else can solve the basic issues of their existence. When people come to know themselves more fully, they are usually more prepared to experience the pain of separation and aloneness – to let go of the Romance, and enter day-to-day reality.

Blame, Withholding and Symptoms

Blaming produces much stress in the blamer. In order to make others wrong, people tighten and withdraw. Such moralizing constriction can produce diverse physical symptoms such as headaches, abdominal distress, arthritic pain, or heart problems, as well as a host of others. One individual who became stressed in his workplace described the evolution of his cardiovascular symptoms:

> *I am the heir of several generations of men who held back their intense judgments, and instead became ill with high blood pressure, strokes and heart attacks. When I am displeased with someone else, I can feel my blood pressure go up, and my chest tightens. I can see how, in a few years, I could develop this withholding of judgments and blame into a full-fledged myocardial infarction. The way out is to own the blame, and to share it with friends, and to breathe, instead of holding back the experience.*

When people are aware, their symptoms can be used as flags, warning them when they have become righteous or defensive. When people see their symptoms as signals of declining intimacy, they can share their experience with partners and friends. Instead of the blaming stance of "You make me so uptight!", it is possible to investigate the meaning of the symptoms with a question like the following: "I notice my symptoms are getting worse; I wonder how I am holding on and perhaps blaming you; have you noticed any clues that I might be carrying some unconscious resentment?"

In this way, instead of becoming barriers, symptoms may be used to open into deeper dialogue.

Bottom Lines

The term *bottom line* is commonly used in business to indicate a limit or a basic requirement for a process to continue. For example, in a business enterprise, a bottom line might be profit; if the bottom line were not met for an appreciable period, the business would fold.

In relationship, the bottom lines indicate limits that people have with themselves and their partners. There are usually very few absolute bottom lines in a relationship. When a bottom line is not met, there is a consequence. For example, an absolute bottom line for some people might be that they would not stay in the relationship if they were struck physically.

Honesty might be a desirable bottom line; yet it might not be an absolute one. For example, if one person is inadvertently lying, and is unaware of this, the partners might discuss this rather than separate.

We recommend as a bottom line that neither partner tolerate violence (which we define as the crossing of boundaries). What constitutes violence is particular to each person; what is judged to be violent for one person and circumstance might be acceptable for someone else. For example, some people seem not to mind wrestling with their partner, while others will not even tolerate verbal chiding. This must be defined by the individuals; what is seen to be acceptable vehement verbal interchange to one couple might be judged as abusive by another.

It is not necessary that both partners have the same bottom line, although it is important for both of them to be aware of each other's limits. One partner might have a bottom line of growth, and the other might have a bottom line of security; they could still live in harmony if they were aware of these bottom lines. Bottom lines can shift; thus, they need periodic updating.

A bottom line can be used for intimacy or for control. Intimacy occurs through sharing the bottom line, and setting out the consequence if it is not met; control occurs if the intention is to threaten and limit the behaviour of the other, rather than simply to provide information. On the surface, these situations may look the same; the difference is in the intention (to get close through sharing information, or to gain control by threats), and the consequences of these intentions in turn will differ.

Sharing Resources

People often become mired in conflict over who is providing more resources to the relationship. This is especially acute when one partner has more money to provide than the other. The superficial glance says that this is not equal, and that one partner should be acknowledged for the greater contribution. This viewpoint is based on a reifying thought process that sees resources only in terms of finances – from this limited perspective, the balance sheet tells all.

Indeed, resources and offerings take numerous forms. There are basically four domains of resources:

1 Money
2 Time
3 Energy
4 Knowledge

It is possible that equal partners in a business enterprise might not put in equal money. Perhaps one partner in a venture has lots of capital (money), but has little time to devote to the new business. To acknowledge the second partner's time and energy, the second partner could own 50 per cent of the business on the basis of "sweat equity."

In marriages, often one person stays at home and devotes time and energy to raising the children and maintaining the household. The other partner devotes much less time to the home, and instead brings home the majority of the money. These partners might be entirely equal.

Energy and knowledge are closely related. Knowledge is the organizing principle, the pattern that contextualizes energy. Energy takes on form and becomes functional through the resource of knowledge and organization. When people have experience, they are able to direct and harness energy in synthetic and creative ways; it is their knowledge that takes disparate materials and organizes them into a structure that has definite function. For example, appreciating patterns and contexts is important in the construction and maintenance of a bridge; knowing the tensile forces and behaviours of the materials, one can build the bridge to withstand the challenges of nature. The more knowledge one has, the more efficiently and creatively energy can be utilized.

Sometimes, older people are able to offer their wealth of experience (their knowledge), accumulated over many years. Their perspective, from having lived long and experimented much, can provide contextual offerings that make or break a relationship venture. Thus, the time and effort they have put into learning are resources that are available to the relationship. Many people misunderstand this perspective as patronizing the elderly, or simply rewarding people for past labours. What this limited attitude does not see is that the knowledge and experience – the context – is a resource, and many times a vital one. In a business enterprise, sometimes outside directors or consultants are paid handsomely to offer the resource of broad-based experience and sage creative process, which they have developed over years of dedication to their field.

Sometimes a younger partner provides the excitement and creativity of seeing things for the first time. This younger person might also do more of the physical labour in a partnership. The older person might be providing more experience and wisdom; this is equal to the offering of the young person, but quite different.

Couples become involved in a Power Struggle when they insist that each person contribute equal amounts of the same kind of resource. On the other hand, this awareness can be used to slothfully not pull one's load; just because one partner is well endowed with a particular resource, this does not mean that the other should not contribute whatever is possible. When people do have equal amounts of a particular resource, they should contribute this resource equally. Basically, in order for both persons to put into the relationship their full effort and dedication, they must offer whatever they have.

In one marriage, the wife was making a full salary but did not contribute any of it to the marriage, because her husband had considerable financial resources. The husband paid all the bills, because he thought that as a man this is what he should do. She used her money for her own interests. This was a parody of this differentiation of resources – with disastrous consequences. This couple did not stay together; they lost each other in the resentment of not having cleared their expectations with each other.

At the beginning of a relationship, partners should discuss their expectations regarding various resources, and come to agreements about what each person will offer. These agreements can be re-negotiated when the conditions change; nevertheless, making the expectations clear minimizes the possibility of future confusion, disappointment and resentment. Although they don't have to contribute equal amounts of each resource, they should contribute what they can. At the beginning of a relationship, it could be useful to keep a tally of the contributions. This may be especially in relation to finances, but couples could also track non-financial inputs (housework, cooking, taking care of children, etc). The issue is for partners to assess their input into the relationship, so that each can have the confidence of contributing equitably.

No Compromise

Generally, our culture expects two people in relationship to compromise, to each give up something in order to find a common middle ground. Such an approach attempts to reduce each person to the lowest common denominator; they become lesser versions of themselves. We find this idea objectionable. In order to learn and grow closer, each person can clarify desires and intentions without having to abandon them. If someone were to ask, "What are you prepared to give up to have a relationship?" the life-giving reply is "Nothing; I'd rather not have a relationship than compromise." In compromise, people give up themselves, and there is less of them to offer. In our own relationship, we will never compromise.

Acceptance of the other's differences without compromise invites harmony. In music, harmony can be between seemingly dissonant notes. There are no bad harmonies; sometimes accepting unusual combinations can give rise to complex and interesting interaction. Very dissimilar partners can co-exist in harmony. As long as they remain curious, acknowledging and accepting the differences without blame or resentment, they can live together without having to change the other, or reduce themselves. Instead of compromise or judging one to be right or wrong, the goal shifts to expanding the appreciation of the new ("dissonant") harmony.

When one compromises, one submits to the desire of the other, becoming reduced and limited. Generally, this is accompanied by resentment of the other, and often a hatred of the self. Harmony comes in working out a solution that incorporates these desires, rather than denying them. We believe each party must acknowledge desires, and try to attain them. This is not a simplistic "follow your bliss" or "go with the energy" approach, which can be irresponsible and insensitive. Rather, partners should respect individual differences, and express their desires openly and clearly. In acknowledging desires, one surrenders to one's life and becomes stronger, with more to share in a growing intimacy.

Once one has acknowledged a desire, one can choose whether to follow the desire or not, without abandoning the self. For example, a person might want to go skiing; however, that same person might decide that he would rather stay home with his partner, who does not ski. He has not compromised; he has made a free choice to value being with his partner more than his desire to ski.

How do I know if I am compromising, or simply being open to the other's wishes? The clue comes with the presence or absence of resentment. If I am happy to go the movie you chose, even though I might have chosen another one, then I have not compromised; I am still aware that I want to see the movie I originally selected, and I probably will see it some time. If I resent you for not coming to the movie I wanted, I have compromised, submitting to your desires. So, no resentment indicates no compromise; resentment and guilt and self-hatred accompany compromise.

Sexual Charge with Others: Desire and Choice

To be in relationship means paying attention to desires, while remaining open and sensitive to the feelings of one's partner. When people know their desires, they can choose to share them with their intimate partner, without having to follow them. We object strenuously to approaches that invite people to "follow the energy" with no regard for the partner. Instead, couples can inform each other about their yearnings, and then can use this as a basis for discussion as to how both parties can get what they want.

It is very common for one partner to have a sexual charge for someone not in the relationship. Because the sexual charge is based in objectification, this is quite normal, and to be expected, as we discuss in Chapter 17. However, many partners believe that they should only have a sexual charge for each other, and that something is wrong when they feel excitement over someone else.

There is nothing in this that needs to be a problem. To acknowledge to the partner that one has sexual feelings for someone else can be an act of intimacy. Because there is such a pressure to suppress such feelings, the sharing can bring new vitality into the relationship; the energy that might be consumed in hiding such information would become available to the partners. Both partners would likely become vulnerable with such a degree of honesty; rather than become defensive or blaming, they could remain open to each other to share the feelings of threat that might arise from such candour. Rather than denying or hiding sexual feelings for someone else, people can share these with their partner, to enhance their intimacy.

Most people will not accept the partner having an affair; however, they might well accept their partners telling them about their attraction toward someone else, with the assurance that they will not act on it. Only in rare couples would one accept the other having the affair, and we do not recommend it; nevertheless, if this were done with full revelation of the entire events to the intimate partner, they could still stay close. Perhaps instead, the partner could role play the desired object, and the desiring one could have some experience of having what he or she wants. We discuss this more in Chapter 17.

Actions Demonstrate Desire

People's actions express their motivations and desires. As the 60s' saying puts it, "If you're doing it, you're digging it!" Denying responsibility for one's actions maintains the Power Struggle; acknowledging one's responsibility for actions invites the dialogue of the Integration stage. Both parties can acknowledge that whatever they are doing, they actually want to do this. Although such desires are often unconscious, there is no room for the ready defence of "I didn't want to do what I was doing." A more revealing statement might be: "I recognize that I was thinking about something else, and didn't listen to what you said; I obviously did not value being with you as much as I valued my thoughts." Although this degree of honesty is challenging, it can help to avoid many unnecessary disputes, and keep the relationship from reverting back to the Power Struggle.

Gossip

Gossip is talking about someone when that person is not present. When gossip is kept secret, intimacy is lessened. This commonly occurs in families, when two people talk about a third; this limits the sharing and interaction that are possible. We maintain that there is no problem with talking about someone when that person is not present, if what is said is reported directly to that person at the first opportunity. When gossip is kept in the open, families, businesses, and friendships can flourish in the atmosphere of openness.

Sharing Violent Thoughts

Violence occurs whenever there is no consent. Hence, for two friends in a karate duel, there is no violence to being struck, as they both agree to such a physical interchange. On the other hand, there can be violence in caretaking someone who does not want attention. We believe that no person or object should ever be injured; hence to us, it is never appropriate to strike a partner. However, in many cases it might be acceptable to use words to describe violence. For example, some couples might not allow physical blows, but might accept being called names in the heat of a disagreement, in order to express all the energy of the interchange.

Couples can agree to describe violent fantasies about the other – for example seeing the partner hurtling through a plate glass window, or imagining administering pain to the other. Sharing the fantasies with permission and agreed boundaries permits the energy of the disagreement to be expressed without any real danger. Furthermore, there can be a vulnerability in actually revealing such thoughts, which are usually considered unacceptable; this vulnerability can work for more closeness when it is respected rather than rejected.

Overcoming Numbness

From time to time, most people find themselves out of touch with their feelings and caring. Even people who are dedicated to the relationship project sometimes close off and become numb, lacking empathy and losing presence with themselves and their partners.

Curiosity and memory can be used to overcome such blunting of feelings. Sometimes the investigation of how presence was lost brings people into touch with some deeper feeling they were avoiding; breathing consciously and looking for unacknowledged feelings often helps. When people don't feel, they can remember that they have previously had feelings. In recognizing that this is a temporary situation, they are less prone to sink into despair over their current numbness; they can relax while they wait to find their way back to feeling again. Also, becoming curious about the other person can overcome dullness of feeling, and return one to a state of presence. Sometimes, the pain in the eyes of one partner (who is missing the dialogue) can summon the other back to presence.

Time Out

Either person can request a "Time Out" rather than persisting in repetitious defensiveness or explosive uncontrolled behaviour. Both parties should honour a request for Time Out, temporarily halting the exchange. The partners agree when they will talk again, before they leave the interaction. After they have had time to consider the situation separately, they can come back to the interchange – hopefully with fresh eyes and less defensiveness.

Five-Minute Cling

In our own exploration of independence and dependence, we made some unexpected discoveries. Jock discovered to his horror that he actually liked to cling like an infant. Having been ferociously independent (he kicked his own parents away when they were diapering him), he opened up to new levels of vulnerability in himself when he began to acknowledge his need to cling and be dependent. Ben's fear was that someone would want to fasten onto him, and thus he avoided situations in which someone would cling to him. Consequently, they both had something to learn.

The solution to this dilemma was *the five-minute cling*: Jock could hang on like a two-year-old for an agreed upon time, and Ben would commit to remaining present with him during this short period. This clinging always required an agreement, as Ben possibly would not be available at the time of the request. In living this through, we each have faced our fears, and have come to more acceptance of our defensive avoidances. Jock can now enjoy clinging without demanding prolonged attention; Ben has learned that he can survive in the face of Jock's dependency without being overwhelmed.

We have talked about this in workshops over the years, and now other people have come to use the five-minute cling principle, too. The clinging partner can learn to accept not having a cling on demand, and can sink into the experience of having one when it is possible. The person who is being clung to can face the fear of being smothered or restricted, realizing that the event is time limited. Just because one partners asks for a cling does not mean the other is obligated; possibly it is inconvenient at the time of the request. Both partners learn a sensitivity to the desires and boundaries of the other by working out these arrangements. By facing the underlying fears and accepting infantile cravings, the charge diminishes in the situation, and both partners gain more autonomy through the process of sharing.

Checking Out

As we have discussed in describing the Communication Model (Chapter 4), checking out with someone else involves sharing one's experience, and then asking questions to find out the other's perspective, rather than merely assuming it. In the process, the initiating person expresses perceptions, interpretations and feelings, and then asks the other person to report his or her corresponding perceptions, interpretations, and feelings. This requires curiosity, and the recognition that one's partner can easily have a different viewpoint on a situation.

Checking out one's impressions is one of the most important tools in developing an intimate relationship. In the fixed attitude of objectification, people continually represent others from their own prejudices and background experience; they believe that they know the experience of another without checking it out. If they do not ask about the perspective of the other, they will often be proceeding on limited or invalid information. When people do not check out their assumptions, they persist in the limitations of Romance and Power Struggle.

When they do check out their assumptions, they invite a dialogue with the other, which can lead to intimate sharing and more Integration.

Clearing Time Each Day

Just as people can adopt an exercise regimen, they can commit to spending time each day to process and become clear in their relationship. This should be done when there are no distractions, because it demands special time, with sharing and presence. This is a time for contact and mutual exchange; partners take an interest in the activities, thoughts, and feelings of each other. With regular time for clearing and contact, people who lead autonomous lives can be in touch with each other's process, even though they still have separate interests and activities. Business partners can meet early before the day's work for clearing; family members can agree to meet over a meal once a day; husbands and wives can agree to uninterrupted time together in the evening.

We recommend that partners endeavour to keep up to date, and stay clear with each other, rather than permitting unspoken information to accumulate. Just as some birds continually clean their nest to keep it tidy, when people stay current with each other, psychological refuse does not build up to contaminate their relationship nest.

Clearing is Not Dumping

When an individual expresses perceptions, thoughts, or feelings without curiosity or regard for the response or feelings of the other, this is a dumping (like having a bowel movement). A dumping is an impulsive catharsis of feelings and judgments, without interest in a genuine dialogue with the other. The other is kept as object, and the self remains fixed in habitual prejudices (literally, pre-judgments). Dumping involves blame and guilt, and hence is frequently used in the Power Struggle stage.

By contrast, a clearing includes acknowledging one's intentions, and curiosity about the other; a clearing involves questions to discover the viewpoint of the partner. In a dumping, both parties are objectified; in a clearing, they are experienced as persons.

Clearing can involve past issues as well as present ones. Often, partners decide to become more intimate after they have been in relationship for a number of years with each other; by this time, they have accumulated a backlog of unexpressed impressions, assumptions, resentments and appreciations. In the present, they can clear up issues from the past, and thus become engaged in their mutual impressions of the events, rather than remain fixated in their own individualistic judgments.

Status Report

Businesses often function with periodic reviews, to see if they are on track with the goals of the enterprise. In raising a vegetable garden, an intermittent check of the condition of the plot is very useful; this would involve checking the moisture of the soil, looking for parasites, and generally assessing the health and growth of the plants themselves.

At any time, couples can request such a review of the relationship garden in the form of a *status report*. This is a particular use of clearing and checking out, where the focus is on determining the state and health of the relationship itself. By periodic review, partners can keep track of ongoing issues and expectations, and evaluate the development of the relationship garden. An in-depth query of each other would include questions such as the following:

"What were we hoping for?"
"Are we achieving it?"
"Where have we failed?"
"What can we do about this?"
"What are we very satisfied with?"

"Where is there room for improvement?"
"What pleasant surprises have we had?"
"What unpleasant shocks have we weathered?"
"How are we feeling with each other in the midst of our relationship project?"

This review would also include volunteering information such as:

"The things you have done that I have appreciated about you are ..."
"The things you have done that I have resented about you are ..."

The Positive Use of Power Struggle

The Power Struggle stage, full of passion and excitement, involves the investment of people's life energy. When people learn to *share* the elements of their Power Struggle, they can come to increasing self-awareness and self-acceptance, moving beyond self-righteous, fixed positions into a genuine curiosity and engagement with others and all of life. In this way, what are usually destructive elements (such as jealousy, possessiveness, control, anger, expectations and blame) can be shared in a responsible, growth-enhancing way. People can come to know themselves and their partners more deeply in a steadily developing Integration of their lives. The elements mentioned in the last two chapters provide some of the major areas that people can address in the development of their relationships.

PART IV

Love, Sex, Family

16 Love, Obsession, and Addiction

Love Is Junk

While in private practice, we commonly saw young people suffering from the termination of relationships. Having lost a loved partner, their symptoms included depression, anxiety, insomnia, weeping, low energy, loss of appetite, withdrawal of interest from normal activities, self-doubt, ideas of being worthless and unlovable, and, often, unpredictable episodes of anger and rage. At other times, we were being consulted by young people withdrawing from drugs such as alcohol or heroin (known on the street as "junk"); remarkably, their symptoms were similar to those recovering from separation from a loved partner. It soon became apparent that the people suffering from loss of relationship were behaving just as the people who were withdrawing from drugs – they were all addicted! Whether people are addicted to drugs or people, they all go through common symptoms of withdrawal. How does this happen?

Becoming addicted is easily done. If healthy people were given insulin over a long period of time, their bodies would shut down self-production of this chemical. After a while, the body would lose most of its ability to make insulin, and thus would be entirely dependent upon outside sources for its well-being. A similar phenomenon occurs when people are fed a high-sugar diet (a quick energy source) for a long time; they lose the ability to mobilize energy from their own metabolism. The process is the same for growing children whose emotional needs are always quickly met and never frustrated. Gradually, they develop a sense of entitlement, believing that they have an inherent right to such care. Being constantly "loved" (or more accurately, given too much attention), their own loving generator is rarely exercised. They grow dependent upon others – rather than themselves – to take care of their emotional needs. They have become effectively "hooked" to outside sources for these needs.

People who emotionally "hook" or addict others to themselves generally do so because of their own sense of inadequacy and lack of real meaning in their lives. In a way, they themselves are dependent upon others depending upon them. This condition is common, beginning when parents "think the world of" their children, rarely allowing them to stray from their sight. Unfortunately for both parents and children, such overly solicitous parenting can be a symptom of obsessing rather than recognizing and highly valuing that person; these parents need the affection, attention, and compliance of their children for their own sense of value in life. Sometimes such an obsession (called "love") over the children is a convenient way for a couple to avoid dealing with very real problems in their own relationship. A cartoon in the *New Yorker* magazine showed a middle-aged couple, their arms around one another's shoulders, looking out of their living room picture window, with the following caption: "Well, dear, now that the children have all grown up and left home, it's just you versus me!"

This obsessive parent-child interaction provides much attention to the children, but little recognition of who they actually are or of what they think and feel. (We write more about the distinction between attention and recognition in *Being: A Manual for Life.*) This attitude frequently results in offspring who are unable to make effective commitments and meaningful relationships. They tend to suffer from a low sense of self-esteem, and worst of all, they can develop high expectations of others and unrealistic levels of entitlement for themselves. When they become emotionally involved with others, they want to control and possess them, and to blame them for everything that happens in the relationship. Unfortunately, these are the kinds of relationships that society has idealized. Love songs fill the radio waves with plaintive proclamations that "I can't live without you" and "You light up my life" so "How am I supposed to live without you?" Our ideal love stories (for example, the story of Romeo and Juliet) would have us kill ourselves rather than face life without one another.

Remarkably, in the subculture of addictions, drug suppliers ("pushers") are sometimes referred to as "mothers" by the addict. Pushers will sometimes offer free drugs at the beginning, until the recipient has become dependent. This process is similar to the sugar example given previously. The body's own mechanisms tend to shut down, allowing the drug to take over those functions that variously provide a sense of well-being, excitement, or relaxation. Once hooked, that person requires a regular external source to feel whole. The drug addict and the person addict have much in common. No wonder that their withdrawal symptoms are often indistinguishable from one another!

Once pushers have succeeded in establishing the addictive pattern of needs, they have the ultimate control. If the pusher determines that some of the addicts' behaviours are inappropriate, the threat of withdrawal of love will soon make them conform. Over time, as the addiction increases, the price of supplies can escalate, and the pusher thus has increasing control over the addict's life. As with all addictions, the person's very soul is eroded and the self is lost. The only recourses the addicts see seem limited and self-abusive. They can threaten to switch pushers, substituting one addiction for another; or they can threaten suicide, either figuratively or through symbolic self-destructive behaviours (such as accidents, physical and emotional illnesses, job losses, or criminal activities).

The Pie Theory of Love

Many people see their love like a pie that can be sliced and exchanged in a variety of ways – a large slice for my partner, perhaps a similar-sized one for the children, a smaller one for work, and maybe even a smaller one for friends. People who live their lives this way keep a wary eye on the size of portions served to each of the parties in their lives and on how much is returned. They become nervous and jealous when they believe that they are not being given their "fair" (meaning "expected") share. They are prepared to barter the amounts, and can go crazy attempting to balance the accounts by the end of the day. As they grow addicted to the slices, they nervously live on the brink of anxiety attacks, in fear of losing the share that they now believe they deserve and need. They seek as much attention as possible to satisfy their craving to fill their sense of emptiness. Their own measure of self-worth becomes tied to the relative size of the piece of love pie that is given to them by their partner, children or friends.

Operating with this theory of love contributes to the creation of obsessions and addiction to others. Such people no longer operate from their own centre; instead, their centre is moved from within themselves to somewhere between themselves and others – or in the extreme, completely in the other person! Their own capability of loving is replaced with a desperate need to be loved by somebody who resembles their "microdot," as we discussed in Chapter 17. To capture the consciousness of the desired object may require submission to that person and an abandonment of the self. Once they capture their prey, they must constantly monitor their victims, to ensure that they will not be able to escape. Thus they create an obsessive life style, in the name of love.

Obsessions and Compulsions

An obsession is a repetitious thought that one cannot dismiss. For example a student often will become obsessed with the ideas that are studied, and cannot shut off the thoughts to go to sleep at night. A compulsion is a repetitious action that is dictated by an obsession; the obsession is the thought, and the compulsion is the action that is linked with the obsession. For instance, one might be obsessed with the fear of germs and contamination; the associated compulsion might be repetitious hand-washing. Often, an obsession is an habitual thought process that provides the security of the familiar; people will often obsess in order to avoid uncertainty. For example, if people devote their time to worrying about the future, they have less time to be anxious in the present. Worry is often a substitute for anxiety.

People become obsessed with another in order to try to overcome the infantile fear of abandonment. At the root of this is the existential condition of aloneness, and the angst of existence. The insecure child becomes obsessed with the parent, trying to capture the parent's attention, in order to avoid being abandoned. The pattern of trying to capture someone else in relationship becomes set; as this individual establishes relationships later in life, the desire to capture the partner will still be operative. Such obsessions give rise to driven activities, such as telephoning the partner numerous times each day, just to check; another compulsion is stalking the partner, watching outside the home, to spy on the partner's activities. The obsessor's life activity can be entirely taken up with the obsession. The movie *Fatal Attraction* is an excellent on-screen depiction of the chilling disintegration of a competent person through obsession, and the disastrous results that can occur.

Hunter and Hunted

This desire to capture the other is often seen as love. In fact, it is quite otherwise – this desire to capture is what kills loving! Because the obsession aims to capture the objectified other, there is no acceptance of the self or the other – and thus there is no loving. Obsession is a prison for the obsessor; the person is not able think or move freely, or be creative. The relationship cannot develop, as all the activity is directed to controlling the other; this is merely a simulacrum of loving. In movies and television, such relationships are seen to be loving, because the parties devote much attention to each other; however, this is not genuine caring, as there is no recognition of the other.

Obsessions and Compulsions Are Deadly

In an obsession, one abandons oneself and bargains away vitality in exchange for the security and charge of the repetitious thought process. The reward (or the aim) for an obsession is twofold: there is the similitude of control and dominance, which provides excitement and charge, and there is temporary relief from anxiety. Obsessions limit people's lives; when people obsess, they don't have room for more frightening thoughts and feelings. They don't have to face death or abandonment or aging or impotence or unimportance; they only have to focus on the obsessions and compulsions. Even though obsessions can seem so intense, they are deadening; people lose themselves and their vitality, and become consumed by obsessions.

Obsessions involve objectification. The Romance stage is filled with obsession and compulsions; people fantasize and obsess about an imagined other that they do not know (the imagined ideal love object), and when they find someone, they devote themselves to this object. In the Romance stage, the relationship is not with the person; people are often addicted to the object of an obsession. In the same way, the sexual charge is a repetition compulsion; in the excitement of pursuing a sex object, people tend towards robot-like repetitive thoughts and behaviours that are diminishing of the person. In this way, romance and sexual charge are similar to other addictive processes; the person is not present. The pursuit of the object is exciting, but deadening!

Dealing with Obsessions and Compulsions

We can be master of our obsessions; they need not master us. By becoming aware of the obsessions, acknowledging and accepting them in a process of sharing, people can find the key to the prison. As people become more familiar with their obsessions, they can become more free with them, able to enter the obsessions for a limited time for excitement and play, without having to become trapped in them. Thus, couples can have a romantic dinner with each other, knowing all the while that the pressures of life still exist; or they can share a sexual fantasy together without having to make it the raison d'être of their lives.

When obsessions are not shared, they tend to intensify in the secrecy; although this might increase the charge (which is addictive), it makes intimacy less possible. As people share their obsessions, the level of intimacy goes up, and the charge diminishes. The key to overcoming an obsession is to become familiar with it and its underlying motive of seeking security. As with jealousy, the problem arises when people try to control their partner instead of acknowledging their insecurity. As people become more aware of their obsessions, they can share these with their partners, acknowledging the motive for the compulsions that accompany them. Thus, they reveal the underlying process, and utilize the awareness to bring more integration in their relationship.

The Empty Bucket Theory of Love

Another common idea of love that governs parent-child relationships is the Empty Bucket theory. In this view, people see their children as coming into this world as empty vessels into which "responsible" (read "obligated") parents must pour their love. The theory supposes that if parents are successful, they will fill their children's buckets sufficiently so that they will have enough in their tanks to be able to find partners into whom they can pour this love. If all goes well, they will be able to have children of their own, for whom they can undertake to do the same.

Because this theory relies entirely on outside sources for the supplies of a commodity – "love" – it sets up ideal conditions for the development of an addiction. The more people depend upon others for love, the less they will generate their own; their love-generator will gradually shut down and they will be totally dependent on others for supplies. In such a way, more love addicts are created. For the pushers, the more they can get others addicted to them, the more secure they will feel in life; they never need to be alone again!

> BEN: *When I was in private (psychiatric) practice, it slowly dawned on me how essential I was becoming in the lives of my patients. Many of them could not function without me. To my horror, I realized that once I had addicted them to me, they were only able to separate from me by replacing that addiction with prescribed drugs. At best, I was able to encourage them to become addicted to others, to work, or to religion. Once I realized this, I hastened to encourage them to withdraw their centre from me and return it to its proper place within themselves. Establishing opportunities for them to have group experiences instead of private, individual therapy helped; but it was important not to provide a group support that would encourage further addiction. Consequently, Jock and I always discouraged the idea of a therapeutic or spiritual community.*

The solution to such addiction is for addicts to take charge of their own lives and well being. As people take responsibility for their own feelings and activities, they are less prone to the manipulations of those who would like to hook them into addictive behaviours. The movement beyond the Power Struggle into Integration involves people becoming the authors of their own lives, thus overcoming their dependencies.

A Wholeness Theory of Loving

Both the Pie and Empty Bucket theories of love have roots in the idea of dependency in relationships; so they are natural precursors to the establishment of co-dependency and addiction. A more wholesome approach involves the concept of personal responsibility with the self and in relationship; this is embodied in the Communication Model that we describe in Chapter 4. Instead of being empty buckets, people are seen to be whole beings that generate all of their own feelings – the hurts as well as the loving feelings – in response to what they perceive and interpret. People's buttons are not pushed by others; it is not even that people *allow* their buttons to be pushed. Instead, we believe, people do the actual pushing of their own buttons! People are never empty; they are always complete, although they keep much of themselves dormant as unrealized potential. When people meet somebody they like, they are stimulated to generate feelings of loving from within their own centre; if they are self-assured, or wish to become so, they will remain open and vulnerable to share such feelings with the other, in this way establishing an intimate relationship. We propose that people *always* have the capability to generate some loving – even though they might choose not to do so out of fear or insecurity. Often, people choose not to love out of a motivation for revenge and anger – even though they themselves, not others, suffer the most!

Contrary to the Pie theory, there is not a finite amount of pie that can be divided among loved ones and friends. Instead, each relationship is a full pie unto itself, into which people are capable of contributing *all* of their current feelings for the other person without lessening in any way their loving for their primary partner or their children. Instead of being diminished and exhausted by loving, people can feel refreshingly expanded. The energy does not belong to the individual, and does not have to be measured out or hoarded; it is universal and ever present as potential that only requires stimulation in order for people to resonate and express in loving.

As people develop a confidence about their own wholeness, recognize that they generate their own feelings, and become more willing to share them, they find an increasing sense of self-esteem and autonomy. In growing children, this is fostered by parental attitudes that encourage responsible, self-supporting behaviour, providing them with experiences of recognition for who they really are as persons, instead of attention for what they do in their roles. In such an atmosphere, people come to realize that they are not empty buckets in search of others to provide them with love; rather, they are full of the possibility for loving. They only need to kick start their loving generators, and to learn appropriate people and places where they can express their love in relative safety. Such learning does not come easily; nor are there many role models for them to emulate. The relationship garden is one place that can support such an education in life.

An Image

Picture a young, fragile, tender sapling growing alongside a strong, straight, well-rooted oak tree. If the sapling develops by leaning on the stronger oak tree, its roots will stay shallow, seeking nourishment only in relation to the oak. Its trunk will be bent from leaning; lacking in robustness, its branches will be short and puny, its leaves sparse and small, receiving little of the bright sunshine. Such a co-dependent relationship fosters weakness in the smaller tree, and occupies much of the energy of the stronger one, thus limiting its potential too.

On the other hand, picture the oak choosing not to support the sapling any more than is necessary, refusing to allow it to lean; the young trunk will grow straight and tall, the roots will be wide-spreading, seeking nourishment from a broad area. This kind of sapling grows in strength, with its branches spreading wide to mingle with those of the oak, its leaves full of colour and richness, dancing with the breezes in the sunshine and the rain. Together, they brace against the storms of adversity, and are cleansed by the gentle rains of compassion. Through the years, they continue to grow in strength and complexity, each fulfilling its own destiny.

Weeding the Garden

In a relationship garden, each person must be true to himself or herself, accepting the nourishment that is there available for all within the garden's boundaries. There are many weeds that need to be identified and removed; the control weed is the most virulent. Control strangles growth, expecting others to become what you want them to be, rather than who they really are. Although there are many obviously negative control weeds (such as manipulation, lying, cheating, withholding, withdrawing, terrorizing, threatening, bribing, blaming, threats of self-destruction, guilt, self-pity, mental and physical illnesses), the less apparent ones are often the most dangerous because they are more confusing. These covert controls include some apparently positive strategies such as being nice, being helpful, taking care, and being supportive. These are ostensibly performed for the welfare of the other, but underneath, they are primarily for the benefit of the caretaker's sense of value.

Before these weeds can be pulled, they first must be identified. This is an important task that is best accomplished through curiosity and an established agreement between the partners. It is most beneficial when each is prepared to openly acknowledge any attempts at control. Healthy dollops of humour and humility really help, as do self-compassion and the

"Five A's" of Awareness, Acknowledgment, Acceptance (of the self as well as the other), the Action required to move beyond fixations, and Appreciation (see page 95). In such a healthy, open environment each person can be nurtured into growth.

A complete sharing between two people is an impossibility, and whenever it seems, nevertheless, to exist, it is a narrowing, a mutual agreement which robs either one member or both of his fullest freedom and development. But, once the realization is accepted that, even between the closest human beings, infinite distances continue to exist, a wonderful living side by side can grow up, if they succeed in loving the distance between them which makes it possible for each to see the other whole and against a wide sky!

– Rainer Maria Rilke[1]

17 Sexuality

Q. What exactly is marriage?
A. When somebody's been dating for a while, the boy might propose to the girl. He says to her, "I'll take you for a whole life, or at least until we have kids and get divorced, but you got to do one particular thing for me." Then she says, "Yes," but she's wondering what the thing is and whether it's naughty or not. She can't wait to find out. – Anita (age 9)[1]

Intimacy Is Not Sexuality

Although many people confuse intimacy and sexuality, they are very different. By intimacy, we mean a deep knowing and understanding of one another's interior lives that is achieved through vulnerable revelation and a shared sense of closeness and caring. Some intimate relationships have no sexual component to them, and yet partners are deeply close. Conversely, many relationships that involve sexual charge and excitement have little intimacy or emotional closeness.

As we explain in this chapter, we understand human sexuality to be at root impersonal, relying heavily on people's capacity for objectification. Because of this, intimacy and sexual charge, by their very nature, tend to work against each other.

The good news is that they don't have to be mutually exclusive. Like salt and pepper, they are quite different, but can be used compatibly. For this to happen, however, couples need to understand how these two aspects of human endeavour occur, and how they differ. Then they will have to work at combining them. We ourselves began our relationship project as two men with no distinct sexual charge for each other, focusing instead on our intimacy together; we have often said that in this way we have had it easier than couples who are trying to balance their sexual interest in each other with their intimacy.

When people pursue a sexual attraction or charge, they often objectify their partners and themselves in a way that makes intimacy very difficult to achieve. One can have an intimacy with a friend or colleague by being open and revealed with that person; generally, this openness does not lead to a sexual encounter. This distinction between sexual charge and intimacy flies in the face of the common euphemism for sexual contact, "having intimate relations." To us, an intimate relationship is based upon relinquishing barriers and defences, moving beyond objectification into profoundly knowing one another; it can be a challenge to have sexual contact be part of such a relationship.

The challenge for intimate partners who are involved in sexual relations with each other is to bring elements that are essentially depersonalizing and objectifying into the intimate engagement. This is definitely possible, and can be a very interesting project. We have often said, "Anything that is shared can enhance intimacy." Although much of sexuality is by its nature depersonalizing, when it is shared, it can be used to enhance intimacy. This is similar to when couples want to share anger with each other; what is often separating and objectifying can also be shared responsibly and openly, and in the process partners can learn to appreciate themselves and each other for the vulnerability of sharing such feelings.

It is usually in the beginning stages of a relationship – when people are relative strangers to one another – that the sexual charge is the highest. As partners get to know one another better, the sexual charge often appears to diminish and may even be lost! Nevertheless, it is possible to have sexual excitement and intimacy with the same person – but not easily or automatically. Indeed, it takes considerable self-awareness and commitment between partners to bring together the sexual charge and intimacy, which seem more naturally to move apart from each other.

Sex, Gender, and Attraction

It is useful in learning about one's self and sharing with an intimate partner to distinguish between sex, gender, and sexual attraction.

Sex is a genetic determination of whether a person is male or female. *Gender* involves individual and cultural notions of masculine or feminine behaviour and characteristics.

The question of who you are *attracted* to sexually is only partly related to either sex or gender. In this chapter we explore the idea of the sexual microdot as a further avenue into investigating this question for yourself.

Often these three – sex, gender, and sexual attraction – are treated as though one flows naturally from another. We think this confusion can be problematic for people and emphasize instead that there are many ways for people to integrate these facets within themselves.

For example, a person whose sex is female might have qualities that are frequently associated with cultural notions of male gender, such as a tendency to dominate or "play rough." This has no necessary connection with whether she is hetero- or homosexual, nor with the particular types of men or women she is attracted to. Similarly, though in a different arena, a man (whose sex is male) may have an interest in articles of women's clothing, and might even want to wear them himself. In this way, he may be expressing a more feminine aspect of his personality (a gender related interest). This same man might be completely heterosexual, turned on to women. People can become very confused if they think their gender-related interests necessarily identify them as either hetero- or homosexual.

A person's sex is biologically based, determined by the chromosomes in one's genetic makeup. A person is male (XY chromosomes) or female (XX); much less frequently there is some variation in this standard coding. In this sense, one's sex is biologically determined, and unchangeable. Even if people undergo a sexual reassignment surgery, they remain genetically the same sex, because their chromosomes do not change. The gonads can be removed, but not replaced. The hormonal balance can be adjusted using external drugs. Many of the secondary sexual characteristics can be adjusted through surgery and hormone administration. The chromosomal level, however, is unchangeable.

Gender is culturally determined and concerns roles and qualities identified as masculine or feminine. So traditionally in modern Western society, little boys have been encouraged to have blue blankets, play with trucks, and learn to be aggressive and play football and climb trees and get dirty. Little girls are given pink blankets and frilly dresses, and are expected to play with dolls and not get dirty. This sets up a dichotomy between the sexes, with culturally expected roles and attitudes. The woman is supposed to wait for the man to take the initiative. Once married, the traditional value is for the male to earn the living and the female to take care of the household and, indeed, to caretake the very relationship. In recent decades, these distinctions have become much less clear-cut, and many variations on the theme are more culturally acceptable in many circles. But the unconscious pressures from the cultural memes regarding gender identity are very potent, and individuals are subjected to expectations that they only partly understand. Boys may feel insecure if they are not big enough, or dominant enough; girls can feel concern about wanting to do things that boys traditionally do.

In traditional Chinese philosophy, human beings have both *yin* and *yang* qualities (*yin* is soft, yielding, enveloping and nurturing – "feminine"; *yang* is hard, aggressive, directed, and initiatory – "masculine"). From a Jungian point of view, all people have both masculine and feminine aspects. The male is taught to suppress the feminine qualities, and to search for a female to complete himself. The situation is similar for females with respect to their masculine attributes.

Thus, people experience themselves as incomplete, requiring someone else to complete them. This is the basis for loneliness, where people are subject to the romance that urges them to find someone special to complete them. They are lonely when they don't have the perfect life partner. This is the main issue in the Romance and Power Struggle stages of relationship; at this period, people have little knowledge of themselves or of others, and they are looking for images to complete themselves.

When people begin to accept themselves and others, they move into the Integration phase of relating. People at this stage are not concerned with being completed by another; they recognize that they are already whole, and find fascination in the ongoing project of discovering themselves and their partners. The project shifts from one in which something wrong needs to be fixed to one in which there is ever-increasing revelation of universal wholeness. Then, people are no longer lonely. Men do not have to look for a woman to complete them; they can search to discover their own feminine nature, which informs the images of what Jung called their *anima* projection (and fuels sexual excitement and romances). In the same way, women can experience their wholeness without depending upon a man to complete them. Whereas Romance and Power Struggle are associated with incompleteness and dependence upon externals, in Integration people can experience themselves as whole, and responsible for themselves as unique expressions of life.

When people become interested in delving beneath their habitual roles, they often discover that they have been trying to get their partner to provide what they themselves could offer. In the grotesque fixedness of the traditional family meme (pattern), the man comes home from work and puts his feet up, while the wife is supposed to make the meal, minister to him, listen attentively to his grumbling, and take care of the children, without ever expecting any of the same in return. Thus, the male is stunted in his nurturing ability, and his ability to relate in a responsive, receptive manner. To become more responsible, people must become aware of these gender prejudices and acknowledge them to their partner; in the process of accepting them, they begin to be able to move through and beyond them. This can be very freeing indeed. Many men find they greatly enjoy some of the roles usually assigned to the feminine gender – cooking, childrearing and shopping. Many women find a great liberation in moving into the workforce and contributing to the family finances.

In most relationships, there will be gender prejudices that were learned from families and culture; when these are understood and overcome, people can become full and integrated – both *yin* and *yang*, masculine and feminine. Much of this can be discovered in sex play between partners who want to learn. This investigation can be intimidating, sobering, and sometimes very frightening, because it questions very basic self-assumptions. But it can also be invigorating and revelatory!

Dimensions of Sexuality

Q. What is the proper age to get married?
A. Eighty-four – because at that age, you don't have to work any more, and you can spend all your time loving each other in your bedroom. – Carolyn (age 8)[2]

The chart on the facing page describes several different aspects of sexuality. These categories are not mutually exclusive. Indeed, all of these dimensions are simultaneously available. In any given individual in a specific situation, there will be varying degrees of expression of these dimensions of sexuality. When a young couple is trying to get pregnant, the biological dimension might be foremost, with them taking great care to have sex at fertile times; in an early stage of a relationship, the sexual charge may be more dominant, and later on give way to the development of aesthetics and spirituality.

None of these zones of interest is better or worse than another. Furthermore, they overlap and flow into each other. None of us is exactly the same; we will have varying degrees of interest in these different aspects of sexuality. People should not try to label themselves or their partners, for example as a "sensual-erotic type." Instead, we hope that knowing about these different dimensions can facilitate understanding of one's self and one another, especially in instances where partners' sexual interest is different.

There are many forms of sexuality. We often say that in a room of fifty people, there are fifty forms of sexuality. This chart can be useful in investigating what areas the reader finds most interesting, and to help individuals understand their partners' interests, which might be different from their own. Hopefully, this can invite much discussion and sharing, some of which can be done in the privacy of the bedroom!

These elements are like the ingredients of a soup, which can be included in varying quantities and intensities. Some soups are heavily laden with garlic; others have a light touch of lemon grass. Some relationships are highly charged, while others are more fragrant with aesthetics or romance. None of the motifs is better or worse than the others. They are simply the components that can go into the multidimensionality of a sexual relationship.

It is important to realize that all of these dimensions of sexuality are in themselves impersonal. It is in the vulnerable sharing of experiences around them that people can make sexuality more personal and a part of a growing intimate relationship.

Dimensions of Sexuality

	BIOLOGICAL	**SENSUAL-EROTIC**	**SEXUAL CHARGE**	**ROMANTIC**	**AESTHETIC/ MYTHIC**	**TRANSPERSONAL**
LOCATION	Physical	Physical	Mental-emotional	Mental	Deeper nature	Higher self
MOTIVATION	Relieve tension	Relieve tension	Overcome helplessness	Relieve anomie	Emotional spiritual	Meaningfulness
MODE	Ejaculatory	Stroking	Penetration/ Fenestration	Image management	Meaning management	Ecstasy
PURPOSE	Reproduction	Pleasure/Pain	Domination/ Submission	Control	Meaning attribution	Union
MEANS	Organic	Sensory	Symbolic	Symbolic	Sensory/ Symbolic	Ineffable/ Inarticulate
INTIMACY	**Impersonal**	**Impersonal**	**Impersonal**	**Impersonal**	**Impersonal**	**Impersonal**

Biological Aspects of Sexuality

The biological aspects of sexuality are generally taken for granted, even though there are many gaps in our knowledge of this very important subject. A common assumption is that the sexual drive is biologically determined, mediated by a complex neuro-hormonal network that affects the mechanisms of behaviour. Simply stated, people are genetically patterned to produce the appropriate chemicals to prepare their bodies for the characteristic sexual functioning and behaviours that drive them toward consummation in the act of sexual intercourse with a person of the opposite sex. The purpose of this is, of course, continuation of the species.

If this assumption is correct, the natural history of sexual behaviour would go something like this. The male has a relatively stable hormonal balance, offering a preparedness for – but (contrary to popular belief) not a drive toward – sexual activity. The female has a complex inner rhythmic cycle of events, a delicate orchestration of hormonal balances. When ovulation is uninhibited, it occurs approximately once a month. In order to enhance the chances of fertilization of the ovum at that time, a subtle chemical intoxicant (a pheromone) is emitted into the atmosphere; if that pheromone can make contact with the male, it will stimulate his sexual neuro-hormonal apparatus, and he will seek out the female. Sexual intercourse would be the result – but only once a month! This is "natural" (i.e., according to nature) sexuality, determined by biology. From this point of view, all other sexual behaviour is considered "unnatural" or "perverse" (meaning "turned in another direction," since its aim is something other than reproduction). Some religions have adopted a moral position based on biological assumptions, claiming that only what is "natural" is morally acceptable. The logical extension of this is that all sexual intercourse other than at the time of ovulation is not only "unnatural," but also immoral! In any case, biological sexuality involves drives that are not specific to humans, let alone to individuals; biological sexuality is therefore not personal. Nevertheless, there are times when this aspect becomes foreground in a couple's experience, for example when trying to have a baby; and it is possible to be vulnerable and intimate with one another in this experience.

The Sensual-Erotic

The sensual-erotic dimension of sexual interest occurs in relation to the organization of the nervous system. The body's neurological apparatus is excited by different stimuli, providing a wide variety of pleasant and unpleasant experiences. Some specific areas (the erogenous zones), when touched or stroked in particular ways, stimulate an excitement or arousal within the person that is described as "sexual." More specifically, it is a sensual arousal to which sexual meanings are attached. The arousal of the senses through touch (stroking, texture, warmth, and so on) is only one of many possible perceptual arousals; for example, stimulation is possible through vision (colour, form, size, lighting and darkness), hearing (music, sounds of breathing, silence), smell (body odours, perfumes), and taste (body tastes, food, drinks). Such arousal through sensual stimulation constitutes the sensual-erotic aspect of sexuality. This is largely mediated through the parasympathetic nervous system, which produces relaxation and a general feeling of well-being. Not all sensual erotic experiences are soft or pleasant or relaxing, however; for example, jumping into an icy cold ocean stimulates the senses in quite a sharp and immediate way, as does a sudden slap or bite.

The sensual-erotic aspect of sexuality is valued to varying degrees by different people. To some, it is the most important aspect of sexuality; to others, it is only the means to a more exciting end. The sensual-erotic experience may have a relatively brief half-life. Being stroked or massaged can even become irritating, as would too many scents or tastes over an extended period of time. Nevertheless, a wide variety of tactile stimuli can be eroticised, ranging on a pleasure-pain continuum from tender caresses and gentle massage all the way to rough handling, pinching, biting, and hitting. The sensual-erotic arousal is not necessarily related to any specific person or object; stroking of the senses is all that is necessary to produce the erotic experience. In this way, the sensual-erotic is essentially impersonal; the specific person that provides that stroking or pinching is secondary.

Sensual-erotic experiences are basically physical, mediated through the neurological sensory apparatus. In the brain, the centres chiefly responsible for integration and experiencing of the stimuli are in the diencephalon, which functions below the level of the thinking brain. Since these brain structures are common to all higher animals, not only humans, these experiences are basically naturalistic, and hence impersonal.

The Sexual Charge

Sex is engaging in the first rounds; what sustains interest in the long run is power.
– Madam Jiang Qing[3]

The sensual-erotic experience can be poetically described as soft and rounded, pleasant, but not compelling. There is another kind of sexual experience that is sharper, more highly charged, more acute, immediate, and driven – the sexual charge. The sexual charge is exciting, tension-filled and urgent, compelling the person to action and creating a physiological flooding of blood flow, increased blood pressure and heart rate, and a hypersensitivity and turgidity of erotic zones in the body. Sexual charge is largely mediated through the sympathetic nervous system (which has been described as the fight/flight/fright system). The sexually charged experience is impersonal – generally in relation to a sexual object. The specific person is secondary, as in the sensual-erotic experience. Unlike the sensual-erotic, however, which is biological and sensory, the sexually charged experience is primarily stimulated by symbols. The process is basically a mental one, involving the cerebral cortex, which functions with symbols. Objects (including language and objectified people) are assigned particular meanings that are then related to specific and highly individualized feelings.

Robert Stoller's book *Sexual Excitement*[4] proposed a number of ideas that we have found very useful in working with people around their relationship with sexual charge. We find Stoller's arguments clever, insightful and thought-provoking, though fundamentally unprovable. Even when we're not completely convinced by his work, his proposals have helped us to clarify our own thinking, especially in relation to notions involving power and strength, control and vulnerability. So, in this section, you are invited to decide for yourself how much of this thinking you want to incorporate into your own view of sexuality.

In the symbolic, charged form of sexual excitement, says Stoller, each individual reflects a combination of influences involving the culture (the cultural romance) and his or her personal history. From an existential point of view, underlying both of these influences are unresolved childhood issues – an ongoing fear of helplessness and annihilation, ruminations of worthlessness and self-doubt, and, ultimately, a fear of abandonment by others that (for the infant) could lead to death. The solution offered by society is for each individual to master survival skills and to control the environment – especially the people in that environment – in order to make life predictable. Thus each individual is caught in a struggle for power. At the same time that one wants to control others, there is a desire to submit, to give over and have someone else take charge. This craving for domination and submission becomes the main theme that underlies the sexual experience at the symbolic level; it is what fires the excitement for the sexual charge.

The chief means of expressing the domination/submission theme in sexuality is through sexual intercourse. The desire is for either penetration or fenestration (that is, being entered or penetrated), which are opposite sides of the same coin. The underlying theme is control – both the dominator and one who submits feel triumphant in being strongly desired and needed by the other. Both experience validation and temporarily lose their fear of abandonment. There is a sexually charged excitement in the pursuit of a desired object-person in the romantic stage of any sexual relationship, on the dance floor or at a cocktail party. There is the thrill of domination when the other person fully agrees, verbally or behaviourally, to do one's bidding. The possibility of failure, of being rejected, only serves to heighten the excitement. There is equal power in submission; many people experience a thrill in being the object of desire or of domination. After a time, the excitement may diminish when the surrender and domination have become commonplace and taken for granted; this occurs in the majority of committed relationships within about five years.

According to Stoller's thesis, the sexual charge involves a sexualized version of an early fantasied power theme, which often involves a reversal of childhood victimization. In the sexual charge, and choice of partner with whom to play out the theme of domination and submission, there is a retelling of a life story. Thus, people do not experience a sexual charge with everyone. There are thousands of components that go into making up the sexual charge (gender, age, size, shape, colouring, voice tone, attitudes, and other personality attributes). One is not sexually attracted to a person; rather, one is attracted to an object that most closely fits the elements in a now unconscious childhood fantasy. The elements in sexual attraction are the components of a theme of power and domination that is seeking realization. Individuals are not attracted to just anyone; they are attracted to people who most closely fit the elements of a character (their "microdot") in their fantasy; by so doing, they are attempting to compensate for earlier experiences of victimisation, traumas or simply a sense of inadequacy. Thus, in every sexual charge there is a story; in the "microdot" is a condensed object-icon that contains elements from earlier life needing reparation. They did not succeed in dominating in their past; hence, they now seek to dominate objects and images that reflect upon their past. In Sartre's words, they seek to "capture the consciousness" of another.[5]

Stoller's view is that the sexual charge involves a revenge theme; individuals choose, not a person, but an object to dominate and control, to symbolically repair the problems of childhood powerlessness. We ourselves don't fully embrace this idea of a revenge theme; nevertheless, we think that much of adult sexuality functions to overcome and balance earlier experiences through the use of control. This is largely a mental phenomenon – although it is experienced physically as a charge, the experience is mediated through the brain, in the unconscious fantasies of the cerebral cortex. This thesis denies the romantic myth that a sexual charge is for a distinct person. Indeed, from this perspective, the sexual charge is not personal at all; it has to do with the manipulation of a symbolized object that represents earlier unresolved incidents and traumas. This has important implications for the place of sexual charge and more generally the exploration of one's sexuality in an intimate relationship.

Romantic Sexuality

For some people the most exciting aspects of their relationship are involved in romantic activities. For them, the actual act of intercourse is less compelling than the events that lead to the bedroom. They enjoy flowers, candlelit dinners, soft music and conversation. Greeting cards and telephone calls heighten their experience of being valued and cherished. They find a quiet dominance in having their partners satisfy these emblems of their ardour. These romantic expressions represent the importance that romantic lovers ascribe to each other; in themselves, they are symbolic, hence not personal.

Romance involves a strong use of one's imagination; thus, it can be a very creative domain of activity. Recreationally, romance is the adult's sandbox – a temporary reprieve from the stark realities of life. At its best, romance opens up the imagination to new possibilities. As an interlude, romances are refreshingly enjoyable. And indeed, romances can be the opening into unexplored possibilities. Becoming obsessed with them, however, puts the possibility of personal growth and intimacy into the background.

Aesthetic and Mythic Sexuality

Some people's main attraction is to pursue beauty and form and grace; they experience pleasure in the aesthetic. For them, the human body and activity are most attractive as art. They become full of pleasure and excitement in appreciating dance or painting or sculpture. Their attraction to a partner is largely on the basis of that person's beauty. People who are stimulated in this way are thrilled with the lines of a body or the particular structure of a face. Graceful movement and transient shadows can also be pleasing in this way. A perfect setting for a meeting, a particular shadow falling across the face, the flickering of candlelight across a bare arm, the tinkling of a deftly played piano – any of these can be sexually stimulating to the person whose charge involves the aesthetic. In this attraction, they are relating to the form, rather than the person; hence this form of sexuality is also impersonal.

For some people, the meaning given to such experiences is mythic in nature. Myths are stories that express deep patterns of existence. In the interplay between mythic characters, universal processes are described and enunciated. When these myths relate to the interplay between the sexes, and to the dynamics of masculine and feminine forces, they describe some common underlying themes in human sexual interactions.

Every society has its myths. They commonly involve stories of infatuation, wooing, and conquest; these are utilized in the creation of characters in plays, movies, art works, and folk tales. There are myths of same-sex friendships (for example, Damon and Pythias), parent-child interactions (such as Oedipus), as well as male-female love relationships. In art and literature of the Western world, depictions of sex and relationships abound – for example, in the stories of Amor and Psyche, the rape of Persephone, Leda and the swan, the myth of Narcissus, and the legend of Apollo and Daphne. The universal tale of lovers defying their parents to be with one another is written into Shakespeare's *Romeo and Juliet*.

In day-to-day sexual expression, these universal aspects are largely unconscious; nevertheless, these deeper elements are probably in operation in many people's sexuality. People who enjoy theatre, ballet, opera, film and literature can tap into this source of sexual arousal. Once again, it is essentially impersonal; and yet can be made personal through sharing.

Transpersonal Dimensions of Sexuality

Like the other dimensions of sexuality we have discussed, the aspect we refer to as transpersonal is essentially impersonal; in this case, the aim is to transcend the limitations of the person. George Bernard Shaw in *Man And Superman*, reflects this view of its basic impersonality:[6]

> DON JUAN: *Do my sex the justice to admit, Señora, that we have always recognized that the sex relation is not a personal or friendly relation at all.*
>
> ANA: *Not a personal relation! What relation is more personal? More sacred? More holy?*
>
> DON JUAN: *Sacred and holy, if you like, Ana, but not personally friendly. Your relation to God is sacred and holy; dare you call it personally friendly? In the sex relation the universal creative energy, of which the parties are both helpless agents, overrides and sweeps away all personal considerations, and dispenses with all personal relations.*

Experiencing a deep sense of loneliness, most people desperately attempt to join with others in numerous ways, including the sexual. For some, fusion or spiritual oneness with another becomes a sexual goal; others aim to achieve ultimate union through what might be called cosmic orgasm.

Rarely in sexual engagements, individuals can indeed profoundly let go, relinquishing personal limitations, to discover a feeling of unity with the universe. This is not an act of joining with another; it is instead recognition of the state of being already joined with the other. Such a peak experience requires moving beyond the fear of aloneness, and the fear of death. It requires a dissolution of the "imprisoning ego," a surrender of the self. Herein lies what some call the divine; others call it oneness or a state of grace.

Some people subscribe to tantric practices, where sexual energy is channelled toward enlightenment. Many find romantic appeal in the notion that sexual practice between loving partners may result in mutual orgasm and thus closer connection. We note simply that such goals, romances and experiences are not in themselves personal, though like any of the other aspects of sexuality we discuss they can be shared in an intimate relationship, as a process of making personal the impersonal.

Making Personal the Impersonal

In each of the dimensions we have named, sexuality is essentially impersonal. The challenge in ongoing relationships is to uncover the sources of interest and excitement and then bring these into the intimate sharing of the relationship, making personal the impersonal. When couples share this private information, they become more vulnerable and known to each other, enhancing their intimacy; as this happens, they objectify each other less. Commonly, partners are interested in different aspects of our chart; so, they have the challenge of how to find satisfaction for both of them. The path to such satisfaction is intimate sharing, with honesty, openness, curiosity and willingness to engage and explore.

As partners become more intimate, their sexual excitement tends to wane as they interact less symbolically, and more personally. Often, sexual experiences become more fulfilling, which for some has an excitement of its own. This "intimacy charge" relates more to excitement over surrendering than submitting (a distinction we discuss in *Being: A Manual for Life*). Some people call this their sexual excitement, and are content with it.

However, some people become dissatisfied with the loss of the charge associated with domination and submission. They may seek therapy or want to change partners. When people want to rekindle sexual excitement in their relationship, they often need to explore creative ways of rediscovering these themes together. Removed from the moral perspective, no act or desire is intrinsically wrong; what can be faulted is insensitive expression of a particular desire. The important word is consent: for growth and mutual benefit to occur, the participants in the relationship must agree on each aspect of the interaction. To transgress consent and personal boundaries converts the sexual experience into an act of violence. Each person should be able to explore the meaning of particular desires and impulses in a context where no one is disadvantaged.

Fantasy, play-acting, stimulation of the senses, and exploration of pornographic stories and movies together are all possible approaches. We say more about these possibilities below. First we want to look more closely at how individuals develop their particular charges and attractions, by exploring further the idea of the microdot.

Ideal Sex Objects and the Sexual Microdot

The elements of a sexual attraction are both cultural and individual. Each society has some objectified ideals that are held to be attractive; because they are arbitrary, they vary from generation to generation, from century to century, and from locale to locale. Currently, in North America (and because of movies, increasingly so in many other parts of the world), the cultural female sex object ideals are such things as blonde hair, athletic body, long legs, pouting lips, and well-shaped buttocks – much of which can be found in the reigning movie stars and singers. Each decade brings a new group of ideal sex objects for the population to dream about and emulate. The male counterparts are often a well-muscled athletic body, boyish face, shy grin, penetrating eyes, flat abdomen, and a devil-may-care attitude. Men and women "turn on" to these stars and emulate them as much as possible.

On an individual level, people's sexual attractions are related to their individual histories. Nobody is turned on to all men or all women. We agree with Stoller's assertion that people encode within their sexual charges their unfinished childhood business. Each person has a particular story to tell in his or her specific charges. If a child grows up wanting to possess or control his blonde mother, perhaps as an adult he will be interested in a partner with blonde hair; or if he finds the association too threatening, perhaps he will convert it and become interested in raven-haired girlfriends. People who did not have enough of father's attention might choose as the object of their sexual desire men whose bodies and/or temperaments are similar to that of their father. Perhaps when they were children their father drank; even though they might have sworn never to become involved with a drinker, they often find themselves unconsciously responding sexually to exactly that kind of man. We do not suggest that these associations always occur; nevertheless, they are frequent enough that we encourage partners to consider these ideas in exploring themselves in their sexuality.

All of these stories, cultural as well as individual, are coded into the *sexual microdot*. We discussed the evolution of this term in Chapter 17. People's life stories are symbolically condensed and contained in a person's subconscious as an encapsulation of what each person will want to pursue. The object is never a full person; it is only parts of a person, or things belonging to a specific kind of person, or personality characteristics related to people upon whom the individual has tended to become fixated. From this perspective, the sexual charge is an indication of obsessions and fixations upon objects dating back from early childhood all the way up to the present time.

This explains the wide range in people's sexual charges – whether the object of desire is skinny, fat, full-breasted or no-breasted, athletic or wasted, tall or short, tight or slack-jawed, hairy or smooth-skinned, with dirty fingernails or surgically clean, talking rough or with sophistication, dressed in lumbermen shirts or basic black with pearls. The underlying stories are legion.

From across a crowded room, or a little ways down the bar, or on the other end of a pew, people are quickly able to spot the object of their sexual charge, thanks to the silent radar that seems to be attached to the internal sexual microdot. The pulse quickens, and they begin to fantasize scenarios that ultimately lead to pursuit, to make the object their very own! These scripts of pursuit and acquisition are themselves written in the microdot, motivating the unfolding of very specific moves that could lead to a capture. Once the object is acquired, people have idiosyncratic ways to relate to it; the particulars of the ultimate interactions will be specific to each individual. All this provides the story line underlying the laments and pleasures of romance; they stem from the internal microdot, reflecting tastes and predilections, hopes and desires.

Sharing Sexual Fantasies

Most of the ideas that follow relate especially to sharing aspects of domination/submission themes of the sexual charge, as in our work with couples we have found these to be particularly important for those who wish to keep sexual excitement alive in their relationship.

However, the sexual charge is only one of the expressions of sexual energy. There is the compulsive energy related to the monthly ovulation cycle, which is designed for reproduction. There is also the pleasure of the sensual-erotic in which all of the senses can be stroked, and the thrill of the aesthetic with perfect form or grace. Furthermore, there is the peak experience of the transpersonal in which one surrenders to the cosmos in sexual bliss. And all of these forms, including the sexual charge, can be romanticized into gross sentimentality. We encourage partners to enjoy and share whichever of these various energies they choose, thus enhancing an intimate relationship.

As we have already said, the exploration of these various themes needs to be done with consent and agreed boundaries. In relationship, capture themes connected with sexual charge can be acted out in sexual games. If there were no limits, no respect for boundaries, the risk of personal annihilation could translate into fear, with a loss of the sexual charge. After establishing limits, couples can discuss, share and role play without devastation. With close relationships – or at the least, trusting ones – there exists a sufficient level of perceived safety to allow the taking of risks, to explore the limits of the danger of losing the self. Without that safety, and without permission being granted, the same acts that can be so exciting for intimate relationships would be acts of violence. It is the permission and level of safety that make it otherwise.

With such agreements, couples can explore novel and exciting sexual games. Many couples enjoy being able to masturbate one another, sometimes whispering sexual fantasies into one another's ears. More risky – and hence potentially more exciting – might be to masturbate oneself in front of one's partner. For many people, this means confronting their vulnerable shame and guilt over voyeuristic and exhibitionist desires. What has been most prohibited could well prove to be most exciting!

There are classic themes in pornographic fantasies, which include the travelling salesman and the farmer's daughter, the soldier on a final date before leaving for battle, a minister and a member of his flock in church, a student and a teacher, a patient and her doctor, an encounter with a rapist or a hostage-taker, an anonymous phone caller talking dirty, a peeper with someone undressing or taking a shower. The more forbidden the fantasies, the more charged they will be. Add to those the array of individually created fantasies, and there will be endless situations that couples can explore in the privacy of their own homes. Permission and safety must always be stressed; it is also important for couples to agree upon some password that would signal that one of the members really does wish to stop the fantasy – a signal that would immediately be respected. Once they embark upon this exploration, the possibility exists that as one level of fantasies is recalled, shared, or acted out, deeper layers of repression will become available for the future. Thus, in that process, each person's history can be revealed and expressed and understood.

An interesting aspect that may emerge is a desire to humiliate or to be humiliated. This is related to a need for revenge rising out of perceived humiliating experiences as a child or youth. This can include such desires as to spank or be spanked, to be tied down, or to be ejaculated on. Telephone sex and other practices that play on an element of anonymity may be highly charged, especially when partners have an experience of apparently controlling one another's sexual excitement; the element of anonymity highlights the depersonalization involved.

Pornography is everywhere these days, on the internet, in magazines, even in subliminal forms being used in television advertising. Whatever the moral and political issues that frequently surround the topic, it is evident that pornography is very, very popular. Many people are aroused by pornography in one or more of its myriad forms. In an intimate relationship, this need not be a problem, even if only one partner is interested in pornography. Problems generally arise when involvement in pornography is a private, secret affair. In couples, the husband sneaking off to the computer late at night to view online images can establish a wall of secrecy and create a distance between the partners. We recommend that partners share all their sexual secrets with each other, and remain present with each other to deal with the feelings of embarrassment, shame, and insecurity as well as excitement and passion that can be revealed. As we often say, "Anything that is shared can enhance intimacy." This holds for pornography just as well as for other areas. If your interest is in pornography, we recommend that you share this with your partner in a vulnerable, revealing way; if you are the partner receiving this information, remain curious and open, sharing your feelings, both positive and negative, in order to come to deeper knowing of your partner and yourself.

Sharing Attractions and Charge

Couples seeking intimacy, who want to connect through loving, are encouraged to identify and acknowledge any impulse toward objectification. In intelligent, highly complex individuals, the sexual object choices can be very variable and exotic. Knowing one another's source of objectifying excitement can enhance the intimacy. At this point, to deepen intimacy, it is important that both agree to share their inner fantasies of excitement, even if the object of that charge is someone (past or present) other than the partner. By so doing, what was impersonal becomes personal. As with all personal information, such sharing may be accompanied by considerable vulnerability and may result in much pain and anger, which also can be shared to further the intimacy even more.

During this kind of sharing, it is important that partners remain as non-judgmental, uncritical (both of the self and other), and curious as possible. As people come to know more and more about their partner's past experiences and sexual orientations, they catch glimpses of that person's inner power desires and feelings of inadequacy. Frequently, during those times, the sexual charge for one another may become strong, and they can bring it into sex play between them. As they become more familiar, they may begin to realize that they have previously really known very little about one another – and what they thought they knew might be revealed to have been only projections upon one another!

With the information revealed about those innermost objectifying secrets, the partners can be co-creative, as in the following experience. In sharing of this sort, Cindy revealed to her partner that often when they were having sex, she had become excited by a fantasy of being seduced in her own home by a travelling salesman. Without telling her what he planned to do, Sam dressed up one day as a salesman and rang the doorbell; when Cindy answered the door, he proceeded to seduce her into the bedroom where they enjoyed some of their most exciting sexual encounters! The exploration of these fantasies with one another is another way to turn the impersonal into something personal and revelatory.

Generally we do not recommend that partners move outside of their primary relationship for sexual excitement. For the rare couple who can successfully operate within these parameters, we recommend that the partners reiterate their commitment to holding their relationship as being primary, and be stringent about always revealing such inclinations, activities and feelings to each other.

Sexual Charge and Passion

The sexual charge with its objectifications, fantasies, obsessions and compulsions produces a sense of electrical excitement, accompanied by various levels of self-doubt and self-hatred, because of its denial of the personal. The accompanying desire to dominate and capture the other makes a victim of both of the parties involved. According to Sartre, such sexual desire is doomed to failure.[7] By this he means that the excitement in objectification is a repetition-compulsion, not regenerative. Thus, over time, the tendency is to seek a new sex object to dominate, rather than deepen with one's current partner. Unless people address their inclinations to objectify, and explore them in the context of a deepening intimacy, they tend not to reach a point of knowing either themselves or others. Most people are limited in how much they share, and thus do not reap all the benefits that can come from an intimate relationship.

On the other hand, as people share their fantasies and objectifications with one another, they may find that they increasingly experience a sense of passion for life. They relate to life energy in a more direct way, beyond roles, idealizations, and objectifications. Their lives might become less exciting, but much more fulfilling and passionate; a whole person should be capable of both excitement and fulfillment.

Submission versus Surrender

The act of submission is related to power. One person gives over control to someone else, yielding to the will of another. The main referent is the other; the self is diminished in importance. However, as in all power circumstances, both the one who dominates and the one who submits are invested in controlling the other, albeit from seemingly opposite ends of the pole. In existential terms, the exciting charge that is experienced over the prospect of submission is related to the flirtation with nonexistence or death – the giving up (or the taking over) of all responsibility through the ultimate dissolution of the will. As we have seen, this theme of submission and domination is characteristic of the excitement of sexual charge.

The act of surrender is related to giving up of control of the self, and its referent is only to the self, not to another. One surrenders (lets go) of one's attempts to control or limit oneself, but not by handing over such control to someone else. In order to survive and be rewarded in society, people need to develop self-control through roles, social conventions and task competency. Such self-restraint is important to the development of one's personality; but at the same time it inhibits spontaneity and involves some loss of sense of oneself. The act of giving up such controls (as in surrender) results in a softening, an exhilaration, a sense of experiencing oneself again, fresh and new.

All relationships involve an interplay between submission and surrender by the people involved. The relative amounts of those experiences determine the nature of a relationship and the possibility for personal growth within it.

In the process of exploring with another the various dimensions of sexuality we have outlined, and perhaps especially that of sexual charge, one may have recurring opportunities to *surrender* to one's own nature. In acknowledging to one's self and another the range of one's sexual being, one may experience a letting go of control, a sense of flow and exhilaration, which some describe as ecstasy.

Taking Responsibility for One's Sexual Excitement

We assert that people are responsible for creating their own feelings – including all of their sexual excitement. Thus, one person does not "turn on" or "excite" the other. Instead, people's passions and sexual interests are generated within themselves, based on their life experience, imagery, and personal tastes. Thus everyone can learn a great deal about themselves when they are turned on or off. But they should not blame themselves or their partners when they are not turned on. They can investigate why they are not turning on, and can learn about their own limitations.

This relieves each partner of performance demands. Instead of the common (and doomed) approach of trying to excite each other, we recommend dialogue between sexual partners to discover what each other finds exciting. People cannot turn their partners on; however, they certainly can increasingly learn about what partners use to turn themselves on, so that they can willingly and lovingly participate in enhancing their excitement and pleasure.

This principle of self-responsibilty is useful as partners learn about the varieties of orgasm they can experience. Although simultaneous orgasm is possible, it can become a limiting ideal. The idea that people should orgasm together is often based on a romantic idea that they will then be joined in a cosmic way. But there is also deep sharing possible in being present for the partner's orgasm, quite independent of one's own satisfaction. And there can be great joy, sharing, and excitement in participating in bringing a partner to climax after having had one's own.

Vaginal, clitoral, and anal orgasms all tend to be different in quality; but one is not better than the other. They are a matter of personal preference, and informed by each situation. If people are free to experiment, they can experience a great variety of orgasms. Some people report that there are orgasms possible without even being touched. And contrary to the myth that men are only able to orgasm once, many men can come twice, and some can let go several times in an hour. The orgasms are often different each time. Sometimes, they are more like what their female partners describe – whole-body shudders of pleasure, rather than an ejaculatory release. Conversely, sometimes women can have an experience more akin to a man's ejaculation. When it comes to orgasms, men and women both are capable of much more than people commonly realize.

One notion that interferes with people having sequential orgasms is the idea that the only valid orgasm involves intercourse. Indeed, often the most exciting orgasms are from manual or oral or anal stimulation, or from masturbating oneself in the presence of one's partner. When people become creative about sexuality, they can openly masturbate themselves; and their partner can have pleasure and excitement in being a witness to this. This relieves great pressure from relationships where one partner has a higher sexual drive than the other; not every sexual feeling needs to result in intercourse or recriminatory pouting! If he is excited, and she is not interested in intercourse, she can be present with him, and share in his pleasuring himself, and vice versa. In this way, one can share sexuality without demanding anything in return. Then partners are freed of the necessity to become aroused every time the other is sexually interested; indeed, with this freedom, people often find that they become aroused by their partner's sharing.

Open communication is the key. Keep talking about how you feel, what you want, and don't want, at any given time.

The Isomorphism of Sexuality with Life

"Isomorphic" means "having the same pattern." The expression of one's sexuality is a reflection of one's entire life. People who are interested in domination/submission in sexuality are likely to have these issues elsewhere in their lives. It is not necessary to act out all the forms of one's sexual interest; the very investigation to discover where attractions, charges, or disgusts reside can provide a key to the basic patterns of one's existence. Thus, sexuality can be an investigation ground for self-discovery. Whatever passions people have in their sexuality can be discovered in other areas of their life. For years, we have made the statement:

As you are in your sexuality, so are you in your life.

This warrants some explanation. What we really mean is that you have the same themes and issues throughout your life, in all the aspects, including the sexual arena. But these themes are handled differently in different zones. For example, a mild-mannered, polite chap at work might be a tiger on the basketball court. The compliance in one situation mirrors the domination in the other. The theme is domination/submission, played out differently in different areas of one's existence.

The same holds for considerations of sexuality. If you are dominant in your regular daily life, being in charge, managing everyone, this does not necessarily mean that this is the form of sexuality you will desire. It just means that dominance is a theme in your life. Indeed, in your sexual play, you might prefer to take a very passive role, and relish the opportunity of having someone else be in charge.

An Opportunity

To us the distinction between intimacy and sexuality is crucial. Confusing the two can lead to much disappointment, as people miss out on the range of what is possible in terms both of intimacy as we define it, and of sexual pleasure and excitement.

Through sharing their unique sexual interests together, couples can enhance their intimacy and find a deepening understanding of themselves. In an ongoing relationship, partners can experience more freedom in discovering all the dimensions of being involved in sexuality, ranging from the profane to the ecstatic. With this exploration they can find growth, self-discovery, appreciation of themselves and each other, an ever-growing closeness, and most of all, a greater personal sense of meaning in life!

18 The Family Garden

Learning how to relate begins in the family garden, where people establish feelings of security and insecurity that they will carry for the rest of their lives. The child is born into the context of the parents' or other caregivers' relationship. Different children in a family can have very dissimilar learning situations depending on what stage of relationship the parents are in when they are born. Each phase in their partnering provides a specific milieu that can either help or hinder the child's personal growth. The best conditions for child rearing occur in the stages of Integration, Commitment, or Co-creativity. More often, however, children are born while the parents are struggling to know the ground of their relationship; then the children may be objectified, sometimes sent away to boarding school or simply ignored at home. When children are born in Romance, they might not learn valuable lessons about the realities of life. The atmosphere for children is most destructive when they are objectified and used as weapons or bribes during a Power Struggle. The milieu is most nutritive when the caregivers have an interest in their own personal development, and are intimate with each other.

We note that there are many instances where children are not raised in the traditional "one mother, one father" milieu. In single-parent families, sometimes the child-raising tasks are shared with other family members, or with close friends of the parent. Our point is that children raised by caregivers who have ongoing honest and caring relationships with each other will have the benefit of growing in an atmosphere where personal concerns are understood and appreciated and respected for all parties.

Being a parent or a caregiver is a very important task – one of the most important ones that life brings. Most of us are not prepared for the unexpected demands of the job, and we are prone to doubt ourselves, or our efficacy. Yet, somehow, as long as we have an intention to provide a nutritive atmosphere for children, even with our mistakes and shortcomings, we usually manage to do an acceptable job. So, to new parents and caregivers, we remind you that you have probably experienced some of the limitations of your own parents' uninformed efforts. You yourself probably didn't have perfect parenting, even though your parents were likely trying hard to provide what was needed. Even in this imperfect atmosphere, you turned out as you did, which probably isn't too bad! So, don't worry about how qualified you are to parent; just roll up your sleeves, and dedicate yourself to learning what is involved.

Parents Don't Have to Agree

Parents do not need to agree on how to raise their children. If they are fully revealed in their attitudes and feelings, they can know their differences without compromising. Once they are clear on the differences, they can learn from one another and decide together how to be consistent in raising the child, with a common purpose and will. If they are open and curious, they can move beyond the righteousness of the Power Struggle to find practical solutions to differences. In a harmonious family relationship garden, these differences can be openly discussed with the children who can participate in the decision-making process.

When parents separate, and share the raising of the child from their separate homes, there are often differences of opinion and style in regard to child-raising principles. This can be confusing to the children involved, and frustrating for the separated parents. We find that children are very flexible and adaptable, and can deal with the different parenting styles when there is respect shown all around. When one parent is willing to say, "I disagree with your mother on this issue, but I respect her, and in her home you are expected to follow her guidelines," without making the other parent wrong, the child gets the message that cooperation is possible even in the midst of disagreement. The other parent experiences respect and is likely more willing to participate in a harmonious way. The situation becomes contaminated when one parent insists on being right, and enforcing the rules beyond the boundaries of one household to encroach on the next. The easiest solution is that the parent where the child is currently residing is in charge of the parenting protocols and guidelines; when the child goes to the other household, then the rules can be different. This is sometimes very uncomfortable, and such arrangements are not always possible; however, when blame is kept out of the situation, and respect and honesty amongst the parties is the ground, everyone can navigate this challenging path.

Roles

At the beginning, as we have seen, relationships are object to object, first in the mother-child paradigm, then expanding to include the father-child, then to the brother-sister objects. The project of *intimacy* involves moving beyond these objectifications to practice relating person to person – to shift from the family situation of *familiarity*, dropping roles and walls to discover just *who* the parents and siblings really are! Families often shy away from doing this because they are unaware of the consequences until it is too late;

and furthermore, parents often have little experience with being vulnerable themselves. For parents to be vulnerable, they would share with their children their true feelings *without control.* In particular, a vulnerable parent would be less inclined to resort to attempts to induce guilt in the child, or to succumb to feelings of guilt within themselves. Instead of trying to be an ideal parent, without fault, a more vulnerable parent would aim to be *authentic* and honest.

In the early years, children need the security of the parent-child objectification, but soon they are capable of shifting gradually to more personal relating. A mother could begin by sharing with her children when she is tired, or angry, or frustrated (since they know anyway), always remembering to own her *responsibility* for those feelings, so that the children are encouraged not to blame themselves. Usually, in families that play roles, children bear the brunt of those parental feelings without realizing the source, which is always the *person* of the parent. Without that link, both the parent and child become embroiled in fostering *blame.* When this condition is acknowledged in open discussion, remembering that *each person is responsible for his or her own feelings*, the child can learn about sharing feelings between people in a responsible and growth-promoting way. In families such as these, the children can learn about intimacy from early days, instead of waiting to clumsily experiment with it with their own future partners or offspring.

Parents often think that they should shelter their children from their own concerns; this is usually because of a family romance or an overall fear of intimacy. Children are able to *feel* the effects of their parents' worry; lacking the information that intimacy could provide, they tend to fantasize about the causes and too often, they take the burden onto themselves. This is a common problem in any relationship where people are playing roles, whether it be friend-friend, student-teacher, or employee-employer. People can only break through these roles into an atmosphere of intimacy when all of the facts are exposed. Hopefully, understanding parents will help their offspring along this path at an early age.

Rules

For the sake of efficiency and safety within the family, rules are necessary. Through rules, a child learns appropriate behaviour and good personal habits that will ensure future social acceptance and success. Unfortunately, rules also promote the establishment of roles and walled defences; although such policies afford protection, they tend to become imprisoning.

Regulations dictate the behaviour of interpersonal relating (the social skills), through which the child can practice and learn about consideration of others; when people rely entirely upon these rules, they lose *sensitivity* to others. Rules should be guidelines that do not take the place of responsive interaction with others. The person with boundaries remains cognizant of the rules, but is also constantly aware of the point of contact, remaining in touch with others. Children can learn this, although teaching it requires a greater awareness and expenditure of time on the part of the parents. Instead of shouting a rule ("Don't hit your brother!"), teaching boundaries would involve having a discussion among all of the concerned parties to help everyone understand any particular incident; in this process, all of them could learn how to acknowledge and appreciate one another's feelings.

Children can benefit from having experience with a variety of walls and boundaries. For example, children may be allowed to designate their bedroom as private space for which they are fully responsible, and which others may not enter without permission (excluding the instances when the room may become a fire or public health hazard!). On the other extreme, the living room may be a space in which only certain behaviour of decorum and manners is permissible; in the more formal atmosphere of the living room, children can learn about limiting their personal expression in such public spaces as libraries and churches. Other common spaces in the home, such as the family room and the dining room, could be areas with fewer rules than the living room; in these common spaces, children would be expected to respect others' boundaries and privileges, being sensitive to the feelings of others (although not controlled by them).

Hopefully, children can experience a shift from being controlled by rules to assuming responsibility for themselves; then parents will apply rules only when a youngster demonstrates an inability or a refusal to accept such a responsibility. Being in charge of their own feelings and being willing to share them in a responsible way helps to prepare children for intimate relationships, in which personhood (rather than roles) can flourish.

Control and Choice

For obvious reasons, children often feel helpless and inadequate. Having a limited array of tools, they soon discover that their most effective ways of getting what they want – to be fed, cleaned, held, given attention – are by crying and expressing hurt feelings; early in their lives, they learn how to control others with such feelings. Because these methods are so effective, people become convinced that they can hurt (and control) others with their feelings, and that others can hurt them. Thus people learn to relate through guilt and blame, leading them to play roles and to take care of one another. These habits are difficult to break later in life, but such attitudes and behaviours must be overcome in order to fully experience intimacy.

> BEN: *One day, Jock and I were attending a picnic on the lawn by the beach. Two six-year-old children of our friends wandered a little way down the beach out of sight of the adults. We surreptitiously watched as the little boy gave the little girl a shove, causing her to fall on her knees. Rising to brush off the sand, she looked around to see if any adults were around. We were out of sight, and no others were close by. So in silence, the little girl began to head for the lawn, crawling over boulders and logs to do so. After a matter of many minutes, she finally arrived at a place in her mother's line of vision. There, she stopped dead in her tracks and began to howl as if in great pain, effectively drawing her mother swiftly to her side to minister sympathy and comfort. It struck us both that the child's hurt (physical as well as emotional) was being used to solicit attention more than expressing pain.*

By quickly responding to hurt, parents unwittingly reinforce the idea that feelings can be used to control others. Children must learn that although their feelings will be acknowledged and respected, others will not be controlled by them. They need to hear such statements as "I can see that you hurt ... I feel with you ... you can have and express your own feelings ... and let's consider the feelings of others also."

Sadly, children often learn that their "hurt feelings" can be useful in controlling the behaviour of others. Sometimes, parents tiptoe gingerly around their children in order to avoid upsetting them, especially if they see their children as particularly sensitive to being hurt. It might be more realistic to acknowledge that in some cases at least the children have learned to control the actions of the family, merely with the threat of their being hurt. In such cases, the net result can often be the development of strong feelings of entitlement and expectations of others, very little sense of being responsible for the self, and little experience at relating at the boundaries with others. This does not serve them well as they become adults who wish to develop close relationships with others.

Children's impulses must be checked so that they can learn to respond rather than react. Responsiveness requires holding back a reaction long enough to consider deeply within oneself what one truly feels and wants to communicate; by so doing, the individual develops a greater capability of self-reflection. According to Ernest Becker:

> *The child must be blocked in his experience in order to be able to register that experience. If we don't "stop" the child he develops very little sense of himself, he becomes an automaton, a reflex of the surface of his world playing upon his own surface.*[1]

So, indeed, parents need to exert control at times, especially for young children. Control is not a bad thing; it is a necessity and a vital part of a parent's role. As a child matures, however, parental control becomes less important and less desirable. In infancy, the child is subjected to the directions and controls of the parents for most situations; as the child learns to relate, and to participate with others, the need for control by the parents will gradually diminish as the child's capacity to make healthy choices increases. The process of growth and development should involve increasing responsibility on the part of the child, and thus, less and less need for control from the parent.

Ultimately, children grow into adults who, for better or worse, consciously or not, make their own choices in life. Parents cannot control what the child learns along the way. The most they can do is to be clear in what they intend, and then try to communicate this clearly to the rest of the family. This is the value of dialogue. Situations degenerate into battles when communication and understanding are lacking, and exertion of will supersedes caring. When people see the family project as a shared one in which they can all participate – a family garden – unexpected and life-enhancing growth can occur.

Consistency and Consequences

Inconsistent responses to children's behaviour can cause all sorts of problems. If youngsters are at different times variously punished, rewarded, then ignored for a certain behaviour, they fail to develop a respect and sensitivity to the wishes of others. Often they become contemptuous, and begin to dismiss the words of others as being irrelevant. How often we hear parents yelling ("I thought I told you not to do that! Now, I don't want to have to tell you again!"), only to find themselves repeating the same phrase over and over again, without any effect. Often, their children learn that *they* are in control, while the parent is frantically trying to maintain stability. The child does not face consequences, and instead is prone to become more entitled and less respectful of the context and wishes of others. Later in relationships, they fail to appreciate that there are consequences to any of their behaviours. We think that an understanding of consequences, and consistency in their application, can be very helpful for parents and children alike.

Consequences should be realistic and explainable, taking into account a child's developmental age. They should be related to the act involved. For example, no dessert if the dinner is not finished is an easily associated consequence; having to go to bed early is not. This common situation where the child does not want to finish a dinner that is provided can be challenging and disruptive for everyone involved. We think that there is the potential for important learning in this situation if it is handled sensitively and in dialogue. We recommend having conversations *outside of the heat of the moment*. One can then refer back to such discussions if necessary when the particular issue arises.

We suggest the parent should explain to the child the situation as the parent sees it. For example, "As your parent, I cook nutritious meals for you that I think are good for you and your growing body and mind. So, I want you to eat all of the meal. If you choose not to eat this nutritious food, I won't make you; but I will not allow you to fill up later on less nutritious food. I know you like dessert; so, if you want dessert, you must first eat up the food that has the building blocks for your health. Then you can have the dessert. But I will not let you have dessert, which is not so nutritious, as a substitute for the main meal. So, if you choose not to finish the main course, you won't get your optimum nutrition and you won't get any dessert."

Handled in this manner, with interest in the child's response, the consequence is not a punishment or a bribe. The child is free to choose to eat or not eat the main course. The parent gives the child clear information and affirms his or her autonomy by respecting whichever choice the child makes. But not getting dessert is a real consequence of not eating the main meal. The child can expect the parents to follow through on this, and will likely respect them for doing so; the child also has an opportunity to learn to make choices on their own behalf.

Parents need to be very clear in their own intention to teach the child, and also to respect if the child does not want to do as the parent wishes. If the child chooses not to finish dinner, so be it. When the parent is overly invested in a specific outcome, the situation can readily degrade into a battle instead of a learning situation. Similarly, children may relentlessly test their parents to try to get them to relax their consequences; when the parents give in, the child wins a battle. They gain control but lose the opportunity to grow.

Another example might help to clarify. We recall a situation when a boy was failing in early primary school, and the teacher told the parent that the only way the child would be advanced to the next grade would be for the child to have remedial teaching in the summer holidays. Wisely, the father did not impose this on the child, but opened up the topic with the child by asking how the previous school year had been. The boy slowly unfolded a story of distress and misery in school, and revealed that he didn't understand the teacher, and felt unsure in many areas of the teaching. With the child's revelation, the father openly told the son about his conversation with the teacher, and passed on the information to the son that a failure to advance was imminent unless a period of remedial work was accomplished. The father said, "You can have a relaxing, fun summer, and repeat grade three next year. Or you can decide to work for two hours every day with me to improve your schoolwork. If we are successful in our work together, you will be able to enter grade four with your friends. The choice is yours; if you decide to work with me on your school work, you must agree to do this every day, and we won't stop until the end of the summer. It will be hard work; but you will have the chance to not stay behind in grade three. Think about it, and come back to tell me what you choose."

The next day, the boy said, "I want to do the work every day." The father affirmed that this decision from the child meant that they would work every day, and this decision could not be revoked. Once they started, they would continue until the end of the summer. The boy agreed. After several days, the boy wanted to stop, and the father reminded him of his agreement: once they began, they would continue daily. This was difficult, but the father held firm, and gently continued the remedial work with the boy, reminding him of the consequence of hard work, which was the possibility of advancing to the next grade. This was very difficult for both father and son; yet, they did persist, based on the boy's informed decision. And indeed, he did succeed in advancing to the next grade in the fall.

In general, children need to have the initiative to make choices, but should be aware of the consequences of those choices, and be prepared to fully accept them. One of the main responsibilities of parents involves teaching their children that our choices *always* have consequences, to give as clear information as possible about what the consequences are likely to be for certain actions, and if the consequences are decided by the parent, to consistently apply them when necessary. We have seen so many problems arise when parents were inconstant in these interactions. The child who has not had to face consequences learns to control the situation by outwaiting the parent's determination to affirm the consequence. We think this brings the parent-child relationship into a control/domination mode, and such children lose the opportunity to learn important lessons about consequences which they could take forward with them into their adult lives and relationships.

Sharing Feelings

People's feelings are like internal weather; they fluctuate, they move and flow and change, and are part of the texture of the individual's inner world. They provide texture, colour and meaningful dimension to everyday activities. As such, feelings are a natural part of human life and need expression. Just as the weather can be either a source of pleasure and variety or a destructive force to withstand, feelings can be either enhancing or interfering to people and their relationships.

In the family garden, it should be possible for each individual to share feelings. When feelings are used for control, the roles and rituals take precedence; when feelings are shared with vulnerability, respect, and sensitivity, all members of the garden can benefit. Parents can share the range of their feelings as expressions of themselves as people; children can learn to express themselves with openness and candour, without blaming or manipulating others. Then feelings become rich soil of interpersonal interaction, which nourishes the growth of each individual in the family garden.

Mirroring and Self-Esteem

The family garden is where people experience their earliest mirroring – that is, they have images of who they are reflected back to them by others, which they tend to carry with them for the rest of their lives. Thus, it is unfortunate that most parents give their children greatly distorted mirroring. Two common distortions are *convex* and *concave* mirroring.

Believing they are helping their children's self-esteem, parents commonly utilize *convex mirroring*, in which the child's image is reflected back as bigger than the person really is. When the child returns home from school to show the parents the drawing that was done that morning, parents are used to saying exaggerated comments ("How wonderful! That's the GREATEST drawing!"), when in fact it is only a so-so work of art.

More helpfully, the parent might say something more realistic ("How colourful!" or "How different!" or "Boy, it sure looks to me like you had fun drawing that! Did you?"). In this *direct mirroring*, emphasis should be more on asking the child about his or her experience ("How did you enjoy painting that?") than on the parent judging the piece to be a great work of art or not. With convex mirroring, children either will have an overinflated idea of their talents, supporting the belief that they do not have to work at school; or if they disbelieve the hyperbole, they can develop contempt for what the parent says, and a belief that they are not seen or recognized for who they really are. Such people often get a rude awakening when they don't receive the same inflated opinion from teachers, bosses or co-workers.

The second common distortion is *concave mirroring*. This kind of mirror reflects an image that is smaller than the original object. Children subjected to this will hear comments such as "Is that all you can do?" or "Why can't you bring home good marks like Sammy does?" Such experiences contribute towards a pattern of self-doubting, self-hating, and low self-esteem, which can haunt these people for the rest of their lives. If such people are fortunate to acquire a partner later in life who is able to give more honest, *direct mirroring*, they often find difficulty in being open to accept it; they have become fixated in the reduced vision of themselves that came with the parental concave mirror.

Children who receive *mixed mirroring* (sometimes inflated, sometimes reduced) can become very confused in their self-image. Youngsters who have parents who are very uninvolved (such as occurs when parents are addicted to alcohol or drugs, and lose touch with the children) have no mirroring, and have difficulty affirming a consistent identity for themselves.

This is another challenge in intimate relationships: to learn to give and receive direct mirroring feedback, and thus construct accurate representations of oneself and one's partner in the present. Through this process of direct mirroring, one learns self-acceptance and self-compassion.

Entitlement Limits Intimacy

Early life experience is often one of entitlement. Children tend to think that they are entitled to their parents' attention and love. Parents often believe that they are entitled to their children's gratitude and time; they are amazed when their children would rather spend time with their friends than be at home with the family. If family members remain entitled, repetitive battles and disappointments will ensue.

When parents are entitled, sometimes their teenagers stay home out of obligation, rather than going out with their friends; in playing the role of good children, the young people often tend to resent the family, and can become distant. On the other hand, when parents realize that they are not entitled to idealized versions of their offspring, and instead are interested in recognizing the nascent personhood of their youngsters, they can become a stimulus for the children to grow with a separate sense of themselves. With such recognition, children can learn to interact in dialogue, valuing both self and other. Everyone can benefit from this atmosphere.

Likewise, parents often experience the burden of their children's expectations for attention. Thus, family members who have fixated expectations of themselves and others can limit the intimacy that is possible within the family. In a similar fashion, husbands and wives can objectify one another, and become invested in roles and behaviours of themselves and each other.

To move through this requires acknowledging entitlements and sharing them without a demand that expectations be met. When people communicate in this way, they are revealed to each other, and can be close. As soon as control is imposed, the opportunity for intimacy fades.

Genes and Memes

Genes are biological determinants of structure, function (and possibly behavioural tendencies) that are located on the chromosomes; genetic material is transmitted from parent to progeny, providing given characteristics at birth. A meme, on the other hand, is a sociocultural pattern that impinges on the individual from without; thus a meme is imprinted or learned by the developing child. Among clinicians and theoreticians, there is much controversy around how much behaviour is determined by heredity and how much by learning. We hold the view that the *possibilities* for a particular behaviour were present at conception. Whether or not that potential is converted into reality depends on whether or not it is stimulated and nurtured by experience. Thus, the evolving person never *changes* – she or he rather *transforms* from one state to another.[2]

Genes and memes provide the context in which people live and die. They are the parameters that structure human experience. Although the dictates of the genes are relatively fixed (for example, you can do very little about your racial characteristics), the memes have much possibility for transformation. The individual can make autonomous choices not to follow the robot-like patterns of inculcated beliefs and rules. Instead, with free will, sensitivity, and choice, people can begin to lead responsible lives of personal participation; in so doing, they can decide not to blindly live out accustomed roles and automatic behaviours. People have the capacity to grow beyond the limitations of fixed beliefs, attitudes, and prejudices that they learned in childhood. For such a daring venture, an ongoing intimate interchange in a relationship garden is a rich medium in which to learn and grow.

For example, there are numerous memes – culturally coded behavioural expectations – around the concept of love. We have already discussed the Empty Bucket and the Pie theories of love, in Chapter 16. We believe that each person is born with the potential to be loving; whether or not that capability is turned on and developed is dependent on life experiences and choices, first in the family garden, then later in schools and out in society. Rather than giving love to their children (as in the Empty Bucket meme), parents can provide stimulation to help their children develop their own capacities for loving. If parents merely imprint on their children a formula of loving (such as telephoning home on holidays, or routinely sending greeting cards on birthdays), the children have been trained to do so, but they will experience little fulfilment in the performance of those duties. Hopefully, if children are stimulated to be in touch with their sensitivity and loving, they might genuinely come to desire to do some of these things, and feel good about doing them; they would not be fulfilling an obligation, but would be acting autonomously.

The Immortality Project

For many parents, their investment in their children represents their lack of acceptance of their own mortality. This is dressed up in language that refers to "family pride," "family honour," and "what will the neighbours think!" At root, such parents are afraid of facing their own limitations and eventual death; they take comfort in knowing that their children might carry on for them after their demise. For these parents, if the children can do well, and ultimately procreate themselves, then they have hope that their lineage will not die when they do. They are mortal; perhaps the family line is not. In this way, grandchildren can be even more symbolic of hope than one's own children. For this reason, people are prone to invest in their children and grandchildren, hoping the next generations can accomplish what they have not. This can be a heavy burden for the children, and a situation fraught with problems of control, rebellion/submission, and disappointments.

Now that we the authors have the experience of grandparenting, we note in ourselves the intergenerational issues of parenting and child raising. Grandparents often have a different position; they don't have the day-to-day duties of the parents, and can have a longer view of the developing life. We propose that grandparents not assume the central role of child raising (unless circumstances make this necessary), but rather act as a counsellor or mentor when the parents wish it. Just as children will try to take control of their parents by dividing them, they often will try to get their grandparents to side with them against the parents. This can be a big problem. The child needs clear guidelines as to who is in charge. We propose that this should generally be the parents, backed up and supported by the grandparents. When there is disagreement, the parents and grandparents can talk this out as a feature of their ongoing intimacy when the children are in bed, or absent. Then they can arrive at agreements that have the best interests of the youngsters' growth and development in focus.

Grandparents are especially prone to give convex mirroring to their grandchildren (and probably concave mirroring to the parents, criticizing their efforts). The optimum situation would be to give direct mirroring to the grandchild, to treat them as human beings (not special objects), being honest and clear with them. Furthermore, when grandparents and parents are involved in a frank, ongoing intimate engagement, they can provide direct mirroring for each other.

Parents Need a Life

In the family garden, when parents devote the majority of their attention to their offspring, they are in danger of giving the children a sense of undue importance. This becomes a burden to young people if they see that their lives are their parents' chief source of meaning and pleasure. Commonly, people make their children most important, and often will stay together in unhappy relationships "for the sake of the children." They are prepared to sacrifice themselves, making the family more important than their own personal happiness or growth. This is dangerous to all concerned, because it can breed complaint, resentment, and weakness. One day, these parents are liable to wake up to discover that they do not know themselves or anybody else, that their lives are devoid of meaning, that they have wasted a lifetime of years fulfilling their obligations without any rewards beyond the assuaging of their own guilt. This is a great (and common) tragedy.

The parents' primary relationship should be with one another; in their intimacy is where everything needs to be revealed and shared. When one parent establishes that primary place with one or more of the children, a rift occurs in the family dynamics, with a danger of some child getting control of the family (a control that the child both desires and dreads!). To be made primary by a parent is too much of a burden for youngsters. When children are made most important, they do not develop the healthy perspective that the world does not revolve around them. When children are made primary to parents, this encourages a sense of entitlement, weak will, and a poor sense of self-directed learning. They suffer from convex mirroring. They become spoiled, pampered children, with an inflated sense of their own importance. These spoiled children are "Little Emperors" or "Princesses" who often dictate to the parents. This objectifying situation of entitlement threatens to lead to stunted, narcissistic development in these youngsters, who are likely to have unsatisfactory relationships throughout life. When they grow up, they are shocked to learn that their spouse or boss does not beam approval upon them with the same kind of reverence that their parents did. Indeed, when others wish to treat them with fairness and equality, such people lack the tools to properly assess their own performance in relationships.

Whenever we are asked what would be the best thing that parents can do for their children, without hesitation we recommend that *parents should get a life of their own!* By that, we mean that the parents should be primary with one another, and that they should have interests of their own quite apart from the children. All individuals within the family are best served in a family garden that considers and provides for the interests and needs of all members. Everybody in the garden, including parents, deserves the opportunity to grow.

Parents Are Not Perfect

Ultimately, children must leave their original family garden to establish one of their own. Hopefully, they will have learned what worked well in the original family garden, and what actions produced undesirable results, so that they can cultivate an even more nourishing relationship garden. As people create their own, it is important that they acknowledge and appreciate what they have been given. As Judith Viorst writes in *Necessary Losses*:

> *There is plenty that we wanted, and did not receive, from our parents. It is time to know, and accept, that we never will ... For now that the world belongs to our generation – not to theirs – we see how little power they ever had. To love us perfectly. To understand us perfectly. To save us from sorrow and solitude – and from death. We see how little power they had, and how little we have now, to build sturdy bridges across the gulfs which separate us. Letting go of our vain expectations as parents and children and spouses and friends, we learn to give thanks for even imperfect connections.*[3]

With this understanding, it is time to close the gate of this important family garden. We hope that you have found some lessons and perspectives that will be useful in the cultivation of your own.

PART V

Loving

19 Aspects of Loving

The Meaning of Love

"Love" is one of the most frequently used words in the English language. People long for love, fight for love, and even die for love. They tell one another that they love each other. Most people assume that love exists between family members. Yet, there is very little agreement about what is really meant by "love!" When the word is spoken, each person assumes that the meaning heard is the one intended. Frequently, that is not the case. Yet, on such misconceptions are built many relationships that are doomed to fail, with all the resulting emotional pain and complications that we know so well! We think it is useful to clarify some different ideas about love and loving.

Loving Is Not a Thing

Too often, love is treated as though it were a commodity, some thing that can be exchanged or bartered, or withheld and used for ransom or control. This is the Pie theory of love we discussed in Chapter 16. When love is seen as something limited in quantity, it must be carefully guarded, and slowly measured out in amounts that do not deplete a person. Such a view of love as object is mechanistic in nature. In this framework people have only so much love to give, and so they must become shrewd investors in order to ensure a healthy return when they dedicate any to another. Children are viewed as empty vessels that must be filled with love so they will have some to give in the future. Parents and children become fixated in the pattern of exchanging love as if it were an object, a commodity to be used for control of one another. "Love," said Abraham Lincoln, "is the chain whereby to bind a child to his parent."[1]

We ourselves distinguish between love and loving. To us, loving is not a thing or an object. It is an *action*, expressing emotion. There is no such thing as love; there is only *loving*. Loving is a process; there is no end point where one finds something called "love." There is only a *journey*, a developmental *project* in life, wherein one can *discover* oneself and others to be in loving relationships. It is a quality of interaction, something that is felt within, that could be shown on the outside by appearance (the "look" of love) and by deed (loving behaviour).

An Energetic View of Loving

Another view of loving is an energetic one in which loving is seen to be the energy of *union* flowing between people, nurturing their growth and providing their pleasure. With such a view, there is a corresponding need to *be loved*: loving without reciprocation drains people of their energy. It is apparent that this definition of love is still mechanistic in nature.

Again, our own view is different. We believe that energy is not transferred or exchanged. Instead, energy within one resonates with the energy within another – all in the context of the universal harmony. What others see as a "love bond" we see as a *meaningful relational resonance*. Thus, there is no need to be loved; people need to discover and activate the energy of their own loving resonance.

When people are finely tuned to one another, a resonant vibration occurs between them. Such loving people are sensitive and vulnerable, willing and able to be in harmony with others. Energy is not lost or passed between them, as the mechanistic views of energy would have. In this state of being, people can allow the energy of the universe to flow within them in an unimpeded way, creating the possibility of being in empathetic vibration, responding with others. In this process, people are *recognized* by themselves and each other. Loving does not join; rather the joining that already exists is revealed, because people are not really separate.

Loving Is Relational

Loving is relational. We disagree with the simplistic dictum that "You can't love someone else until you learn to love yourself." Indeed, this notion has led to much self-involved indulgent behaviour, where people waste their time waiting for love to arrive, and fail to develop into their potential fullness and depth. People don't have to be loved first; as they learn to take an interest in others, they can discover their own feelings and responses. As they learn to experience empathy with another, they will be activating their own loving potential. Rather than having to first be loved, they need to exercise their initiative and courage, to take the risk to enter into a loving relationship.

Loving provides people with a way of seeing beyond their defences, masks and roles, making visible what hitherto has been invisible. Loving is not the glue that holds together their personality, as the mechanistic view would have it. Rather, it is a way of *illuminating*, *revealing* and *locating* a person in the overall scheme of things.

Development of Loving

As people grow and mature, the meaning of loving changes. This change is not sequential in nature, but cumulative. Infants have a need to be loved in a way that is nurturing and protective. As they grow, that need grows less important, but never entirely disappears. Other meanings of loving unfold, with various degrees of importance at different times. The more a person matures, the more encompassing and complex loving can become.

Loving is not a constant entity – rather it is a *process* that is different in different situations and at different times. An infant in its mother's arms experiences different loving from the mother who is the co-participant. And that same mother means something different when she says to her husband, "I love you." And the same woman means something different again when, as an adult, she says "I love you" to her own aging parent.

Loving develops as the individual grows and gains experience. The quality of loving changes at different ages; furthermore, loving is different at the same age in various relationships. So, you can love pizza, your dog, Mozart, your child, your husband, yourself, or God. Each "loving" is different, even though in the vernacular, the same word "love" is used to describe them all. Much as the Eskimo people have dozens of words to describe various qualities of snow, there probably should be dozens of words to describe the variations in loving.

Developmental Aspects of Loving

The following are aspects of loving we believe can occur in developing mature relationships with others, with oneself, and with life.

1. *Loving Is Supportive*
2. *Loving Is Enstrengthening*
3. *Loving Is Enlightening*
4. *Loving Is Valuing the Person*
5. *Loving Is Pleasuring*
6. *Loving Is Recognition*
7. *Loving Is Being Vulnerable and Intimate*
8. *Loving Is Accepting*
9. *Loving Is Sharing*
10. *Loving Is Co-creating*
11. *Loving Is Eternal*

Note that these aspects of loving reflect stages of development (hence our references in describing them to early experiences of being taken care of and so on) and that they are additive and cumulative. Although they tend to proceed in order from the top to the bottom, they are like elements in a rich tapestry of experience, rather than strictly sequential phenomena.

At any point in time, depending upon the level of maturation, adults may have the capability of loving in a great variety of ways. They choose the way their loving will be expressed, depending upon their personality and circumstances.

1. Loving Is Supportive

Dependency

At birth, the infant is helpless. Anxious, frightened and needy, the baby is dependent upon parents or other caregivers for survival, for comfort, and for reassurance. When these basic physical and emotional needs are met, the child experiences being loved. Parents express this loving by caretaking; infants experience this loving as the recipients of the care.

It is this basic kind of interaction – this "taking care of" and "being taken care of" – that is most universally interpreted as love. For infants, it is an essential transaction, as they live with a vague but very real fear that not to be loved would be to perish; if they were not loved, they might be abandoned, which would make survival impossible. Whatever natural bonding exists between a mother and her child is reinforced by this *mutuality of dependency feelings*. Such strong bonding is indeed a matter of life and death to the child in all aspects – physically, emotionally, and spiritually. The physical is of less importance to the parent; however, the emotional and spiritual needs can be even stronger in the parent than in the child.

This aspect of "love" remains part of each person's experience throughout life. With maturity, people come to recognize their ability to take care of themselves; indeed, each person has an increasing capacity to be independent, to separate and make individual choices. However, no matter how mature people become, they will always carry this infantile feeling of dependency, which can never be erased. As people grow, they can learn to more freely *choose* when, how and with whom that feeling is expressed.

This view of love as involving need and dependence has been mythologized in the romances that people see as role models, such as the story of Romeo and Juliet. Underlying this great love story is a theme of two people not being able to survive without one another; they sacrifice themselves in the name of their "love." Most people seem to yearn to participate in some version of this romantic (and tragic) tale.

Security and Control

In the immaturity of such dependent "love," people attempt to control the loved person to maintain a base of security. Such control is established between "loving" persons in a great variety of ways. Placating, manipulating, threatening, being pleasing, or becoming indispensable to the other – these are some of the more socially acceptable ways of gaining control, and hence, feeling secure.

In both children and adults, such a dependent "love" is usually accompanied by feelings of possessiveness and entitlement; people think they "own" their loved ones. Jealousy occurs when that ownership is threatened. Too often, in their fear of being abandoned, people use their jealousy as a means of control of the loved person.

Obviously, this is *love objectified*, not loving. In such fixation upon dependency and ownership, people do not come to recognize each other; hence genuine loving cannot flower.

Pleasing the Other

Children learn to please their parents because of their insecurity and fear of abandonment; this sets the basic motif for the relationships that follow. As they grow, youngsters continue to look outside for support and attention, and try to be pleasing to keep this security intact. As they enter school and establish relationships with peers, pleasing continues as a theme. People continue this motif in trying to please teachers; this appears later on with employers, and in their spousal and partnering relationships. Oddly, parents are often confined by their intense need to please their own children. All of this pleasing and desire to be protected relates to an ongoing infantile fear of abandonment; this theme lurks under the surface of most adult relationships.

Sharing Neediness in Intimate Relationships

Most everyone has these unresolved infantile dependencies. They only become a problem if they are the central motif in relationships, because the relationship will be limited by them. Indeed, in a developing relationship, this theme of loving as support is an important building block. Not only is this a necessary early stage of relational development, but this stage also involves feelings relating to personal vulnerability. When people make each other important, they are afraid to lose that person, in the same way infants are afraid to lose their parents. People can share much intimacy with each other in working through this dependency to more autonomy. As long as one partner does not try to control the other with this felt need, there can be nutritive times of mutual pleasure and satisfaction when such feelings are shared. As Shakespeare wrote:

> *Love comforteth, like sunshine after rain.*[2]

2. Loving Is Enstrengthening

Enstrengthenment, Not Empowerment

In earlier writing, we titled this next phase "Love is Empowering." Now we recognize much confusion exists for people in distinguishing between power and strength. We ourselves confine the use of the word power to situations of domination, submission, and control. People have power over one another. Strength, on the other hand, originates from within, asserting the person's genuine autonomous self; it involves self-awareness and responsible choices and actions that are not "over" anyone else. We have written at length elsewhere on making the distinction between power and strength.[3]

Recognizing that the use of the term empowerment seems to perpetuate much confusion, we do not use this term any longer. For us, more distinct meaning can be associated with the term "enstrengthening."

When people become empowered (accumulating power), they remain tied to the very thing that they are gaining power over. Enstrengthenment (growing strength) comes with an embodied sense of self, where people have their own viewpoints, perspectives, values, thoughts and feelings. In expressing strength, there is no need to oppose, or to move away from anyone or anything.

Self-Reliance

As a child grows, it naturally develops the skills it needs to become increasingly self-reliant (first grasping, then crawling, then walking and talking). The mastery of these skills affords the child a sense of confidence and a feeling of self-worth (which others have called "personal power"). The better these skills are developed, the less the child will have to rely upon others for survival. Anxiety and fear are reduced as the youngster becomes increasingly self-reliant. During this process, the child anxiously checks out the reactions of the parents or caregivers, upon whom survival depends.

As youngsters experiment, they constantly check back with parents, looking for reactions of approval or disapproval for newly found independence. If parents have a need to be needed, then their children will get the message that it is not OK to go out and explore; these children will tend to remain emotionally tied to their parents, and develop guilt feelings to keep them from pursuing their natural desires to explore and learn. In this overprotective environment, the parents are using the children as a means to not face their own insecurities. They have made their significance to their children so important in their own minds that they find it unthinkable that their children can grow and develop on their own.

This is often expressed as overprotectiveness when the children are young. When the children are older, the parents frequently give rules and admonitions "for their own good" that serve to keep the children tied to the parental view of the world, rather than encouraging the young people to develop their own views. This excessive control also occurs when little children bring a school project to the parent; parents often make suggestions as to what their child should draw, or write about, thus inhibiting the development of the youngster's own creativity. If parents were able to say, "What do *you* want to do?" rather than "Here's an idea for you," children could become stronger with their own viewpoints and initiatives. Such parents will encourage the children's ever increasing steps toward autonomy and independence.

Parents Who Won't Let Go

Some parents themselves have not developed beyond the belief that to love is to take care of another. When these parents are possessive or controlling, they are usually expressing their loving as they know how, through offering support and protection and control; because this tends to foster dependence, it can be very limiting for both parents and children. At some unconscious level, these parents experience a fear of losing their dependent children. Aware of this fear in the parents, children can react in a variety of ways. They can believe that it must be dangerous to become independent, and so can lose interest in acquiring the tools of self-sufficiency. On the other hand, when children want to be independent and do not feel supported toward that goal, they can feel resentment, anger and defiance.

In adult relationships, people are often attracted to one another in a desire to support and be supported. When either becomes interested in growing as a separate person, the security of the dependent relationship is threatened. The other person can often feel anxious, hurt, angry, and may blame and try to regain control over the other in some way. To feel loving and supportive of another's growth as a separate individual seems beyond that person's comprehension. When people persist in such control, they can become alienated from each other and feel neglected. These relationship dynamics often began in the nuclear family with overprotective parents.

Roles

Roles are based on expectations of performance that demand adherence to rules and conventions, rather than valuing the growing independence and autonomy of both parties. Seeking security, needy persons often want their partners to fulfil roles rather than explore their own interests. For example, the husband might expect the wife to stay at home as a homemaker, even though she might prefer to be out in the work force; conversely, the wife might expect the husband to go out and work, even though he is more interested in being the homemaker. Mature, loving individuals take pleasure in witnessing their loved ones becoming more of themselves as persons, full of their own strength, and less needy of the approval of others.

Autonomy

In an intimate relationship, partners can recognize, acknowledge and learn to let go of their impulses to caretake and control. When loving is enstrengthening, both partners are recognized as separate individuals; in their mutual solitariness, they can embrace each other without leaning. Thus, both persons become strong in their own individuation.

> *Love consists in this, that two solitudes protect and touch and greet each other.*
> – R.M. Rilke[4]

3. Loving Is Enlightening

Order out of Chaos

To the infant, both the inner and outer worlds of experience seem senseless and anxiety-producing. Through developing personal abilities and skills, a child acquires particular viewpoints, with individual likes, dislikes and aspirations. Loving that child involves an offering of stimulating experiences that will sustain that learning, to cast a light into the shadow of ignorance. The child feels the loving of those *enlightening* situations that help to bring order into this chaos. As the child continually grows and learns, the enlightenment becomes more extensive. Such a child shines with the increasing awareness of self and others.

Children have a natural inclination to learn and to discover the world; they become illuminated as life is revealed. One aspect of loving is related to this illumination: as parents witness the light in a child's eyes as the little one learns something new, they light up, too, with loving. Curiosity is a natural function, which can be lost or underdeveloped when parents do not appreciate their children's native ability to learn.

Learning throughout Life

People have the ongoing capacity to further develop and strengthen their curiosity, through investigation of the world and themselves. Life provides the possibility to learn unceasingly. People can have a strong sense of fulfilment from learning, acquiring mastery of their innate potentials. Strength accumulates, as people become more of themselves. Learning is not an accumulation of facts; rather, it is a process of relating to the world, incorporating and responding dynamically in a way that brings the whole self to bear upon circumstances. Through learning, one is fulfilled in relationship to self and others.

When people come to enjoy learning, they can have enlightening relationships throughout life, with spouses and children, partners and friends. Such people take pleasure in seeing their partners learn, grow, and become fulfilled; they themselves continue to expand their vision by learning to see the world through the eyes of others.

Indoctrination and Discovery

Not all knowledge is freeing. Too frequently, information is taught in a way that is controlling and enslaving. In schools, children often must agree with and conform to what is taught. Such *indoctrinated* knowledge – albeit useful and perhaps even essential to that person's successful adjustment in society – is not enlightening. It is convenient to create and maintain roles, but it does not help people to discover themselves. In accommodating to this inculcation, people's essential nature can often become stifled.

In mid-life, an urgency often develops for self-expression. This frequently occurs after a person already has established a relationship based on a mode of mutual dependency. The thrust toward self-awareness and creativity becomes a disruptive force to the set patterns of such a relationship; yet, such a disruption can be revitalizing to both parties. If they can learn to enjoy each other's creativity and learning, couples can enter the new territory of loving as enlightening.

Mirroring

We discussed the various types of mirroring in Chapter 18. Providing direct mirroring facilitates the growth of autonomous persons; distorted mirrors often occur in power-based or romantic encounters.

Every person's growth as an individual (*individuation*) involves an ever-increasing awareness and knowledge of the self. A loving person provides information, experiences, encouragement, and feedback in a caring way. Parents who are loving in this way recognize that their children are individual entities, capable of their own growth and independence – like plants in a garden to be tended, watered, and allowed to grow – stimulated by such practices as *direct mirroring* by the parents and other people. Too often, feedback is not provided lovingly; it can be critical, disapproving, and controlling, fostering compliance and impairing the person's self-esteem.

Many times, parents are invested in their offspring becoming what the parents want. Often, they care mostly about social position and what others think of the children (and by association, the family), and are less concerned for the welfare and learning of the youngsters. Some parents see their children as their chance for immortality; when parents believe that they have failed in life, they can heap unrealistic expectations upon their children to achieve what they have not. In this atmosphere, the children are seen as tools to fulfil the parents' ambitions, rather than as individuals who have their own interests and who can learn about the world from their own vantage points.

When parents offer *distorted mirroring*, they reflect back images where the children experience themselves as smaller than life (*concave mirroring*) or larger than life (*convex mirroring*); both of these faulty mirrors fail to provide an opportunity for the child to learn a realistic sense of self and a harmonious perspective on the world. When parents praise excessively, or criticize harshly, the children do not learn accurate self-assessment.

If children are given *direct mirroring*, with honest, uninflated feedback of thoughts and feelings from guardian figures, they will be able to learn about themselves and the world around them without a distorted viewpoint. This direct mirroring provides a nutrient atmosphere for realistic learning and enlightenment.

In a relationship that values direct mirroring, people encourage their partners to have greater self-awareness, and, toward this end, they provide loving, honest feedback. In most relationships, feedback is not given lovingly, or with any concern for the feelings of the other. It is usually delivered and received with resentment, for the purpose of control.

> *The value of the personal relationship to all things is that it creates intimacy … and intimacy creates understanding … understanding creates love … love conquers loneliness.* – Anaïs Nin[5]

4. Loving Is Valuing the Person

Ways to Value Children

Parents have children for a great variety of reasons – to fulfil their own need to find meaning, to avoid their own loneliness, to provide a mutual project for relationship, to find pleasure in taking care of someone, to solve an inner need for immortality, and numerous others. For each of these reasons, the parent values the child in a different way, each way transmitting a particular emotional message to the child; most of these messages are called "love."

A baby peering into a parent's eyes is looking to see how the parent values the infant. If children are valued as possessions, their behaviour will develop accordingly, and they will tend to base their sense of self-worth on their ability to please others and meet their expectations. When children experience being valued as persons, they can learn to value themselves in the same way. When children are cherished, they are helped to believe that they count, that their existence is of consequence and that their being is of some importance in this world!

Possessive Love

Some parents value their children as possessions; they "own" their children, who must behave in particular ways to please the parents. Little regard is given to who the children are as individuals, or what they themselves might desire. They are seen as "good" children to the extent that they conform and achieve. The child's self-esteem is dependent upon how much the parent is pleased, and ultimately, how pleasing the child can be to all parental authority figures. As the child develops, self-esteem continues to be directly related to being able to please others, rather than stemming from internal assessment by the self.

> *You love me so much, you want to put me in your pocket. And I shall die there smothered.* – D.H. Lawrence[6]

Such possessive "love" often is often highly valued. Much of our socio-cultural achievement is related to it. A lot of people's desire to be in relationship, to raise a family and to work hard to provide for them stems from this urge to own, to caretake, and to improve others; this helps to establish a base of security. When people are "loved" in this way, they feel worthwhile; unfortunately, in this circumstance their self-esteem is dependent upon the valuation of others, rather than their own. Many children are unable to meet the expectations of their parents and teachers who love in this way. They spend their lives feeling inadequate, inferior, unacceptable, unworthy, insecure, and at the mercy of the approval of others.

Roles and the Ideal Self

Commonly, children are raised as *objects*, and grow up playing *roles* (good daughters, successful students, loving fathers). Generally they do not have much experience in being valued for the persons they are. Youngsters are expected to manufacture and match an ideal, rather than be appreciated for their beingness (their authentic self). People raised with rewards for these roles will tend to objectify themselves, and lose touch with their deeper nature. Thus, they are prone to self-hatred, and lack the self-awareness and self-acceptance that would bring them back to their essential being.

Self-Esteem

In the adult years, the issue of self-esteem is central. In relationships, many people only feel worthwhile to the extent that they have the approval of others. These field-dependent people seek the company of others who will hold them in high regard, and are happy to be pleasing in return. This stance works well until another's expectations are not met. Then resentment, anger, and rejection become real possibilities, often followed by depression.

People can, however, learn to value themselves as persons, supported by experiences with parents and friends who value them in this way. When rejected, such people will not crumble into helplessness, or react with defensiveness, violence or punishment. They will be able to clearly see the important issues at stake for what they are – nothing more, nothing less. They tend to remain vulnerable, and do not shy away from feeling emotional pain. They remain responsible for their own feelings and are less likely to blame others.

Valuing the Person

This aspect of loving involves valuing people beyond their roles and accomplishments. Each party in a relationship is seen as an autonomous being, separate and whole. Because partners are appreciated as persons, not objects, there is no ownership between them; instead, they grow together in their separateness.

5. Loving Is Pleasuring

Taking Pleasure in Loving

A loving person takes enjoyment in seeing pleasure in another. Parents are in touch with a spark of life that is noticeable in the eyes of their children. When this spark is present, they see it as a sign of connection with life and with them that is pleasurable, comfortable, and desirable. Much of a parent's child care is unconsciously determined by such signs. In return, many of the child's reactions are aimed to see or feel a similar sign of delight in the parent. When this spark is present on both sides, they participate in a *loving state*, which has been created by both of them.

A word of caution: it is important to note that the other person is not the source of pleasure. In the loving state, both parties are responsible for their own pleasure, which is stimulated by being in the presence of another loving person. Many people become fixated in the belief that their pleasure is dependent upon someone else – that they can only be happy when they are loved by that other person or persons. They lose touch with their ability to feel their own pleasure, making others responsible for it. By being so field dependent, they are prone to be pleasing and placating in order to control others, and to avoid being rejected. The end result is often a loss of strength and autonomy. In loving, each person grows and is greater for it; whenever the self is reduced, then loving has been lost.

In adult loving relationships, the pleasure is in the loving itself. Loving people have pleasure when their partner has pleasure. People's loving does not cause the pleasure in their partners; because each is a distinct person, capable of growth and autonomous development, everyone's pleasure is self-generated. As most people carry within them the childhood desire to be loved, there is indeed a comfort and pleasure in being loved. However, the more profound pleasure for each person is in *being able to love*, to feel the expansiveness and exhilaration of loving itself.

> *The pleasure of love is in the loving. We are happier in the passion we feel than in what we arouse.* – La Rochefoucauld[7]

6. Loving Is Recognition

Revelation and Knowing

When defences are relinquished, people are open to themselves and to each other. When the walls are down, both parties are able to see and witness each other. In this process, each is *revealed* to the other. As people come to know one another in this way, they become increasingly able to be close, in harmonious contact with themselves and each other.

One is recognized in being revealed; so too, one is revealed in recognizing another. The word recognize comes from the Latin *recognoscere* (literally, to know again). When people recognize their partners, they also recognize themselves, as they can only know in another what they know in themselves. As people know their partners to be an expression of life, they too can feel their own profound sense of participation in life. In recognizing each other, partners may find a new understanding of their place in the harmony of things, and come home to the union of themselves with each other and with the universe. Life shines forth, and events are seen with deeper meaning – a spiritual dimension opens. Some people experience this as a manifestation of God.

> *Every relationship, from the intense closeness of parent and child or partners in marriage to the more distant connections with coworkers and business acquaintances or even the driver of the bus we take daily to work, is an entanglement of souls. The gift of this entanglement is not only intimacy between persons, but also a revelation of soul itself, along with the invitation to enter more deeply into its mysteries.* – Thomas Moore[8]

7. Loving Is Being Vulnerable and Intimate

Defences and Roles

During the developmental years, most of children's training is to prepare them for security and survival. Education and parenting thus promote *defences* – through the teaching of roles, achieving, and compliance to authority. Children learn social niceties and acceptable moralities at home, school, and church. People learn to contain their emotions, to overcome their impulsiveness, and to control themselves and others. Thus, a pattern of relationships is established wherein manipulating others and controlling the self are encouraged and rewarded.

People defend or protect themselves to assure the integrity of their own organism and being. This is necessary for survival. Psychological and emotional survival is just as important as the physical variety – to lose any of these seems like losing all. Each person may use a variety of defences to this end. The particular array of defences creates much of that individual's personality and uniqueness; in this way, such a system of defences is not only necessary, it is desirable.

Unfortunately, those very defences that ensure survival also work to inhibit the full expression of the self. People who are fully themselves risk censure, rejection, and abandonment. To the child such rejections are seen as a threat to existence; adults often retain significant anxiety in relation to possible rejection, probably stemming from their earlier experiences. So people learn to function in roles that are effective for survival but involve a closing down, a contraction of the energy body. The self is "put into cold storage with a secret hope of rebirth,"[9] safe from the judgments and possible rejections of others. Then people find difficulty in being exposed either to others, or to themselves. They are unlikely to be vulnerable in relating to others.

Letting Go into Vulnerability

For personal growth – to discover an essential meaning in life – each person must ultimately *let go*, to experience spontaneity, to feel the outer limits of existence and the fullness of one's own inner space. That can only happen when the personal defences are set aside, or made transparent, or abandoned altogether – when the person is *vulnerable*.

Children are vulnerable at the beginning; in face of the threats and vagaries of life, they soon learn to develop necessary defences and roles. If they were to fail in this, they may be seen as handicapped and ineffective in life. Thus, sadly, social pressure works for young people to cover over their innocence. It is possible however to regain lost innocence in the context of a loving, honest, intimate, sharing relationship.

Loving Is Offering Vulnerability

To be loving is to offer this vulnerability, to reveal the self openly, innocently, without guile and without control. In so loving, the person is able to experience the self in its most authentic form, without the usual restricting defences. It is a fresh, open, and exhilarating emotional state. The self is expansive, and able to experience the outer reaches of its own boundaries. In this way, a rare opportunity occurs – to become reacquainted with the self, to become fully *present*, past all the defences.

Being Vulnerable

When people are intimate, they desire to share themselves with others, to become recognized. However, to be recognized, people must shed their habituated defences and roles. By the time people reach adulthood, these defences are so ingrained that this becomes a difficult (nearly impossible!) task.

When people present themselves in a defenceless way, they are revealed – becoming available for intimate contact, without guile, deception or manipulation. Hence, their relationships can be authentic; their loving involves an extreme vulnerability. In this situation, people might feel anxious and uncertain; however, they are also present, revealed, and available for genuine contact.

Without vulnerability, relationships involve roles and habituated behaviours, and the persons remain unknown to each other. So many marriages and long-term partnerships are between two roles; the two individuals might never be revealed to each other. Personal growth becomes possible through vulnerability; such loving offers recognition and the opportunity for intimacy.

This loving occurs in relationships in the Integration stage and beyond. In Romance and Power Struggle, there is limited vulnerability. When vulnerability increases, along with curiosity about the self and the other, the state of Integration opens more fully.

> *Where love rules, there is no will to power; and where power predominates, there love is lacking. The one is the shadow of the other.* – C.G. Jung[10]

8. Loving Is Accepting

Accepting

In relationships where roles and obligations are paramount, people do not come to know each other sufficiently to experience loving as accepting. When partners become more curious and less defended, opening to each other in the Integration stage, they become aware of themselves and each other beyond the limited images of roles and objectifications. As they reveal this to each other, they can embrace and accept previously unacknowledged aspects of themselves and each other. As this process of curiosity, awareness and acknowledgement becomes established as a consistent theme in a relationship, partners can grow to know and accept both themselves and each other. This process of accepting self and other progressively deepens, and is continually translated into new actions of growth, awareness, and further acceptance. As the relationship matures, each partner becomes more personal and more individuated.

Beyond the Power Struggle

In the Power Struggle, both persons remain hidden within defences and roles, and cannot be known; hence, there is little opportunity for accepting themselves or each other. Instead of being curious, people become fixated in blame, guilt, and contempt. When people move beyond the limitations of right or wrong to accept their thoughts, feelings, and attitudes, a new dimension of loving opens; more and more, they are willing to acknowledge these in interchanges of revelation. In this process, people can overcome the limitations that accompany blame and can move to a deeper loving acceptance of their partner; at the same time, this process of acceptance operates to overcome self-hatred, and their own self-worth grows.

In a dialogue of mutual acceptance, couples can accept their current situation, rather than complaining or wishing for something different. They have metaphorically "rolled up their sleeves" and are fully engaged in the relationship project, interested in whatever comes to light. This curiosity and willingness to face any turn of events is a characteristic of the Integration stage. As the relationship deepens, both individuals become fuller in their loving acceptance of each other, and in their self-acceptance and self-loving.

9. Loving Is Sharing

> *A good marriage is that in which each appoints the other guardian of his solitude.*
> – R.M. Rilke[11]

In the early phases of relationships, partners are often defended in their objectifications of each other. Both are hidden behind their defences and walls, and unavailable for genuine dialogue. When they begin to experience Integration, they are more curious than defended, more available than hidden. In the atmosphere of exploration and curiosity, they become revealed to each other, vulnerable yet strong. Each becomes more individuated and autonomous, and yet capable of much deeper closeness because they can accept their separateness. When partners are willing to be open and vulnerable with each other, free of expectations, blame, guilt or defence, they can share their feelings in a loving way.

Taking Care of Another, or Caring about Another

Sharing is not loving when it has an expectation in return. Frequently, parents do things for their children in order to control them, to have them do their bidding. That is not wrong; it is understandable, probably even desirable. It is a way of training a child for the future, a means of behavioural control. It is an element of *taking care of* the child. But, as the child grows, the parent should be able to do less of that, and become more able to *care about* the personhood of the child. In this way, parents can become less "parents" and more persons with their children.

By not remaining fixated in the caretaking role, people can become more free within themselves, and more able to share themselves with others; this is especially important in primary intimate relationships. Taking care of one another reduces people to dependent objects, encouraging arrestation of personal growth and producing a relationship that is static and inhibiting.

Caring about others respects their individuality. When parents love their children in this way, they can take delight in the persons, the individuating selves that are emerging, and at the same time share themselves more personally. When partners in a primary relationship can share without fostering dependence, they can experience a true communion.

Individuation

When partners share in this way, they express more of themselves, and become more individuated; each is separate, yet sensitive to the other. They do not have to become distant in order to be individuals; they can be close in their interaction, through establishing an *interdependence* (a collaborative co-mingling of separate autonomous people). When sharing is impaired (as it is in most families), the children need to rebel to become *independent* and *individualized*. Sharing helps to establish boundaries and autonomy; caretaking and obligations establish dependency and walls.

Anything that is shared can enhance intimacy. For example, anger can be shared in a responsible manner, not blaming the other for the anger, and keeping the expression of the emotion boundaried so that there is no threat of violence or control. In the same way, jealousy, possessiveness, guilt, blame, expectations, resentments, and sexual charge can all be shared with a partner to bring further closeness.

Learning to Share

The task in learning to share is to move beyond the limitations of one's own perspective. People can learn to recognize that their partners have valid (and often very different) points of view. In sharing, people can learn to really listen, and hear what their partners hear; in the same way, they can learn a new seeing, to witness what their partners' viewpoints offer. In this way, people grow beyond the narcissistic self-bound attitudes of childhood into more mature empathetic responses, sensitive to each other's feelings and perspective.

> *Nothing we do, however virtuous, can be accomplished alone; therefore, we are saved by love.* – Reinhold Neibuhr[12]

10. Loving Is Co-Creating

> *The most visible creators I know of are those artists whose medium is life itself ... the ones who express the inexpressible – without brush, hammer, clay or guitar. They neither paint nor sculpt – their medium is being. Whatever their presence*

> *touches has increased life. They see and don't have to draw. They are the artists of being alive.* – J. Stone[13]

When people become *co-creative*, they share their acceptance and awareness in joint engagement with life. In such loving, people's lives become a creative process in dynamic interaction with others around. This results not only in fine art works, but also in inventive expression in all aspects of life (a "flourish" in home decorating, or a tasty flair in cooking). Evidence of this co-creativity manifests in people's work, family life, and leisure activities. A remarkable quality of life is revealed that comes forth in the activities and interactions of the persons involved – newness, freshness, and vibrancy are evident, even in small things. In the mutuality of their relationship, such people are inclined to approach all aspects of their life as creative endeavours.

The Spirit Child of the Relationship

When loving is shared, something new is created. Some people call it a "bond"; some refer to it as a "spirit child." Any name is an attempt to describe something ineffable. In this vulnerable state of mutual sharing, caring, and revelation, each person becomes more fully present to the other, offering the fullness of the self innocently and without guile. Each experiences the expansiveness and authenticity of the self, fresh and without defences. Each is in tune with the other; some experience what they call a "joining of the souls." It is as though boundaries have been erased, and a union of two separatenesses has been accomplished.

In actuality, the surrendering to loving does not extinguish the boundaries between people. Rather, those boundaries become more clearly defined. One often has the sharp pain of recognition that oneness with another is not possible. Each person will continue to be separate. However, both will know themselves more distinctly, and will know one another more intimately. It is a state of *recognition*. Because partners know each other's experience so well, separating boundaries seem absent. Union does seem possible. This is a characteristic of the *loving state* that is created between people sharing their loving.

> *Let there be spaces in your togetherness.* – Kahlil Gibran[14]

The Inspirational Quality of Co-Creation

What Co-creative people do, and how they are together, influences their environment and the products of their joint labour. Not only do others recognize such loving, but more, they are often profoundly affected by it.

They are inspired to enter into their own loving project of individuating and sharing!

All mankind love a lover. – Ralph Waldo Emerson[15]

11. Loving Is Eternal

Loved Ones Are Never Lost

Possessions are soon forgotten; people never are. Things that are held closely to the self remain passively uninvolved, even though they might appear to be highly valued. People who are loved become part of a dynamic relationship in which both parties are transformed. The parts of one another that have been possessed more than loved will fade and disappear. But the *essence* of what has been involved in loving is forever.

Such loving does not involve the imposition of one personality on another. Rather, it is like two musical instruments that are capable of many resonances; when the presence of the other is imminent, previously unrevealed harmonies come into flower. People are not so much *changed* by loving interactions as *called forth* into the fullness of their own nature. When this has occurred, it is never again undone – the harmonies themselves are timeless and eternal.

Thus, when one person dies, the loving does not stop. Indeed, often the intensity of the loving increases when the physical presence is gone. A friend lost her son to a sudden automobile accident; when we saw her, we asked her, "Do you feel closer to him now that he is not in the body?" She was at first shocked by this question; however, a few days later she reported that this perspective came to be very sustaining to her, to realize that her connection to her son is not dependent upon the bodily presence or the anticipation of his return. She realized that her loving for him is eternal.

We ourselves are facing this as we age together. We keep death as a current topic of conversation – with ourselves, our children and our friends. We want to face this challenging prospect – that one of us might leave before the other – while we are together, rather than after death brings its finality.

The Harmony of Loving

We agree with the perspective from Chinese philosophy that the basic life energy is not related to time and space. When people are more authentic, they are joined to the universal vibration, and hence are connected and related to all of life. In this way, the essence of people is eternal (not related to time) and infinite (not related to space); at the same time, we are distinct and individual and finite. This is the deep spiritual nature of people: each individual, though mortal, participates in eternity and infinity.

Universal Loving

In the Resonance Model we described in Chapter 3, the universal wave energy of the universe could be called "God" (other words are Dao, universal energy, or universal loving). The individual person springs up as a distinct being, emanating from the substrate of universal energy. Each person appears separate and distinct in time and space; yet the mortal being is an expression of an eternal process. When people touch their authentic nature (by self-compassion, by breathing, and in dialogue with others), they resonate in harmony with the loving state of the universe, where they are eternally related one to another. "Loving is eternal" acknowledges the oneness of all.

For us, this is the *transpersonal* dimension to loving. As partners discover more of themselves and each other, they are *transformed* – in their appreciation of both their uniqueness and the wholeness of which they are both expressions. This is *not transcendence*, where one rises above the body, and disidentifies with worldly existence; the very raw stuff of each individual has been transformed through the crucible of the dialogue in a loving relationship. This state of loving involves *reunion* with cosmic energy; the partners experience profound closeness, not just with themselves and each other, but also with all of life. They reunite in harmony with the all, through touching each other.

Joined beyond Time and Space

When people open more fully to themselves and their partners, they begin to glimpse a deeper dimension, in which they are indeed joined, and not bound by time or place. In this way, loving is eternal and infinite. The experience of eternal loving involves the *revelation* of our connection with the wholeness of the universe. When people vibrate with life, they move beyond social roles, which separate them by colour, race, creed, and social class; in this *reunion*, they find themselves at one with themselves and life itself, rejoined with the harmony of the cosmic vibration. Some call this God, though we ourselves do not find it necessary to name it in this way.

> *If we can find the whole world in a grain of sand, we can also find the soul itself at the small point in life where destinies cross and hearts intermingle.*
> – Thomas Moore[16]

Persons Fully Alive in Loving Relationship

In a mature relationship, people will experience many of the dimensions of loving described in this chapter. In the dialogue and appreciation of themselves and each other, the project goes on without cease. At the beginning of our friendship, Ben gave Jock a copy of the following poem, which has continued to have perpetual meaning for us both ever since.

THANKS TO A FRIEND

You loved me first in a way strange to me
As the air is strange to the fledgling bird,
Giving support but demanding the use of wings.
And as I trusted you,
As I was compelled in my whole being to trust you,
You accepted my trust in trust.
You received my love and my dependence
In trust for what you trust.
You taught me to look beyond you, see what you see,
Hear and proclaim the voice you hear and proclaim,
Which is your voice, and mine.
I fly in the air of the spirit of perfect love
And whistle the dewfall song of the truth of love
And eat forever the fruit of the Tree of Life
Because you did not love me to possess me,
Because you did not labour to convince me,
Because you belong to the life that I belong to
And you, knowing it, made me know it too.
And now, what thanks have I
That I might offer in a golden bowl
To you?
This only: that what you gave, and give,
I give and will give and forever.
As it is with you, so shall it be with me,
That all may know – and may come to rejoice in knowing,
The worth of a true friend.

– Theodore Black[17]

20 The Harmonious Garden

A garden would be easy to develop and maintain if it contained only one kind of plant – but it would also be boring. Fortunately, gardens can be seeded with all manner of inhabitants, each with its own desires and requirements for growth. One kind of watering or fertilizing will not be appropriate for all. Some plants (like cucumbers) require space to ramble and expand, while others (like carrots) will stay put where they are planted; some need to climb toward the sun while others like to creep under some shade. A well balanced garden will afford the ideal opportunities for each plant to have what it needs.

Like the vegetable garden, a good relationship garden provides for the varying conditions required by each of its inhabitants. One person may like time alone in privacy, while the other may be garrulous and social; one may like classical music, while the other may prefer heavy rock. It is important to recognize that none of these choices is wrong – they are merely *different*. Because people generally feel insecure and threatened by differences, they often judge those dissimilarities as being wrong, and set into motion (subtly or grossly) a series of strategies to change the other person; this underlies many power struggles in relationships. The desired outcome in such struggles is for one person to abandon what he or she wants in order to become more like what the partner wants.

The turnip dreams longingly for an entire garden of only turnips, and generally feels more at home with vegetables, such as carrots, that are like itself. Because of these similarities, the turnip thinks they can sing in mellifluous harmony. The presence of other inhabitants in a garden would create a state of tension. The greater the difference, the more dissonant the harmony.

In any relationship, however, there are likely to be many differences; the harmony will sometimes be discordant. At first, people devote much energy toward changing one another. For the sake of peace, one or the other (or sometimes both) abandon what he or she wants, in order to reach a *compromise*. In such instances, what has been abandoned remains buried somewhere deep within the person, generating unspoken resentment that, like pus in a carbuncle, must ultimately come bursting forth. In this manner, partnerships and nations create treaties for temporary peace, setting the stage for the next eruption. But for a while, they both sing the same song or some harmonious variation of that song.

Instead of submitting to being reduced to one another's wishes in order to hum a pleasing harmony, it is possible for both of the involved parties to continue with their individual songs, producing what initially seems discordant. Then, instead of changing the harmony, both might expand their consciousness to be able to appreciate the divergent melodies and the dissonant harmonies produced by the differences. Such an appreciation would not be a *tolerance*, which retains a belief in the wrongness of the other; the goal is for a true acceptance and appreciating of the different harmony. According to Richard Bernstein, "Deep attachment to culture is one of the things that prevents different people from understanding one another."[1]

BEN: *When I was younger, I recognized a strong dislike for pieces composed by Bartok; I found his music to be dissonant and unpleasing to my ear. In my mind, Beethoven and Chopin were the real composers because I liked their harmonies; Bartok was wrong! But even away back then I was aware that there was a large body of people who thought the world of Bartok's music. I wondered then about the possibility that there was nothing wrong with his music; perhaps the fault was my own inability to appreciate it! Being convinced about this fact, I set about to listen and relisten to such music, always looking into what I could like about it. The process has been a long and sometimes arduous one, but it has opened me up to appreciate a much broader band of music. Instead of narrowing my world, I have learned the possibility of increasing my consciousness and awareness to incorporate so many different kinds of experiences. And it all began with Bartok, for whose music, to this day, I still have a limited liking!*

Our world has become increasingly aware of *diversity*. Unfortunately, this diversity is generally viewed through political eyes instead of personal ones. In the power arena, diversity produces hierarchies, with some differences being preferable over others. In democratic communities or families, the majority rules. However, the minorities fight back with resentment and victim politics; their positions become the causes aimed at correcting the faults suffered at the hands of those in power. Like the French Revolution, such causes begin with good intent, but through a process named *dérapage*,[2] this aim gradually slides into the opposite. In a similar way, relationships that begin with all good intent often deteriorate from something healthful and helpful into a destructive environment. This is especially so when important issues are ignored – swept under the rug and denied – rather than exposed, addressed, and ultimately appreciated.

These principles of relationship are directly applicable to the world stage. Centuries of recorded history have shown that treaties will not ensure a lasting peace. Repressed hostility just builds up over the years, waiting for an excuse to erupt into the use of force and conquest to wrestle the world into a sameness that is thought to be secure. Indeed, lasting peace is not possible, since peace is built upon tolerance and ingrained morality. More could be accomplished by diverting all the resources, time, and energy that are spent in the pursuit of peace to a project of expanding the consciousness of the involved parties. Then, a true appreciation of the different harmonies could lead to a world in which all of the divergent melodies would have a place.

A healthy garden would be a riot of colours, shapes, and sizes; so would a healthy relationship. With intact boundaries, each person (or group or nation) would have a place in the sun, with a right to be different. Sameness that has been achieved through denial and repression begets future strife. It is preferable to make room in our hearts for differences that can be sustained only through an expansion of our consciousness. The harmonies of the differences can arouse our curiosity instead of our fears and judgments. Only through repeated exposure to those differences are we able to expand the range of our regard. This attitude in relationship furthers growth and strength while our horizons are being expanded. Such are the conditions of a healthy relationship garden.

The mysterious and unsought uprising of love is the experience of complete relationship with another, transforming our vision not only of the beloved but of the whole world. – Alan Watts[3]

Epilogue: The Garden Revisited

These 43 years have been full for us – full of learning, of experiencing, of loving. From simple beginnings when we first asked what intimacy was, through the original experimental design and its early frightening prospects, our relationship has been nurtured by our caring for one another and the gifts of love given so freely by others. Early on, we had no idea what we had planted – we only knew that there was something within each of us that wanted to gestate and burst forth with life! And burst forth it did, but not in the ways or directions that we had originally fantasized.

All we knew at the beginning was that we each had come through marriages wherein our authentic natures had been suppressed. This was neither the fault nor intention of ourselves or our previous partners; all of us were swimming in a social matrix that expected conformity, obligations, and rules. Having studied the field of psychiatry and sought marital counselling for ourselves, we discovered that we were all expected to give up many things (desires, wishes, hopes, and dreams) in order to make our relationships work. It quickly became evident that we were all expected to reduce the two members of each relationship to the lowest common denominator through sacrifice and compromise.

Having already abandoned much about ourselves for the modicum of success that we had achieved to that point, both of us recoiled at the thought of any further submission. Thus began our intimacy project. Even with all of our other obligations, we created the time for our investigations; as we prepared the ground for it, we soon imaged ourselves to be tending a garden in which each of us could grow. At that time, the words from the Broadway musical *The Fantasticks* rang in our ears: "Plant a radish, get a radish, there's never any doubt ... every plant grows according to the plot." Growing up in families and relationships full of expectations, radishes might never know their full potential. We early decided to discover what each of us could be if we dedicated our energies into the cultivation of this relationship garden.

Over the years, we have run into a wide variety of weeds of our own and others' making, which seemed common to most relationships that we knew. Attempting to stomp them out of existence or to turn our backs to them only made matters worse; we soon learned that we had to carefully assess each weed, know it intimately, pull it, and then carefully watch for its re-emergence. We also discovered that our relationship garden could not tolerate inattention; we needed to devote daily periods of time for routine tending. All of this we did with an ever-present fear of being captured somehow when we least expected it.

To our great delight, each us grew sturdy and full. All the while, we were discovering the exigencies of stormy relationship weather, the threats of flooding from the hurricanes of indulgent feelings and self-pity, the dangers of burning up from arid contempt, and the effects of the chilling frost of withdrawn feelings. Along with the ever-present possibility of neglect, we weathered all of these threats by rolling up our sleeves and ceaselessly attending to anything that came to light. To our great satisfaction, everything flourished!

To our astonishment, we were not the only ones to benefit from our garden! Our children, our friends, and our clients all appeared to thrive when they visited for a while. Indeed, many of them were inspired to cultivate their own relationship gardens. Over a long period of time, we began to see that others could indeed learn what we had learned, to grow themselves *in relationship!*

We did not imagine our professional journey would take us from our early medical and psychiatric careers into personal development seminars, then into running a conference centre and developing a school for life learning at The Haven. We were gratified that so many others wanted to continue the teachings and learnings that we had found important. Then, when we were ready to pass ownership of the school into the charitable foundation, we had another unexpected professional experience as global management consultants and world travelers, which continued until an illness process necessitated our slowing down, and staying home. Now retirement, and the experiences of aging, decline and losses of loved ones, bring forth some of the darknesses of life; these we now embrace as gifts and challenges along with the lighter aspects, which include the unexpected joys of grandparenting, renewed awareness of the importance of family and friends, and our ever-transforming knowing of each other.

This brings us to the end of the tour of our relationship garden. Our work is not over; our garden continues to require our attention. However, we notice that we can take longer periods of pause during which we can look lovingly and appreciatively at one another, content over what we have cultured and what each of us has grown and learned.

This book is one such pause. We hope that it has proven to be as interesting, pleasureful, and nutritive to you as it has been for us. We will close with one of our favourite poems.

To Edith

Through the long years
I sought peace.
I found ecstasy, I found anguish,
I found madness,
I found loneliness.
I found the solitary pain
that gnaws the heart
But peace I did not find.

Now, old and near my end,
I have found you,
And, knowing you
I have found both ecstasy and peace.
I know rest,
After so many lonely years.
I know what life and love may be.
Now, if I sleep,
I shall sleep fulfilled.

– Bertrand Russell[1]

Appendix and Notes

Appendix

Jack Sproule's Foreword to the 1996 Edition

This piece appeared as a foreword in the original edition of The Relationship Garden. *We are including it here as an appendix; it represents a decades-long relationship between ourselves and Jack Sproule, wherein we have bridged between very different fields of work. Jack Sproule was a Roman Catholic parish priest, who visited and taught at The Haven over many years. Although he worked primarily within the confines of the Church, he was always concerned with the personal welfare of his parishioners, beyond simply religious issues.*

With Jack, we had a meeting of minds. We ourselves do not have theological concerns or "God language" at the forefront of our thought; nevertheless, across the gap between Jack as a priest and ourselves as secular humanists, we found a lot of common ground in regard to meaning and spirituality. We included some of Jack's thinking in The Illuminated Heart.[1] *His writing illustrates how divergent views can find compatibility when there is decency, consideration, and willingness to listen to each other.*

I am a Roman Catholic priest working in the area of spirituality and religion. Religion for me must be about real life, about deepest convictions and ideals. Religion must always be grounded in my own experience. I believe all religious traditions can be traced back to one common experience of belonging that is expressed in diverse ways. This is what it means to be fully human and united to others.

Over the years some very special people have managed to touch my life. They are people who possess the uniqueness of this present age, but in their own lives are able to penetrate and personalize more deeply and freely than others. They are artists of human beingness. Ben and Jock are such people.

Much of this book has been worked out in the unique relationship of these two men. They are not the kind of people who are cautious about every comma. They want us to recognize what they have seen, because it has brought them a life of love and joy, a range of wholeness not commonly experienced.

Each moment from all sides rushes to us the call to love.
We are running to contemplate its vast green field.
Do you want to come with us?
This is not the time to stay at home,

But to go out and give yourself to the garden. The dawn of joy has arisen,
And this is the moment of union, of vision.[2]

For me, Ben and Jock's relationship (which grounds this book) does not fit ordinary categories. It allows a multifaced wholeness to emerge in response to personal and archetypal experiences. It suggests that countless configurations are inherent in each individual soul. My own insights, and the insights of others to whom I minister, are illuminated by delving into the wealth that Ben and Jock have found in their own relationship. I myself am just beginning to discover the boundlessness of human spirituality that can occur in the kaleidoscope of patterns in human relationships.

Several years ago Ben and Jock invited me to rethink, to revision, and to re-imagine my religious belief system. This enterprise invited me into new life. With them I discovered a spiritual vitality that has lifted me up, taken me out of myself, and made me present to myself and others on a level of being I did not know before. My relationship with them became a vehicle for a life, which continues to unfold. We learned from one another what we already knew in our hearts.

The Relationship Garden is not a religious book. Instead, it is a practical, all encompassing, culturally neutral, spiritually profound work, for people of all sorts, who are willing to challenge abusive understandings, of life in general and the spiritual in specific. In contemplating a new vision, people can move from limited concepts (of perfectionism, guilt, fear, violence, sin, sex, threats of hell, superiority, exclusivity, black/white values, power, submission) and take a journey into humanness, wholeness, the right to choose, the strength to bend, personal responsibility, and especially the Divinity within.

The Relationship Garden is a book of faith, not beliefs. Religion and beliefs are what people hold to be true because someone else experienced it. To me, faith comes not from indoctrination (words I pour into myself), but from the Spirit of God bursting from inside me. Faith is experiencing myself actively on a journey; it is a way of life, of confidence and curiosity. Beliefs are what are seen or imagined along the way, gleanings from the fields passed by on the journey. The heart of becoming fully human is faith, not beliefs. The "Garden" that Ben and Jock write about continues to be explored by them as they walk the journey with faith.

In this book Ben and Jock awaken me to the common territory of this garden – an experience that differs in depth for each of us. Their real function is not to provide maps, but to sharpen our own sense of direction so that when we really get going we can travel without maps.

Religious traditions can point beyond themselves and their churches toward this larger territory. Each uses its own imagery for description. Christianity, for instance, names it and explores it as the "Kingdom of God," a place of becoming fully human, a way of life that is soul making, a place of renewal; similarly, Buddhism points to enhanced dimensions of awareness, rooms where consciousness is enhanced.

When Ben and Jock speak of strength and grace in relationships I hear them speak of God. For myself, because I work in the field of personal and institutional transformation, this book is a wonderful tool. Dualisms, as traps, as alienating language, are laid to rest as I listen to these men speak passionately of the human/divine strength that brings humanity to life. In their writing I see, touch and taste this strength – this God as me.

In this book my senses come alive; relationships become vehicles of grace calling me into strength and the "seat of God" within me. There I discover the clues, the inspiration, the grace of God grounded in me. This is pure experience, not doctrine, not something laid under a tree, but the tree itself. Each religious tradition finds imagery to express this. In Christianity this experience is called "conversion" or "metanoia," a deep glimpse at a new awareness, a turning around, a shift, a constant confirming of one's own self as a personal life reality, not just an idea. The authority for this is placed in the hearts of those who choose the journey. Thus people already know about it as they stand on their own two feet. I believe Jesus touched people to awaken them to their self-respect and deepest possibilities for relationship, precisely by reminding them this was never lost.

At one time I became very involved in social justice issues. Gradually I realized that the very cultural lifestyle that kept me from knowing myself as a "gardener" also perpetuated injustice in the world. I've learned we are all linked, and to whatever extent I realize and express what wants to manifest through me, the world will unfold. This book invites us to take seriously what many would call "simply personal," as a base for anything later labelled as social or political. Joseph Campbell suggests that if you really want to help this world, what you really will have to teach is how to live in it.[3]

Laughter, for me, is holy and important to the spiritual life. Its gift is a therapy of the heart. When we can laugh around man-made institutions, claims and moralisms, we can realize that the facts of the world within and without are never the end of the matter, never the last word. The laughter present in this book and in the authors' seminars is an experience of faith, a way "back to the garden."

My religious training has taught me very little about sexuality; basically it has ignored sexuality, or treated it negatively. In the seminary I heard it as suffocating and alienating. In this writing of Ben and Jock I experience a great rediscovery of the body, of embodiment, of a manifestation of the life power that enters into everything one does, especially in relationships.

Jesus said, "I have come that they may have life and have life in fullness" (John 10:10). This tells me all areas of life are to be cultivated and savoured – poetry, music, painting, sculpture, imagination, relationship, passion, fantasy, sexuality – all contributing to new fire leading me beyond to see a new world. There is the dark as well as the light to befriend.

Ben and Jock are mystics who enjoy their connection to the divine and so love the sound of human life as much as the silence of God.

> *Welcome, O life! I go to encounter for the millionth time the reality of experience and to forge in the smithy of my soul the uncreated conscience of my race.* – James Joyce[4]

Notes

TITLE PAGE

1 Pierre Teilhard de Chardin, from "The Evolution of Chastity" (1934), as quoted in E.H. Sell, *The Spirit of Loving* (Boston: Shambhala, 1995), preface, p. 6.

Part I: Contexts

1 OUR RELATIONSHIP PROJECT

1 Carl Whitaker (1912–1995) was a psychiatrist and pioneering family therapist who taught at The Haven in the 1980s. His approach was iconoclastic, and he sometimes shocked participants with unexpected statements that frequently cut through to the heart of the matter. His assertion that individual psychotherapy is "emotional incest" is an example of such a comment. He refused to see people individually, believing that the only worthwhile approach was within the entire family and social system of the client.

2 Ezra Pound, "Cantos LXXXI," in *Selected Poems of Ezra Pound* (New York: New Directions Publishing, 1957), p. 174.

3 RESONANCE AND THE NATURE OF LOVING

1 Paul Tillich, *Love, Power and Justice* (Oxford: Oxford University Press, 1954), p. 25.

4 INTIMACY AND COMMUNICATION

1 J. Traupman, *The New College Latin and English Dictionary* (New York: Bantam Books, 1966), p. 156.

2 J.P. Sartre, *Being and Nothingness* (New York: Washington Square Press, 1972), p. 36.

3 Ben Wong and Jock McKeen, *Being: A Manual for Life* (Gabriola Island: The Haven Institute Press, 2013), Chapter 1.

4 Ibid., Chapters 2 and 3.

5 Lama Anagarika Govinda, *The Psychological Attitude of Early Buddhist Philosophy* (New York: Samuel Weiser, 1974), p. 121.

6 William Nicholson, *Shadowlands*, from Plays International, Vol. 5, No. 5, December 1989, p. 49.

5 SHARING FEELINGS AND EMOTIONS

1 Jock McKeen and Bennet Wong, *A Book About Health and Happiness* (Gabriola Island: The Haven Institute Press, 2005), Appendix A.
2 George R. Bach, *The Intimate Enemy* (New York: William Morrow and Company, 1969).
3 Joann Peterson, *A Book about Anger, Boundaries and Safety* (Gabriola Island: The Haven Institute Press, 2006).
4 Rollo May, *Love and Will* (New York: W.W. Norton & Company, 1969), pp. 29–30.

6 FROM OBJECT TO PERSON

1 Cited in Morris Berman, *Coming To Our Senses* (New York: Bantam Books, 1990), pp. 32–34.
2 Ibid.
3 For more on object relations theory and the problem of the self, we refer you to our *The Illuminated Heart: Perspectives on East-West Psychology and Thought*, especially chapters II.3 and V.5. We have had longstanding, sometimes fervent dialogues on this topic with Gerry Fewster and Geoffrey Carr. Both these practitioners are steeped in the academic study of child development, and both maintain that we have leaned too heavily upon the perspective of the object relations approach. At their prompting, we have investigated the research that suggests earlier development of some form of recognition of others as "persons" and noted that our granddaughter has illustrated evidence of inclusive behaviours from a very early age. Currently, we see that the two approaches are different, yet compatible. The notion that children are in union with mother, and very interactive with others from early days, is an essentialist approach; Stern's idea of a pre-emergent potential is like Jung's notion of archetypes, and Hillman's idea of the acorn. The concept that each is born alone, in a separate body and needs to develop perceptual and intellectual systems in order to achieve objectification and then proceed to inclusion is a more existentialist approach, which we find useful too. For ourselves, each system has a use, albeit in different contexts.
4 D.H. Lawrence, *Aaron's Rod* (Harmondsworth: Penguin Books, 1950), p. 200.
5 Martin Buber, *I and Thou*, trans. Walter Kaufman (New York: Charles Scribner's Sons, 1970), p. 62.

Part II: The Relationship Cycle

7 THE RELATIONSHIP CYCLE

1 William Blake, quoted in Thomas Moore, *Soul Mates: Honorinq the Mystery of Love and Relationship* (New York: HarperCollins, 1994), p. 43.
2 Susan Campbell, *A Couple's Journey* (San Luis Obispo, CA: Impact Publishers, 1980).
3 *The Illuminated Heart: Perspectives on East-West Psychology and Thought* (Gabriola Island: The Haven Institute Press, 2012), Chapters II.14 , IV.2.
4 For more on the difference between aloneness and loneliness see p. 127 and *Being; A Manual for Life.*

8 ROMANCE

1 David Heller, *Growing Up Isn't Hard to Do If You Start Out As a Kid* (New York: Random House, 1991).
2 Ernest Becker, *Denial of Death* (New York: The Free Press, 1973).
3 David Heller, *Growing Up Isn't Hard to Do If You Start Out As a Kid.*
4 Ibid.
5 Robert Stoller, *Sexual Excitement* (New York: Pantheon Books, 1979).
6 D.H. Lawrence, *Women in Love* (Middlesex, England: Penguin Books, 1960), p. 212.
7 For more on the distinction between hope and faith, see *Being: A Manual for Life*, p. 50.

9 POWER STRUGGLE

1 David Heller, *Growing Up Isn't Hard to Do If You Start Out As a Kid* (New York: Random House, 1991).
2 Edward Albee, *Who's Afraid of Virginia Woolf?* (New York: Pocket Books, 1964).
3 I. Prigogine, quoted in J. Briggs & F.D. Peat, *Turbulent Mirror* (New York: Harper and Row, 1989), p. 138.
4 J. Ford, quoted in J. Gleick, *Chaos: Making a New Science* (New York: Penguin Books, 1987), p. 314.
5 Rollo May, *Love and Will* (New York: W.W. Norton & Company, 1969), p. 33.
6 Bennet Wong and Jock McKeen, *In and Out of Our Own Way* (Gabriola Island, BC: PD Publishing, 1995), pp. 34–35.
7 Thomas Moore, *Care of the Soul* (New York: Harper Collins, 1992), p. 262.

10 INTEGRATION

1 David Heller, *Growing Up Isn't Hard to Do If You Start Out As a Kid* (New York: Random House, 1991).
2 Martin Buber, *I and Thou* (New York: Charles Scribner's Sons, 1970), p. 14.
3 Paul Tillich, *The Courage To Be* (New Haven: Yale University Press, 1952), p. 175.
4 M. Csikszentmihalyi, *The Evolving Self* (New York: Harper Collins, 1993), pp. 178–79.
5 Rainer Maria Rilke, quoted in E.H. Sell, *The Spirit of Loving* (Boston, MA: Shambhala Publications, 1995), p. 47.

11 COMMITMENT

1 For our views on the impossibility of change (and opportunities for transformation), see *Being; A Manual for Life*, Chapter 17.
2 Bennet Wong and Jock McKeen, *In and Out of Our Own Way* (Gabriola Island, BC: PD Publishing, 1995), p. 131.
3 Note that this is quite different to the notion of manifestation popularized in the book and movie *The Secret*. We discuss the difference in *Being: A Manual for Life*, Chapter 21.
4 J.W. Goethe, translator unknown. Original German quoted in *Goethe's Faust, Gesamtausgabe* (Frankfurt am Main: Insel Verlag, 1976), p. 142.

12 CO-CREATIVITY

1 Walter Tubbs, "Beyond Perls," *Journal of Humanistic Psychology*, 12(2), Fall 1972.

Part III: Moving through the Cycle

13 CHAOS AND RELATIONSHIPS

1 Dean Black, *Inner Wisdom* (Springville, UT: Tapestry Press, 1990), p. 42. For more on chaos, see *The Illuminated Heart: Perspectives on East-West Psychology and Thought*, Chapter V.8.
2 We discuss this process in depth in *Being: A Manual for Life*, Chapter 1.
3 Martin Buber, *I and Thou* (New York: Charles Scribner's Sons, 1970), p. 14.
4 *The Illuminated Heart*, Chapter II.1, II.2.
5 Dean Black, *Inner Wisdom*, pp. 119, 120.

6 Richard Wilhelm and Carey F. Baynes, translators, *The I Ching, or Book of Changes*, 3rd ed. (Princeton, NJ: Princeton University Press, 1967), p. 17.

14 FROM POWER STRUGGLE TO INTEGRATION, PART I

1 J.M. Russell, "Sartre's Theory of Sexuality," *Journal of Humanistic Psychology*, 19(2), 1979, p. 41.
2 D. Fitzpatrick, personal communication.
3 Fritz Perls, *Gestalt Therapy Verbatim*, 1969. 2nd revised ed., Gestalt Journal Press, 1992.
4 Paul Zweig, quoted in R. Bly, *Talking All Morning* (Ann Arbor: University of Michigan Press, 1980), p. 177.

15 FROM POWER STRUGGLE TO INTEGRATION, PART II

1 Bennet Wong and Jock McKeen, "The Walking Wounded: A Way of Life," *Journal of Child and Youth Care*, 7(3), 1992, pp. 79–89.
2 Bennet Wong and Jock McKeen, "Memories of Abuse – A Call For A Balanced Perspective," *Journal of Child and Youth Care*, 10(3), 1996, pp. 67–81.

Part IV: Love, Sex, Family

16 LOVE, OBSESSION, AND ADDICTION

1 Rainer Maria Rilke, *Letters of Rainer Maria Rilke* (New York: W.W. Norton, 1945), p. 52.

17 SEXUALITY

1 David Heller, *Growing Up Isn't Hard to Do If You Start Out As a Kid* (New York: Random House, 1991).
2 Ibid.
3 Madam Jiang Qing, quoted in *Time* March 21, 1977.
4 R. Stoller, *Sexual Excitement* (New York: Pantheon, 1979).
5 J.M. Russell, "Sartre's Theory of Sexuality," in *Journal of Humanistic Psychology*, 19(2), Spring 1979, p. 41.
6 G.B. Shaw, *Man and Superman* (Baltimore: Penguin Books, 1952), p. 163.]
7 J.M. Russell, "Sartre's Theory of Sexuality," p. 41.

18 THE FAMILY GARDEN

1 Ernest Becker, *The Denial of Death* (New York: The Free Press, Macmillan Publishing, 1973), p. 263.
2 We discuss this distinction between change and transformation in *Being: A Manual for Life*, Chapter 17.
3 Judith Viorst, *Necessary Losses* (New York: Simon and Schuster, 1986), p. 234.

Part V: Loving

19 ASPECTS OF LOVING

1 Abraham Lincoln, quoted in E.M. Beck (ed.), *Bartlett's Familiar Quotations* (Boston, MA: Little, Brown and Co., 1980), p. 524.
2 W. Shakespeare, "Venus and Adonis" (line 799), in W.J. Craig (ed.), *The Complete Works of William Shakespeare* (London: Oxford University Press, 1957), p. 1082.
3 *Being: A Manual for Life,* Chapters 2 and 3.
4 R.M. Rilke, *Letters to a Young Poet*, quoted in *Bartlett's Familiar Quotations*, 15th ed. (Boston: Little, Brown and Company, 1980), p. 756.
5 Attributed to Anaïs Nin, source unknown.
6 D.H. Lawrence, *Sons and Lovers* (Middlesex: Penguin Books Ltd., 1948), p. 506.
7 François, Duc de La Rochefoucauld, *Reflections*, quoted in *Bartlett's Familiar Quotations*, 15th ed. (Boston: Little, Brown and Company, 1980), p. 293.
8 Thomas Moore, *Soul Mates: Honoring the Mystery of Love and Relationship* (New York: HarperCollins Publishers, 1994), p. 259.
9 H. Guntrip, *Psychoanalytic Theory, Therapy, and The Self* (New York: Basic Books, 1973), p. 152.
10 C.G. Jung, *The Psychology of the Unconscious,* vol. 7 (1943), quoted in *Bartlett's Familiar Quotations,* 15th ed. (Boston: Little, Brown and Company, 1980), p. 755.
11 Attributed to R.M. Rilke, source unknown.
12 R. Neibuhr, *The Irony of American History* (1952), quoted in *Bartlett's Familiar Quotations*, 15th ed. (Boston: Little, Brown and Company, 1980), p. 823.
13 J. Stone, "Artists," www.jstonecards.com.
14 K. Gibran, *The Prophet* (New York: Alfred A. Knopf, 1966), p. 15.

15 R.W. Emerson, "Love," *Essays: First Series* (1841).
16 Thomas Moore, *Soul Mates*, p. 259.
17 Attributed to Theodore Black, source unknown.

20 THE HARMONIOUS GARDEN

1 Richard Bernstein, *Dictatorship of Virtue* (New York: Vintage Books [Random House, Inc.], 1994), p. 6.
2 Ibid., p. 3.
3 Alan Watts, *Nature, Man and Woman* (New York: Pantheon Books, 1958), p. 29.

EPILOGUE

1 Bertrand Russell, *The Autobiography of Bertrand Russell* (Boston, MA: Little, Brown and Company, 1967), dedication page.

APPENDIX

1 *The Illuminated Heart: Perspectives on East-West Psychology and Thought*, Chapter V.10.
2 A. Harvey, *The Way of Passion: A Celebration of Rumi* (Berkeley, CA: Frog Ltd., 1994), p. 314.
3 Joseph Campbell with Bill Moyers, *The Power of Myth* (New York: Doubleday, 1988), p. 149.
4 J. Joyce, *A Portrait of the Artist As a Young Man* (Middlesex: Penguin Books, 1960), p. 253.

Index

Printed in Great Britain
by Amazon

64533985R00149